ONE PARENT ONE LANGUAGE

STUDIES IN BILINGUALISM (SiBil)

Volume 3

Susanne Döpke

One Parent One Language

ONE PARENT ONE LANGUAGE

AN INTERACTIONAL APPROACH

SUSANNE DÖPKE
University of Melbourne

JOHN BENJAMINS PUBLISHING COMPANY
AMSTERDAM/PHILADELPHIA

1992

Library of Congress Cataloging-in-Publication Data

Döpke, Susanne.
   One parent, one language : an interactional approach / Susanne Döpke.
      p.   cm. -- (Studies in bilingualism ; v. 3)
   Includes bibliographical references and index.
   1. Bilingualism in children. 2. Language acquisition--Parent participation. I. Title. II.
Series.
P115.2.D66   1992
404'.2--dc20   92-26142
ISBN 90 272 4103 1 (Eur.)/1-55619-346-7 (US) (Hb; alk. paper)   CIP
ISBN 90 272 4107 4 (Eur.)/1-55619-535-4 (US) (Pb; alk. paper)

John Benjamins Publishing Co. · P.O. Box 75577 · 1070 AN Amsterdam · The Netherlands
John Benjamins North America · 821 Bethlehem Pike · Philadelphia, PA 19118 · USA

Table of Contents

Figures and Tables

Preface

My interest in bilingualism goes far back into my own childhood when I first made the acquaintance of some bilingual children in my hometown, Berlin. Having lived in an entirely monolingual environment up to that point I dearly wished I could speak another language as well. And it was this interest that motivated me to become engaged in the study of childhood bilingualism.

On my way down the East coast of Australia towards the city of Melbourne, which would become my home for the duration of my PhD work and beyond, I talked to very many people who all had some story to tell about children with parents of non-English speaking background. Unfortunately, nearly all of those people cautioned me against the impossibility of a study on bilingual children because the children, they said, hardly ever become proficient in their parents' language.

Hence my focus shifted from how a child becomes bilingual, to how one can make a child bilingual. I was now wondering what differentiated families who were successful in raising their children to speak their home language, from those who were not.

Consequently, this study turned out to be about parents more than about children. It is about parents and it is for the benefit of parents. And most of all, it is for the benefit of myself as a parent of a bilingual child, who now grows up in much the same fashion as did the children described in this book.

I am much indebted to the people and institutions which made this work possible for me. I am grateful to Alice, Keith, Jacob, Agnes, Fiona, Trudy and their parents for the hospitality and friendship extended to me. Without their generous cooperation, this book could never have been written. Moreover, the parents' help with the verification of the transcripts was invaluable for the analysis of the data.

I wish to thank Dr. Toni Cross for her inspiring criticism during the early stages of data collection and analysis, Dr. Anne Pauwels for her continuous support and interest, and most of all Professor Michael Clyne for the many years of encouraging supervision, his sensitivity to his student's needs and the immediacy of his response whenever asked for help.

For stylistic corrections of the typescript I owe great thanks Ms. Gwelda Weghorn. Her needs-tailored instruction in English academic writing contributed significantly to my becoming a more balanced bilingual than I was before.

For the first three and a half years, I was supported by a Monash Graduate Scholarship, without which I would never have been able to embark on this project and probably would never have come to Australia. The professional and personal opportunities which were thus opened to me are much appreciated. The production of the book was made possible through technical support from the Department of Linguistics and Language Studies of the University of Melbourne.

Susanne Döpke
Melbourne, 1992

1. The Acquisition of two Languages in Early Childhood

1.1 Introduction

An often referred-to principle of bilingual upbringing is that of 'one parent–one language'. This form of raising children bilingually is increasingly chosen by middle class families in the Western world. Hence, it has been termed 'elitist' bilingualism by its critics and at times not found worth the attention it has been receiving during the last fifteen years. However, parents who choose this form of bilingual upbringing for their children often find it a difficult path to go.

The degree of bilingualism achieved by the 'one parent–one language' principle varies considerably and can be disappointing for parents. The very fact that families who follow this principle tend to belong to the higher socio-economic classes and that they raise their children bilingually by choice rather than out of necessity, produces very specific problems. These families are usually well integrated into the mainstream society and isolated from other bilingual adults and children. Consequently, the children's exposure to the minority language is limited to a few interlocutors, often only the parent who speaks the minority language. Moreover, decades of negative attitudes towards bilingualism, distorted perceptions of bilingual children's social adjustment and academic performance as well as discouraging advice from authorities, often lead to parents abandoning the 'one parent–one language' principle prematurely and with much emotional discomfort to the various members of the family.

Those families not succeeding in raising their children bilingually tend to be puzzled by others' apparent success, particularly in the absence of any overt differences in the families' linguistic situations, such as live-in grandparents or frequent trips to the country of the minority language. In this book I will attempt to find some explanations for parents' varying success with the 'one parent–one language' principle. I will take a very close look at what happens during interactions between parents and their children in 'one parent–one language' situations and relate this to general principles of first language acquisition.

In this introductory chapter, I will firstly attempt to define what "bilingualism" entails or what bilingual children should be able to do, and then look at the source of people's negative or sceptical attitudes towards bilingualism in the past and present. I will also provide some general background information on the most prevalent topics in child bilingualism: the developmental effects of early bilingualism on the growing person, the course of the linguistic development with special regard to possible deviations from the linguistic development of monolingual children, and the aspect of mixing the two languages. A different approach with regard to the significance of the two languages will be suggested. Secondly, a number of case studies of children who were exposed to two languages via the 'one parent–one language' principle will illustrate the range of bilinguality to be achieved by this approach and give insights into the difficulties which parents have in establishing active bilingualism. Finally, I will introduce my own empirical study on the relationship between parent-child interaction and the establishment of active bilingualism.

1.2 Bilingualism in early childhood

1.2.1 Definition of bilingualism

By no means does the simultaneous acquisition of two languages ensure equal proficiency in both languages, or what is called 'balanced bilingualism'. On the contrary, one language usually dominates. This is due to the roles which the languages play in the bilingual's life: a language which is used in a wide variety of contexts tends to become dominant over a language which is used less often or in less significant circumstances. Such is the case where people speak one language in school, at work, in contact with members of the wider community, but speak another language at home and with close friends. In fact, many people in our predominantly monolingual Western societies who were exposed at home to a language other than the language of the majority acquire good comprehension of the minority language, but never learn to speak it, or they forget their rudimentary productive skills long before they enter adulthood. Such individuals who can understand (and possibly read) the minority language are called 'receptive' bilinguals or 'passive' bilinguals, whereas those who can talk (and possibly write) in both languages are called 'productive' bilinguals or 'active' bilinguals.

Although some people may be inclined not to consider receptive bilinguals to be bilingual at all, this distinction between active and passive bilinguals is a useful one in the context of young children acquiring two languages in the home. Young children naturally learn to comprehend language long before they learn to express themselves in words. Infants who are exposed to two languages may initially use words from one language only, but continue to develop their understanding of both. Alternatively, they might start out using words from both languages, but favour one linguistic system over the other as their verbalizations become structurally more sophisticated. Since young children do not stop acquiring important receptive and productive language skills until several years after they have started school, it would be premature not to consider those receptive bilinguals to be bilingual, provided they are still regularly exposed to the less favoured language and therefore have age-appropriate passive skills. Experience has shown that passive language skills can easily be activated when the linguistic environment changes and a real need for speaking the minority language is experienced by the child.

1.2.2 Attitudes to bilingualism

People's (and researchers') tendency to define bilingualism very narrowly is a relic from the rejection of bilingualism in the 19th and early 20th centuries. Philosophically the mother-tongue was often compared to religion in its importance for the character and moral development of a person (Schmidt-Rohr 1933; Weisgerber 1966). Consequently, two languages were believed to be unnatural, mind-splitting, "almost indecent and best to be avoided" (Dodson 1983:403). The human brain was not thought to be fit to learn more than one language, therefore, bilingualism was acquired at the expense of other things. The bilingual child was expected to do poorly in school, and as a result, feel inferior and frustrated, and become either aggressive or extremely submissive (Jespersen 1922; Dodson 1983:402).

Many of the negative attitudes towards bilingualism were due to people's reactions against newly imposed languages in annexed or subjugated regions between or after the two world wars, or resulted from prejudices against immigrant groups. Bilingual children's performance in school and on intelligence tests reinforced these negative attitudes: the children's intelligence appeared to be diminished and their language development disturbed (Peal and Lambert 1962; Porsché 1975).

A change in attitude towards bilingualism was brought on by Peal and Lambert's pioneering study in the early sixties, which drew attention to the fact that sampling methods had been lacking in accuracy and had created biases against bilingual children. Most bilingual subjects were from lower socioeconomic classes and could therefore be expected to do less well in school than middle class children anyway, and many of the children sampled as bilingual were in fact monolinguals with an ethnic-sounding family name. Moreover, the tests tended to compare only one of the bilingual's languages with the verbal skills of monolinguals and did not consider the children's total linguistic proficiency. The change in sampling and testing has since proven that bilingualism does, at least, not create a disadvantage for the individual, but more likely brings about an intellectual challenge for the infant (Beck 1985) and certain intellectual and social advantages later on (Dodson 1983).

An alternative extreme position has since been taken, claiming that children can learn two or more languages as easily as one (Penfield 1967); in fact, many researchers and lay-persons expect a child to become actively bilingual as a matter of course when exposed to two languages. Arnberg (1979) suggested that parents do not always have realistic expectations as to the degree of bilingualism which can be achieved with the 'one parent–one language' principle, and that this causes them to be discouraged and to give up prematurely.

The majority of parents and educators today view bilingualism as desirable intellectually, socially and economically, but have not quite forgotten previous scepticisms against it. They are, therefore, watching bilingual children's language development much more closely and much more critically than that of monolingual children. The most common fears are a late start in speaking and interference between the two languages. Due to lack of knowledge of the developmental pace and linguistic difficulties found in monolingual children of either of a bilingual child's two languages, parents and educators are only too prepared to abandon the minority language at the slightest sign of what they perceive as a developmental irregularity.

1.2.3 Developmental effects

Ever since Peal and Lambert's (1962) revelations with regard to the short-comings of earlier studies on bilinguals' intellectual capabilities, a never ending row of researchers has undertaken to prove or disprove Peal and Lambert's results, namely that bilinguals performed at a superior level on intellectual tasks, due to their, as the authors believed, more diversified set of mental abilities.

Bilinguals have since been attributed with greater metalinguistic awareness and greater adeptness at divergent thinking. The former is usually expressed by an early separation of sound and meaning and the greater ability to evaluate non-empirical contradictory statements than found in monolingual children of the same age; the latter is tested through tasks such as "Think of X and tell me how many things you can do with it". A child's adeptness at divergent thinking is taken as an indication of his/her verbal creativity. This advantage was found to increase with age.

Few studies have reported any negative developmental effects due to bilingualism during the last twenty years, and if so, then factors other than the bilingualism of the child are likely to have caused those negative effects, such as the socioeconomic status of the family, prejudices against the language, the social group the bilingual individual lived in, or the self-image of the child (Dodson 1983). A number of researchers claim that there is no relationship between bilingualism and cognitive development *per se* (cf. Rosenblum and Pinker 1983), neither positively nor negatively.

Since this book is concerned with bilingual families who pursue the 'one parent–one language' principle, Bain and Yu's (1980) cross-cultural study on the cognitive consequences of this principle is of particular interest. They found that, although the differences between bilingual and monolingual children at 22 and 24 months of age were statistically not significant, bilingual children aged 46 to 48 months typically performed ahead of their monolingual age-mates on language related tests of cognitive maturity. Arguing along the lines of Luria (1961), Bain and Yu (1980) suggested that it is the very principle of 'one parent–one language' which facilitates the mastery of the four interrelated functions of language, *i.e.* separation of sound and meaning, differentiation between meaning of the communication and the communicator, abstracting the general category from the particular experience, and self-control of one's own cognitive dynamics, which in turn is "the key to voluntary cognitive control" (Bain and Yu 1980:312).

1.2.4 Linguistic development

Of major concern to parents and researchers is the question of whether the simultaneous acquisition of two languages takes longer than that of one language only. There are very few studies which address that point, and those that do are limited to a very restricted range of features, like onset of speech or isolated grammatical structures. The results of these studies are generally inconclusive.

Differences in the developmental rate of two languages have been conceptualized with reference to Slobin's (1973) Cognitive Complexity hypothesis. Slobin suggested that simpler forms are acquired before more complex forms in any language and that the age by which a particular grammatical item is acquired depends on its saliency. Thus, what is acquired early in one language might be acquired late in another language.

In general, one must keep in mind that onset of speaking and rate of language development varies greatly among monolingual children as well as among children from different linguistic and cultural backgrounds. The limited evidence so far does not suggest any delay in language development due to exposure to two languages. Bilingual children who are exposed to two languages through the 'one parent–one language' principle usually compare well with monolingual children of the country they live in, but might lag behind when compared with monolingual children of the country in which the minority language is spoken (Saunders 1982b; Taeschner 1983; Fantini 1985). Their use of the less widely used language often appears to be halting and semantically and idiomatically less varied (Saunders 1982b; Arnberg 1987).

1.2.5 Mixing and interference

Another area of great concern to parents and educators is the linguistic confusion which bilingual children might suffer. The mixing of elements of both languages on the word or sentence level and the switching from one language into the other at the constituent or sentence boundary are often taken as evidence that the child is overburdened by the simultaneous acquisition of two languages.

Research reports vary with regard to the extent of interference found in their bilingual subjects' speech. This is due to the varying ages of the subjects (1;5 to 6;0 years of age[2]), the direction of interference examined (the majority language interfering in the production of the minority language or vice versa), and the range of interferences studied (lexical, syntactic, semantic, morphological, phonological), as well as environmental conditions such as lack of language separation by the parents. Some agreement has been reached with respect to the decreasing frequency of interference with increasing age of the child. The debate as to the cause of this has, however, not been settled yet.

Most researchers agree that there is hardly any interference on the phonological level (Leopold 1939; von Raffler-Engel 1965; Taeschner 1983). Deviations in pronunciation are usually similar to those found in monolingual children (Leopold 1947, 1949; Ruke-Dravina 1965).

Morphological interferences have not been studied very much in child bilingualism, but where so, they were found to be rare (Burling 1959, Foster-Meloni 1978; Taeschner 1983). Taeschner (1983:175) suggested that "their purpose is to make the lexical interferences conform to the language in which they are inserted".

Semantic interference refers to the over-extension of a semantic concept in one language to a similar but not identical semantic concept in another language. The verbs "to bring" in English and "bringen" in German, for example, though very similar, differ in the interactional direction they imply: "to bring" is unidirectional whereas "bringen" is bidirectional. Semantic interference between the two happens easily. Closely related languages are more susceptible to this kind of interference than are more divergent languages.

Syntactic interference is probably the type of interference which occurs most often after lexical interference. Taeschner (1983:183) argued that "the form they take can be traced to the way in which sentences are planned in the other language. Since the sequence of a sentence just said or heard is still fresh in the child's mind, and since this sequence forms a perceptive Gestalt, the child is merely replacing items from lexicon A with items from lexicon B, and leaving the structure intact". Another type of syntactic interference is due to the child still being in the process of separating the two syntactic systems. Volterra and Taeschner (1978) provided evidence that separation on the syntactic level is accomplished only after the languages have been separated on the lexical level.

Not only are interferences between the two languages considerably fewer in number than is generally believed, it is important to view them relative to the monolingual child's acquisition strategies. As argued convincingly by Dodson (1983), monolingual children, too, have preferred words, and avoid those which are more difficult to pronounce or just less appealing to them. Bilingual children simply have a greater range to choose from: instead of choosing between "bow wow" and "dog", they can choose between "bow wow", "dog", "wau wau" and "Hund", for example. Preferred words from two languages easily lead to mixed structures at an early age. Just as the monolingual child may say "bow wow gone" or "dog gone", the bilingual child can say those two or "Hund weg" or "dog weg", or any of the other combinations. Semantic overextensions are also extremely common in young monolingual children and believed to be a necessary developmental step in children's acquisition of their first language (E. Clark 1979). Qualitatively they are not different from semantic interferences in young bilingual children. Likewise, syntactic interferences resemble monolingual children's strategy of imitating chunks of just heard sentences and integrating them into their own linguistic productions (R. Clark 1974, 1977) as in the following example cited in Taeschner (1983:184):

> Adult: We're all very mucky.

> Child: I all very mucky, too.

The issue of interference and separation is as much a sociolinguistic one as it is a linguistic one. While language mixing by the parents usually results in a lack of language separation or a delay in language separation by the child, temporary interferences occur when one language is used in circumstances usually reserved for the other language. It has been found that children were quite capable of separating their languages when faced with monolingual speakers of either language, but they continued to mix them when talking to bilingual speakers.

Young children appear to go through stages of hypothesis building regarding the function and distribution of the two languages. The adult notion of language systems is a very abstract one and can only be mastered when enforced heavily by sociolinguistic cues. Arnberg and Arnberg (1985) suggested that a certain degree of explicitness on that matter might help the child to master the task more quickly.

The direction of interference, however, is not random. Dodson (1983:416) suggested that "the preference a baby actually shows for one or more words depends to a large extent on the relative number of times he hears particular words in either language as well as on the amount of pleasure or the satisfaction of other needs the baby can gain by using them". In other words, a qualitative or quantitative imbalance of the two languages makes the dominant language interfere in the production of the weaker language. As the child grows older, it is usually the language spoken in the wider community which becomes dominant and causes deviances in the weaker language due to the more extensive use of the former and because of its higher prestige in the community (Katchan 1985).

The most comprehensive model for the simultaneous acquisition of two languages in early childhood, so far, has been proposed by Taeschner (1983)[3]. She distinguishes three developmental stages in the bilingual children of her investigation. During the first stage, the children had only one lexicon consisting of items from both languages, and hardly any equivalents in the two languages. Therefore, they used both languages to everyone, basing their language choice on the pragmatic conditions in which they had first learned to name a particular object or event. The children progressed from single words to vertical constructions and incomplete nuclear sentences in both languages. A few complete nuclear structures also appeared. Morphological and syntactic structures did not appear during the first stage.

During the second stage, the children realized that their parents spoke two different languages. They started to acquire equivalents in the two languages and oriented their language choice on the language used by the interlocutor. Thus, when the parent switched into the other language, the child followed the switch. However, it was at some time during the second stage that the children had begun to speak the majority language only. This caused the mother to introduce the communicatively effective language switching technique of asking "what?", the result of which was that two months later the children spoke the minority language with their mother exclusively. Complete nuclear sentences became more frequent, and amplified, complex and binuclear sentences all started to appear simultaneously in both languages. The children acquired the first morphosyntactic markers in both languages in the same way that monolingual children do in either of the languages. The word order was correct, but half way through the second stage examples of intra- and inter-linguistic overextensions occurred. Both morphological and lexical interferences were observed.

During the third stage, the children adhered rigidly to the 'one parent–one language' principle. They continued to acquire lexical equivalents in both languages. The most important complex and binuclear sentence structures were now used with connectives. Both word order and morphosyntactic markers tended to be over-extended incorrectly on the intra-linguistic level as well as from one language to the other. Towards the end of the third stage, interferences and overextensions decreased considerably. The children were now able to base their language choice on the interlocutor's entire language system. Consequently, their rigidity weakened and they were able, yet again, to respond in whatever language they were addressed (cf. Taeschner 1983:228-229).

1.2.6 Code switching

Code switching is a very different matter from language mixing. The closest that code switching comes to language mixing is probably in the case of borrowing of lexical items. Borrowing takes place when the bilingual speakers lack or do not recall a particular word in the language they are using at the moment, when a semantic concept can be expressed more easily in the other language, or when the word from the other language fits better into the structure of the sentence as it has developed up to the particular point at which borrowing takes place. Speakers are usually conscious of a code switch and can give reasons as to why they chose to switch. Moreover, code switching is often marked - verbally or non-verbally - and only takes place in socially appropriate situations, that is, in interaction with other bilingual speakers.

In most cases, a code switch involves more than just one word and is functional for the particular situation or the particular conversational move. Code switching can arise as a result of changes to the participants in a conversation, the setting, the discourse type or the topic, or by the speaker's need to emphasize or clarify a point, to attract or retain the attention of the listener, to quote somebody, or to exclude or include parts of the audience. All of these functions of code switching have been found among bilingual adults as well as in bilingual parent-child dyads (Oksaar 1976; Garcia 1980; McClure 1981; Gumperz 1982; Harding and Riley 1986).

Thus, code switching is a highly differentiated interactional tool and not a sign of incompetence or confusion. Studies on adults (Poplack 1980) and children (McClure 1981) have shown that there is a positive correlation between bilingual competence and linguistic complexity of code switched discourse.

The amount of code switching in which individuals engage depends very much on the social norms of the community to which they belong. The effect of extensive code switching on the language development of young children, and especially on their ability to separate the two languages, has not sufficiently been studied yet. One can, however, expect that children will acquire code switching as the communicative norm in interaction with habitually code-switching bilinguals and non-code switched discourse as the communicative norm with monolingual speakers of either of their two languages. Provided monolingual interactants are available to the child, the two linguistic systems will be separated in due course; if not, separation is likely to be delayed until a later point at which non-code switched language behaviour becomes a necessity.

1.2.7 A different approach

I would like to go one step further and compare the bilingual's ability to function in two languages with the monolingual's socially diversified use of language. It has been convincingly shown that monolingual speakers adjust their style of speaking to the setting, the participants, the discourse type, the topic or the particular interactional goal as well. Such adjustments have been termed "register" and are believed to be a relatively universal sociolinguistic phenomenon.

Children start acquiring different registers at a very early age. Gleason (1973:163) argued that the "earliest variation is simply between talking and not talking" due to "the presence of strangers". Children's use of whining is also very selective, usually reserved for the mother or some other very close adult. Even the father is often addressed differently from the mother (Gleason 1975; Gleason and Weintraub 1978). By four years of age children differentiate linguistically between their peers and babies, are more polite and more explicit to strangers than to familiar adults, and know how to modify their speech in order to make their mothers do something for them (Gleason 1973, 1975; Shatz and Gelman 1977).

As argued in the preceding sections, the bilingual speaker can perform the same interactional functions by switching from one language to the other as can the monolingual speaker by using more than one register. Differentiation between registers as well as between languages is a cognitive process triggered by sociolinguistic cues. Swain (1972:4) pointed out that "in the case of the 'bilingual' individual (....) the switches made are simply more obvious to the listener than in the case of the monolingual individual. To the user of the code, whether the code is a language, a dialect, or a variety of a dialect, it is not at all clear that the bilingual/monolingual distinction is a useful one"[1].

1.3 Establishing bilingualism in the home

A number of case studies shall illustrate how the 'one parent–one language' principle can be put into practice and the degree of bilingualism which can reasonably be achieved that way.

1.3.1 Patterns of exposure

Bilingual families who follow the 'one parent–one language' principle typically fall into one of the following patterns:

1) The parents have different native tongues, and the language spoken in the wider community is the same as that of one of the parents. Each parent speaks his/her own language to the child.
    a: The parents speak the language of the wider community to one another.
    b: The parents speak the minority language to one another.
    c: Each parent speaks the language they speak with the child when addressing each other.

2) The parents have different native tongues, neither of which is spoken in the wider community. Each parent speaks his/her own language to the child.
    a: The parents speak the language of the wider community to each other.
    b: The parents speak one of the minority languages to each other.
    c: Each parent speaks the language they speak with the child when addressing each other.

3) Both parents are native speakers of the language spoken by the wider community. One parent chooses to speak a language other than his/her native language to the child.
    a: The parents speak the language of the wider community to each other.
    b: The parents speak the minority language to each other.
    c: Each parent speaks the language they speak with the child when addressing each other.

4) Both parents are native speakers of the same minority language. One of the parents chooses to speak the language of the wider community to the child.
    a: The parents speak the language of the wider community to each other.

b: The parents speak the minority language to each other.

c: Each parent speaks the language they speak with the child when addressing each other.

In all four cases, the 'b' alternatives guarantee a more extensive and more diversified exposure to the minority language than the 'a' alternatives. In the majority of families, however, the 'a' alternative is a necessity. The 'c' alternative is rarely chosen.

Pattern 3 may appear somewhat unnatural but in spite of some scholars' warnings against it (*e.g.* Kielhöfer and Jonekeit 1983), there are convincing examples available showing that productive bilingualism can be achieved that way without any loss of family cohesion (Saunders 1982b). After all, in terms of linguistic interaction within the family, Pattern 3 is not any different from Pattern 4, which immigrant families may choose or may be advised to choose in order to install simultaneous rather than consecutive bilingualism in their children.

The 'one parent–one language' principle does not only present an intellectual challenge to the child, but also fulfils needs of parents: the need to interact with their children naturally in the language they heard as children themselves, the need to maintain and develop a much loved language, or the need to practice the language of the new country. Family cohesion may or may not be affected by the use of different languages by different people of the same family, depending on the degree of bilinguality of the adults, their personal temperament and their level of knowledge on the subject. In fact, barring others or themselves from speaking one's native language to the child might not be any more conducive to family cohesion than is the happy use of different languages (cf. Zierer 1977).

1.3.2 Cases of young children becoming productive bilinguals

The earliest recorded case of a young child associating a different language with each of his parents was that of Ronjat (1913). Louis Ronjat and his parents lived in Southern France. His mother spoke German to him and his father addressed him in French. In front of Louis - and for his benefit - the parents spoke German to each other (Pattern 1b). Ronjat, who was a linguist himself, kept a diary record of Louis's language development until he was five years of age, the analysis of which showed that Louis spoke both languages like monolingual children in France and Germany at the end of this period.

The parents were very conscious of their roles as language teachers for their young son. They were extremely consistent in their language choice. If Louis asked the father for a German equivalent of a French word, the father would refuse the information and send him to the mother. The mother was not quite that strict when asked for a word in French. The father corrected Louis's French regularly and even corrected utterances addressed to the mother for mixing of French and German or grammatical mistakes in German. He did not do that directly of course, since that would have violated the principle of "une personne–une langue", as it was called in Ronjat's book, but did so by asking the mother not to allow Louis to use a French word or a wrong case in German.

The Ronjats were an affluent family who could afford to have a number of servants in the house, some of whom were German. The family also visited the mother's relatives in Germany frequently. Both parents spent a lot of time with Louis. The father reported that he took the child for walks, told him stories and repaired his toys (cf. Porsché 1983:75).

The American linguist Leopold (1939-49) also raised his child bilingually. He, himself a native speaker of German, decided to speak German to their daughter Hildegard while the mother spoke English with her. The medium of communication between the parents used to be English before Hildegard was born, but thereafter the parents pursued the 'one parent–one language' principle even in interaction with each other (Pattern 1c). Except for short periods of time, when the family was residing in Germany, Hildegard was always dominant in English, but could express herself in German and did so in interaction with her father. However, speaking German was reportedly more laborious for her and interferences from English to German were not uncommon.

Leopold was not nearly as rigid as Ronjat. He spoke English when monolingual visitors or playmates of Hildegard were present and answered her questions regarding words in English readily. After a stay in Germany, an attempt at making German the only language in the home was made (Pattern 1b), but the mother gave in to Hildegard's preference for English, and the attempt was abandoned. Hildegard was also corrected less frequently than was Louis, and her inconsistencies of language choice as well as her mixed German-English utterances were often ignored.

Nevertheless, the father never grew tired of modelling correct German utterances for her and apparently spent much of his free time playing and talking with Hildegard. Given that he was virtually her only source of German until the family spent half a year in Germany, when Hildegard was five years old, whatever motivation Hildegard had to use German actively must have developed during father-child activities.

Much more recently, Saunders (1982b, 1988) published an account of his children's bilingual development in Australia. Although both parents are native speakers of English, Saunders's excellent command of academically acquired German and his professional orientation towards linguistics and language teaching provided the opportunity to raise the children bilingually. This family also followed the 'one parent–one language' principle, with the father speaking German and the mother speaking English to the children. The parents spoke English to each other (Pattern 3a). The children's language development was recorded manually, on tapes and through tests until the sons were twelve and thirteen and the daughter was six years of age. The children seem to have gone through the three stages of bilingual development as proposed by Taeschner (1983). They are now fluent in both languages, but clearly dominant in English.

The father always addressed the children in German regardless of monolingual adults or children being present. Rather than moving away from the principle of always using German to his children, he would say something twice, once to his children and once for the benefit of the monolingual participants, or he would encourage the children to translate in order to keep everybody included in the interaction. When the children tried to speak English to their father at around 3;5 (the older boy) and 2;7 (the younger boy), he pretended not to understand them. The ensuing difficulties in communication with their father must have convinced the boys of the relative usefulness of German. This rigidity was felt to be of great importance since the family naturally does not have any German relatives who could have supported the father in his efforts, and frequent trips from Australia to Germany are not necessarily an option - not even for the "elitist" middle class family. Since the father was the children's only source of input in German, allowances for a departure from the normal pattern of language choice were made only for quotations from English speakers, role play and 'untranslatables'. The mother was much more tolerant of German being addressed to her and employed certain German words and phrases herself at times, since there was never any danger of the exposure to English being too limited.

It is obvious throughout Saunders' books that the relationship between father and children was a very special one in this family. The many hours of playing and reading, the outings designed to enrich the contact with German, and the father's enjoyment in conversing with his children in German created an environment for German which was rich, stimulating and pleasurable, and probably therefore able to motivate the children to speak German, even when

German did not come to them as automatically as their dominant English (Döpke 1984).

Only a year later, Taeschner (1983) published the description and analysis of the bilingual development of her two daughters. The family lived in Italy and employed the 'one parent–one language' principle there. The father, a native speaker of Italian, spoke Italian to the children, and the mother addressed them in German, which was her native tongue. The parents always spoke Italian to each other (Pattern 1a). The children were studied from the ages of 1;6 to 5;0 and 4;0 respectively, although some mention was made of instances up to nine years of age. The girls were found to develop in both Italian and German very similarly to monolingual children speaking either of the two languages. Except for a short time during the second stage of their bilingual development (cf. 1.2.5), when they were reluctant to speak German, and Italian became clearly dominant, the two languages were always much in balance, swaying only slightly towards Italian or German depending on which of the languages was used more intensively around them at the time. By seven to nine years of age the older daughter's output in both languages was described as good, with Italian being lexically somewhat richer.

Both parents were very consistent in their language choice: the father because of his very limited knowledge of German and the mother because she, again, is a linguist and was highly aware of factors which support the active acquisition of a minority language. While she spoke Italian in the presence of monolingual speakers at first, she gave that up once the girls had become reluctant to speak German, thus increasing the German input on a day-to-day basis considerably. At the same time she started to insist that the girls spoke German to her and pretended not to understand if they did not (cf. 1.2.5), the effect of which was the same as that in the Saunders family: the children soon found that the communication with their mother was much easier when they spoke German. By the time the children realized that their mother did not really fail to understand Italian, the habit of switching to German when the mother asked "wie?" ("what?") was well established. Overt corrections of grammatical mistakes, *e.g.* word order, were not very successful, and therefore hardly ever used. Instead, correct models were given in the form of repetitions and expansions. Gaps which occurred in German were attempted to be filled with the help of direct teaching strategies.

In addition to the teaching oriented linguistic input, the mother also provided the girls with regular contact with German monolingual and bilingual speakers. Bilingual children in the neighbourhood, visits to Germany as well as visits from German relatives, holidays in the bilingual German-Italian region of Northern Italy, a German kindergarten teacher who was hired to play with the girls for a couple of afternoons each week, and later on, a full-time German housekeeper, all enriched the German input and helped to establish and maintain bilingualism. Unfortunately, Taeschner specifically focused on the quantity of exposure to the minority language as a determining factor for fluent bilingualism, and further conclusions concerning the quality of interaction between mother and children as a motivating force for the children to speak German cannot be drawn.

Far less academic, but directed instead at advising parents who want to establish bilingualism in their home is the book by Kielhöfer and Jonekeit (1983). The children of one of the authors provided the illustrative material used to answer questions and concerns readers may have. The data is presented anecdotally, and no analytic information can be drawn from it.

These parents also employed the 'one parent–one language' principle. The mother, who is a native speaker of French, lived with her monolingual German husband in West Germany (Pattern 1a). Still a student when the first child was born, she collected diary-type data until the two sons were five and four years of age. The children appeared to have acquired French and German on a relatively parallel basis, with only some more complex grammatical areas in French, *e.g.* the pronoun system, being acquired later than in German. Interferences were generally unidirectional from German to French. The assumption was that French was the boys' weaker language.

Until the children commenced kindergarten (age unspecified, but probably around three years), they tended to spend their days exclusively with their mother. The mother reportedly played, read and sang with them a lot. Very frequent trips to the grandparents in France further supported the boys' active development in the minority language.

The authors argued strongly for the importance of strict separation between the two language systems by the parents, for positive attitudes towards bilingualism and towards the particular second language by the community, and for a good emotional relationship between the children and the parent who is the transmitter of the minority language, all of which seemed to be given in the case studied by Kielhöfer and Jonekeit. No reference was made to the three-stage-hypothesis (Volterra and Taeschner 1978; Taeschner 1983), and these children did not seem to have gone through a period of reluctance to speak French.

A much shorter account of yet another parent-linguist's attempt at raising, in this case, a trilingual family was presented by Hoffmann (1985). The parents lived in England, but neither of them was a native speaker of English. The mother spoke her native German with the children, and the father addressed them in Spanish, which was his native tongue. The parents spoke Spanish to each other (Pattern 2b). The period studied ended when the two children were eight and five years of age. The children had developed fluency in all three languages, but the dominance pattern had changed frequently due to changes in intensity of exposure. Although English was introduced much later and not spoken to the children inside the home, it finally was dominant over German and Spanish.

The mother professed to have taken conscious steps to create a rich environment for German "backed up by cassettes, songs and stories", since she was the sole interlocutor for German in the home and had to counterbalance the effects of Spanish being the family language as well as the language spoken by the majority of au-pairs who lived with the family. On the other hand, visits to Germany were much more frequent than to Spain. Hoffmann concluded that it was both social and psychological factors which made the establishment of trilingualism in their home a successful endeavour.

Cases of bilingual children raised by parents who are not professionally involved in linguistics are, although frequent, not usually reported in the literature. Arnberg (1987) gives one such account of a trilingual Finnish-Kurdish-Swedish family living in Sweden. The mother spoke Finnish to the children, and the father spoke Kurdish to them. The parents did not know much of each other's language and, therefore, spoke Swedish together (Pattern 2a). The pattern of 'one parent–one language' was employed very consistently, even in front of monolingual Swedish speakers. The parents were reportedly very aware of the extra work which would be involved in being the children's only interlocutors for Finnish and Kurdish respectively, and provided a rich language environment by playing, reading and talking intensively with the children. The children acquired both Finnish and Kurdish actively at home, and learned Swedish later from other children and through the day care centre. When the children were five and two years of age, the father had to move to a different part of the country and only saw the children infrequently from then on. Consequently, the children's use of Kurdish deteriorated, and the children soon became reluctant so speak it. Finnish was now the only language spoken in the home.

Harding and Riley (1986) reported another case of a non-linguist family who successfully established active bilingualism through the 'one parent–one language' principle. The family lived in France. The mother spoke her native French with the child, and the father, an Englishman, addressed the child in

English. The parents spoke French to each other (Pattern 1a). "The father (was) very conscious of his role as 'source of English' in the family and admit(ted) to 'bombarding' his child (...) with conversation, records and songs and rhymes" (Harding and Riley 1986:84). The child only started to speak English at 3;9, but was a fluent bilingual at eight years of age when the family was interviewed.

Due to the relative proximity of countries in Europe, the children from both families had been to the homelands of their minority languages and in the case of the Finnish-Kurdish family in Sweden, had support for Finnish through mother-tongue maintenance programs in the day care centre and through Finnish-speaking peers in the neighbourhood.

1.3.3 Cases of young children becoming receptive bilinguals

Cases reported in the literature overwhelmingly demonstrate the successful establishment of productive bilingualism in young children. This contrasts strongly with most people's direct experience. In the majority of families who set out to raise their children according to the 'one parent–one language' principle in monolingual Western societies, the minority language is met with considerable resistance by the children. As the language spoken in the wider community develops faster during the second stage of the child's bilingual development, the minority language is used less and less and the developmental gap between the two languages widens[4]. Parents usually watch this process rather helplessly, but are not really surprised, since that is exactly what others had foreseen. Depending on their personal reasons for speaking the minority language in the home and their determination to transmit it to their children, parents may or may not continue with it. In the latter case, the children will soon forget whatever bilingual proficiency they had acquired up to that point. If parents, however, persist in addressing their children in the minority language, the children will continue to develop their passive knowledge of that language and become receptive bilinguals.

Arnberg (1981c) observed the children of four English-Swedish families in Sweden for one year, starting when the children were 1;7 to 2;1. In all four families, the mothers spoke their native English with the children, and the fathers addressed the children in Swedish. The language spoken between the parents was different in each family: in one family it was mostly Swedish (Pattern 1a), in another it was mostly English (Pattern 1b), in the third family mother and father would speak either Swedish or English when conversing with each other, and in the fourth family they continued with the 'one parent–one language' principle even when addressing one another (Pattern 1c). Two of the children also had older siblings, who always spoke Swedish to the younger ones as well as to their English-speaking mothers. The mothers' consistency in language choice varied from only English, over mostly English, to equal amounts of English and Swedish. Outings and the presence of monolingual Swedish speakers tended to cause shifts towards more Swedish in the speech of the mothers. All mothers admitted to some language mixing.

The children's use of English was very limited. During the first six months of the study, spontaneous occurrences of English in purely English utterances or mixed English-Swedish utterances made up only six to eight percent of three of the children's total verbalisations to their mothers, and about 17% in the case of the fourth child. The first three children visited an English-speaking country during the summer holidays, the effect of which was considerable in the case of one child, whose percentage of utterances with spontaneously occurring English elements jumped up to 64%, but was very moderate in another (21%) and negligible in the third (9.5%). "In general, most of the mothers were disappointed with the results regarding the dominance of Swedish in the children's language development" (Arnberg 1981c:78).

Søndergard (1981) described his son's "failure" at becoming bilingual retrospectively. Originally, the mother spoke her native Finnish with the child, and the father addressed him in Danish. The family lived in Denmark, and the parents spoke Danish with one another (Pattern 1a). By the time the child was nearly three years of age, he had learned to understand both Danish and Finnish, but was reluctant to use Finnish, *i.e.* he only spoke Finnish when prodded and asked for translations. The parents also felt that he was late in his development of Danish. Consequently, they discontinued the use of Finnish in the home, hoping that the son would become bilingual at a later stage.

A monograph-size account of a young child's bilingual development was published by the parent-linguist Porsché in 1983. The father, a native speaker of English and married to a German woman, interacted with the child in English, while the mother used German. The family lived in West Germany, and the parents spoke German to each other (Pattern 1a). The child's linguistic development was analysed intensively at 2;3 and 2;7, and a short description of the further development until age 10 was given.

It appears that the child's use of English declined from the first to the second recording from 11.6% to 6.6% English tokens, of which about 60% were imitations at both times. This did, however, not include mixed German-English utterances. Mixed utterances increased considerably from the first to the second recording - most likely due to an increase in two-word utterances - and if included, they keep the proportion of English stable at around 13% total or 8% spontaneously uttered contributions.

During his pre-school years, the child spoke partly German, partly English with his father, but returned to German more or less completely once he went to school. The father continued speaking English and the child further developed his understanding of the language. When he was ten years old, he visited an English-speaking country for the first time and converted his so far passive knowledge of English into active production within a couple of days. After the return to Germany, however, German was once again the only actively used language. In contrast to other authors, Porsché did not try to create the need for continuous use of the minority language: "We encourage (the children) if they want to speak English, but do not try to force them; after all they also have other interests apart from practising a second language" (Porsché 1983:183, Clyne's translation 1985:43).

One further bilingual child with receptive rather than productive skills in the second language was described in Arnberg (1987). The mother was Polish, and the father was Swedish. The family lived in Sweden. The parents each spoke their native language to the child, and spoke Swedish to each other (Pattern 1a). The family had hardly any contact with other Polish speakers. At two and a half years of age, the child answered in Swedish only, about which the mother was very disappointed. The lack of Polish in the child's speech made it difficult for the mother to be consistent in her language choice. Interestingly, the mother reported that she was a rather quiet person herself and that she found it difficult to engage in much verbal interaction with her daughter regardless of the language she chose. Nevertheless, the mother persisted speaking Polish, and the child continued to develop receptive skills. A couple of years later (no exact age was given, but the daughter seemed to have been a preschooler still), a visit from monolingual Polish relatives proved that the child could in fact express herself in Polish.

1.3.4 Difficulties in establishing productive bilingualism

It has become clear from the cases of bilingual families described above that bilingual education in the home can be a difficult task for parents in a society where the environment predominantly speaks one language, and one of the parents is the main or only source of language input for the child. From an environmental point of view, the difficulties in establishing productive bilingualism in the young child are due to the lack of contact with the minority language and the lack in variety of contact best provided through a number of different interlocutors. Moreover, children growing up with the 'one parent–one language' principle are usually isolated from other children with whom they could speak the minority language. Frequent trips to the monolingual homeland seem to be most effective in establishing and maintaining productive bilingualism, but they are not necessarily feasible financially. By the same token, employing monolingual housekeepers or nannies who would speak the minority language with the child is restricted to only a very few of these so called "elitist" bilingual families.

In the cases reported, parents differed considerably with respect to their consistency in following the 'one parent–one language' principle, indicating that a lack of consistency in language choice correlates with the children's reluctance to actively use the minority language. Arnberg (1984) suggested that the child's lack of motivation to actively use the minority language may also stem from the child's knowledge that the parent understands the stronger language. This was successfully overcome by Taeschner (1983) and Saunders (1982b), who both pretended that they did not understand when the child used the majority language, but most parents did not seem to have taken such steps or, in fact, stated the opposite (cf. Porsché 1983). Thus, the necessity to use the minority language actively was minimal for some of the children.

From a psychological point of view, the prestige of the minority language internationally would be a promoting or deterring factor in establishing productive bilingualism (Porsché 1975). The cases of English-Swedish families in Sweden (Arnberg 1981c), however, showed that this aspect was irrelevant for the children. It is likely that the local prestige of a language, as created in the family and the immediate community, is of greater importance to the young child than the much more abstract and remote, probably unknown, international prestige. The more immediate prestige of a minority language is very much due to the attitudes towards bilingualism within and outside the family (Fantini 1985).

Arnberg (1981b,c) found that parents who spoke the minority language to the children had difficulties coping with being the only speaker of another language in the family and in the immediate community. Particularly stressful were situations in which the children answered in the majority language, usually leading to the minority language being spoken less by the parent as well. Most parents are uninformed about the course which the young child's bilingual development is likely to take, and they are unprepared for the periods of reluctance to speak the minority language during the second stage. Consequently, they are disappointed with the child's apparent failure to become bilingual, and they give up prematurely (Saunders 1982b:29) to either insist that the child uses the minority language actively or to speak it themselves.

A child's failure at becoming a productive bilingual is commonly rationalized with a lack of aptitude for learning languages in the family or with a child's lower intelligence as compared with children who succeeded in the endeavour (Leopold 1949:152, 1957:251).

From an interactional point of view, one might want to argue that all children are naturally equipped to acquire languages, but that the verbal input which children receive in the minority language from their parents varies with respect to its richness. The accounts of successful establishment of productive bilingualism presented above differ from those which documented the settling for receptive bilingualism or the abandonment of the attempt altogether in that the former all made a point of mentioning their special efforts in creating a rich verbal environment through extensive conversations with the child, as well as the provision of books and records, excursions and overt teaching approaches. Arnberg (1979, 1981c:16) suggested that, "although it is not impossible to raise a child bilingually where the only source of second language input is from the child's family, this requires greater efforts from parents than was previously recognized".

1.4 Aims of this study

The divergence in attitudes to the degree of bilingualism which can reasonably be achieved through the 'one parent–one language' principle is striking. On the one hand, children are claimed to acquire two languages simultaneously as a matter of course of being exposed to them, on the other hand, there is an overwhelming number of parents who report that their endeavours were unsuccessful because their children never progressed past a limited amount of actively used words and a set number of rehearsed phrases in the minority language. The aim of the present study is to analyse this discrepancy more closely, and to see whether parents can further their child's active development in the minority language irrespective of the availability of other minority language speakers (grandparents, adult friends, child's peers) and material affluence (trips to the homeland of the minority language, home help who speaks the minority language). For that purpose, a sample of six German-English families who all followed the 'one parent–one language' principle was studied in detail.

The objectives of the study were the following:
– to gain some measure of the children's relative proficiency in the two languages;
– to establish a correlation between parental consistency of language choice and the child's willingness to adhere to the 'one parent–one language' principle;
– to determine whether the force with which parents insist on responses in the minority language makes a difference in the children becoming productive bilinguals;
– to examine the possibility that less exposure to the minority language can be compensated through quality of interaction;
– to examine the influence of overt and covert teaching techniques;
– to test the notion that mothers at home will automatically achieve higher degrees of bilingualism than working fathers;
– to contribute to the debate on the direction of verbal influence going from the parent to the child or from the child to the parent.

Four hypotheses were put forward. Firstly, it was hypothesized that in line with principles of first language acquisition and the 'motherese' hypothesis the input in the minority language must be of a type that is conducive to language acquisition. Secondly, the child's active acquisition of the minority language was expected to be related to the intensity with which the minority language parent makes use of overt and covert teaching techniques. Thirdly, in order to overcome the possible rejection of the minority language during the second stage, it was thought to be necessary that parents insist on the minority language being used by the child. And lastly, a mother at home who speaks the minority language to the child does not automatically have an advantage over a working father in transmitting the minority language to the child, instead the quality of interaction (hypotheses 1 to 3) outweighs the quantity of interaction.

The next four chapters are an account of my own empirical investigation regarding the degree of bilingualism in families who employ the 'one parent–one language' principle. Chapter 2 describes the collection and processing of the data and analyses the children's proficiency in German. In Chapters 3 to

5, the parents are compared with respect to the linguistic input they provided for their children. Parallels between type and quality of linguistic input and the children's proficiency in German will be drawn constantly.

Chapter 3 examines the language environment on a macro-level: it describes the extent of contact with German, the parents' attitudes to bilingualism, and the degree of consistency of and insistence on the 'one parent–one language' principle. Chapter 4 represents the main body of this study: there the discourse structures in which each mother and each father engaged in interaction with their children are analysed. Chapter 5, then, looks more specifically at the teaching techniques which the parents employed.

Each of these chapters comprises a theoretical part in which the relevant literature is discussed. Chapters 3 to 5 also contain discussions of each family individually and interim conclusions with respect to the particular aspects analysed.

Integrated conclusions will be drawn in the final chapter and a follow-up of the children's further development in German will be given.

2. The Sample

2.1 Introduction

This chapter is devoted to the introduction of the empirical data on which the present investigation is based. I will first describe the means by which the data were collected, and then the ways in which the data were processed. A major part of this chapter will be taken up with the description of the children's language choice and proficiency. It seemed best to do that as part of the presentation of the data because the analysis of the data will be concerned with the relationship between the children's degree of bilingualism and the linguistic environments created by the parents throughout the rest of the book. Finally, the basic aspects of the analysis of the data in the forthcoming chapters will be discussed.

2.2 Data collection

The sample consisted of six bilingual German-English families, who fulfilled the following selection criteria: the children lived in nuclear families, were first born, and their parents had decided to raise the children bilingually from infancy by exposing them to both languages regularly on a 'one parent–one language' basis. The criterion of regular exposure since infancy made it actually quite difficult to find suitable subjects; hence it was not possible to match the children on the basis of their linguistic performance. Instead, they were matched by age. No attempt was made to control the sex of the children or the transmitter of the minority language. Young boys and girls have hardly ever been shown to differ significantly in their linguistic proficiency (Klann-Delius 1980); instead, parents have been found to differ in how they interact with boys and girls (Kavanaugh and Jen 1981; Masur 1982; Pieper 1984). Possible differences in the intensity of the verbal stimulation the children received are the focus of this investigation.

Four of the children were aged two years and eight months (2;8) and two of them were aged two years and four months (2;4) at the time of the first recording. Among the older children, there were two girls, Alice and Agnes, and two boys, Keith and Jacob. The two younger children were girls, Fiona and Trudy. Only Alice and Jacob did not have a younger sibling. All of the children were being cared for mainly by their mothers at home. The parents ranged in age from late twenties to mid-thirties. The parents' educational standards were assigned to either of two groups: very high or high. In the group with very high educational standards both parents held higher university degrees, in the group with high educational standards one parent held a basic university degree and one parent a degree from another tertiary institution. In five of the families, it was the mother who spoke German to the children; only Keith was spoken to in German by his father. All of the English-speaking parents were native speakers; three of the German-speaking mothers were native speakers, two were second-generation speakers, and Keith's father had learned German as a foreign language. Table 2.1 summarizes the basic characteristics of the sample thus far.

Table 2.1: The sample

	Keith	Alice	Jacob	Agnes	Fiona	Trudy
age	2;8	2;8	2;8	2;8	2;4	2;4
sex	male	female	male	female	female	female
siblings	yes	no	no	yes	yes	yes
age of parents	early 30's	late.20's	late 20's	mid.30's	early.30's	mid.30's
education of parents	inter-mediate	inter-mediate	inter-mediate	high	inter-mediate	high
German-speaking parent	father	mother	mother	mother	mother	mother
parent's acquisition of German	foreign language	second generation	native speaker	native speaker	native speaker	second generation

Initially, each set of parents was interviewed about the history of their child's linguistic development, about the family's extent of contact with German-speaking people, cultural activities, media etc., and about the parents' experiences as bilinguals in general and as a bilingual family in particular. The information drawn from these interviews will be presented in Chapter 3. Within a week after the initial interview, each family was visited for one whole day and two half days in close succession. It was intended that during the first day, parents and children would become more familiar with me, the researcher, and become accustomed to my presence. This was also a time for me to learn about the family's routines, to test the equipment and to accustom the child to wearing the radio-microphone.

During the first day, a translated version of the auditory comprehension test of the *Preschool Language Scale* (Zimmermann, Steiner and Pond 1979) was administered in order to test the level of the children's comprehension in German independently of situational or parental decoding clues. I am well aware of the problematic nature of such a procedure, especially with regard to the numerical outcome of the test. In fact, the children achieved unexpectedly good results. I attributed that partly to the lag in time and cultural setting between standardization and present usage. Some of the items tested as developmental milestones seemed to have gained popularity as objects of conscious teaching among the parents, thus allowing the children to perform well in areas which were formerly believed to be beyond the children's capacity at that age. The translation from English to German has, of course, further diminished the representativeness of the test in a broader scope. The results will be discussed in section 2.5 of this chapter.

Since lay-people at times attribute children's successful acquisition of active language skills in a minority language to temperamental characteristics of the child, the parents were asked to fill in the *Toddler Temperamental Scale* by Fullard, McDevitt and Carey (1978). The evaluation of the scale indicated that all but one child were easier than average in temperament (see Table 2.2). Again, the results of such a test have to be treated with caution. Nevertheless, they demonstrated the temperamental differences between Jacob and the other children in the sample (cf. 2.5.4).

Table 2.2: Toddler Temperamental Scale

Keith	Alice	Jacob	Agnes	Fiona	Trudy
intermediate low	easy	difficult and slow-to-warm-up	intermediate low	easy	easy

The actual audio recordings commenced on the day of the second meeting. The child was wearing a radio-microphone of the type Unisound LM-78. All recordings were done with a small portable radio-recorder. The recordings took place on both the second and the third day. They began in the middle of the afternoon and continued until the child was put to bed for the night. This way a good selection of family activities was recorded, including some play in the afternoon, mealtime, bathtime, dressing and bedside routines.

Six months later, the auditory comprehension test and the audio recordings were repeated in order to determine whether progress or regression had taken place in the children's acquisition of German and to ascertain the parents' relative stability in the ways in which they interacted with their children. The families were again visited for one day in order to re-establish familiarity between researcher and child. The auditory comprehension test was administered on that day. The following day, the family's general activities during the afternoon and evening were recorded.

The researcher was present throughout the recordings, supplementing the taped material with her own observations and information provided by the parents. In all cases, she was welcomed into the families as a friend, and she tried to behave as such as much as possible.

2.3 Processing of data

The information gathered through the initial interview and from the observations during the recordings provided the material for the description of the sociolinguistic situation of each of the families in Chapter 3. Chapters 4 and 5 are based on the analysis of the audio recorded material. A substantial part of continuous family activities was transcribed for each family at both times of recording (cf. 2.4). DuBois et als.' (1988) notational system was chosen for the transcriptions. However, some modifications had to be introduced, current with the demands of the bilingual texts.

By and large, words were noted according to the orthographic rules for either English or German. If a word could not be identified as being either English or German by the way it was written, phonetic symbols following the International Phonetic Alphabet were used. Likewise, consistent phonetic diversions or recurring non-words were noted in phonetic transcriptions. Pauses were measured in tenths of seconds. The absolute length of a pause, however, received its significance for the ongoing interaction in relation to the speed with

which the individual speaker talked and to the speed with which the participants in the conversation usually took turns. Unmeasured pauses were very
short in relation to the speaker's speed of speech, *i.e.* usually shorter than two
tenths of a second. The symbols used throughout the transcriptions are presented in the Appendix.

2.4 The transcripts

In each family, the transcription commenced just before dinner and lasted until
the child was put to bed. If the interaction between the child and one or the other
parent proved too limited during this period, another stretch of interaction
between the child and that parent was included from earlier in the afternoon.
In the case of Agnes, no cohesive stretches of verbal interaction took place
during the afternoon. Consequently, the transcription made from the first recording in Agnes's family was with 57 minutes considerably shorter than the
transcriptions made for the other five families. Table 2.3 indicates the length
of time transcribed from interactions between parents and children in each
family, the intensity of verbal interaction in each of the families as well as the
varying distribution of verbal interaction in the father-child and mother-child
dyads.

Table 2.3: Length and distribution of verbal interaction during the first recording

	Keith	Alice	Jacob	Agnes	Fiona	Trudy
length of recording	129 min.	110 min.	150 min.	57 min.	138 min.	141 min.
total moves	1738	1608	2592	577	1437	2439
moves per minute	13.45	14.59	17.26	10.08	10.40	17.29
moves/min.: F–C	11.02	6.26	4.15	7.13	3.40	6.84
moves/ min.: M–C	2.43	8.33	13.11	2.95	7.00	10.45

The length of the verbal interaction transcribed from the second recording again varied considerably with 53 minutes in Agnes's family and between
112 and 132 minutes in the remaining five families. Wherever possible, the
transcripts covered the same types of activities as those during the first recording. In order to adjust the transcripts for length and to balance the interaction between mother and child and father and child, additional stretches of interaction were included from the afternoon. This was impossible again, however, in Agnes's family. Table 2.4 presents the length and distribution of the

verbal interaction transcribed from the second recording. A short description of the contents of the transcripts from each of the families follows.

Table 2.4: Length and distribution of verbal interaction during the second recording

	Keith	Alice	Jacob	Agnes	Fiona	Trudy
length of recording	132 min.	112 min.	123 min.	53 min.	128 min.	124 min.
total moves	1111	1312	1304	612	1209	1269
moves per minute	8.38	11.70	10.57	11.55	9.42	10.70
moves/min.: F–C	4.93	5.54	3.05	2.74	4.96	5.03
moves/min.: M–C	3.45	6.16	7.52	8.81	4.47	5.14

In <u>Keith's family</u>, the activities during which transcription for the first recording took place began just before dinner and lasted through dinner and bathtime. Since Keith went to bed very late on that occasion, the recording of the period between bathing and going to bed was not transcribed. This time was spent with further play, similar to that which took place before taking a bath. For practical reasons, the final going to bed sequence had to be transcribed from the tapes of the following day. During and after dinner, when both parents were present, Keith tended to address predominantly his mother, but was addressed and responded to mainly by his father. Before bathing, the father spent some time reading and playing with Keith, then gave him his bath. The mother put Keith to bed. The transcription from the second recording commenced with the beginning of the family dinner, followed by some playtime during which Keith and his father read books and assembled puzzles. The mother gave Keith and his brother a bath and dressed Keith. Afterwards, Keith spent some more time playing with his father before the mother took him to bed and read him a story.

The transcription of the first recording in <u>Alice's family</u> covered dinner time, bathtime and going to bed, in that order. The father conversed with Alice mainly over dinner, whereas the mother gave her a bath and put her to bed. The activities which were transcribed from the second recording were taken from both days of researcher presence. Since the father did not come home from work until after dinner on the day which was supposed to be used for transcription, most of the recording from the previous day was transcribed. The activities covered the preparation of dinner on the second day, and dinner, story time and going to bed on the first day. Mother and child prepared dinner together, and the father read Alice a few bedtime stories. During dinner and while going to bed, Alice was involved in interaction with both her parents.

In Jacob's family, the activities transcribed from the first recording included a play session between father and son in the middle of the afternoon. They began again shortly before dinner, lasted through dinner, but were interrupted for the following forty minutes of play between mother and child. They started again with their last twenty minutes of play, continued through bathtime and ended when Jacob was put to bed. During the second recording, Jacob fell asleep over dinner. Therefore, a substantial part of the activities during the afternoon had to be transcribed. The transcriptions began in the middle of the afternoon with the father helping the child to start a string of beads. They were interrupted for the following fifty minutes, during which mother and child watched a children's program on television, but recommenced when, firstly, father and child played for a short while, and then mother and child continued to play; they fed the guinea pig and ate some fruit. Later, Jacob was trying to help his mother with the preparation of dinner, then he played with his father, and finally he helped his father clean the barbecue outside. During dinner, Jacob mainly talked to his mother.

In Agnes's family, the activities transcribed from the first recording commenced some time before dinner and continued through dinner, bathtime and going to bed. The father performed more of the child-care tasks than did the mother. The activities were kept relatively short by the parents, thus yielding only little conversational data. The verbal interaction taped during the afternoon was scarce, limited to only short exchanges and difficult to understand. It was therefore not added. The transcription from the second recording started in the early evening with Agnes's bathtime. She then had something to eat all by herself and was taken to bed by her mother. This time, the mother was more involved in child-care tasks than was the father. The activities were as short during the second recording as they were during the first recording. Moreover, hardly any verbal exchanges between parents and Agnes took place during the afternoon. Agnes spent most of the time playing on her own or with a neighbour's child while the parents conversed with each other or, later on, with the neighbour. Additional material from the afternoon could, therefore, not be included.

In Fiona's family, the activities transcribed from the first recording started in the late afternoon with some conversation between father and child. Subsequently, the mother gave Fiona a bath and prepared dinner while Fiona kept her company. Fiona was put straight to bed after dinner. Most of the child-care activities were performed by the mother, whereas the father mainly conversed with Fiona in the afternoon, during dinner and at bedtime. For the second recording, the transcribed activities commenced in the middle of the afternoon with mother and child packing suitcases, were interrupted until the father came home and conversed with Fiona about the imminent trip to Europe, then continued through dinner, but were interrupted again for a researcher induced play session which was not used for the analysis. Transcriptions were resumed when father and child started tidying up after the play session and continued until Fiona had gone to bed. Both parents were equally involved in the child-care tasks during the second recording.

The activities which were transcribed from the first recording in Trudy's family started shortly before the father began to prepare dinner, continued through dinner, bathtime, and ended when Trudy was put to bed. Both mother and father took part in the child-care activities. The father prepared dinner, supervised Trudy's meal and gave her a bath. The mother dressed her and put her to bed. For the second recording, the activities which were transcribed started in the late afternoon with mother and child playing and talking, continued through dinner and bathtime and ended when Trudy had been put to bed. Again, both parents took part in the child-care activities. The mother gave Trudy dinner and dressed her, and the father bathed her and put her to bed.

2.5 The children's language

The children's language proficiency forms the basis to which the analysis of the parent's verbal behaviour in the major part of this book will be related. In the following, the children's performance in the Auditory Comprehension Test by Zimmermann, Steiner and Pond (1979), their language choice and their linguistic progression from the first to the second recording will be presented, as well as two cases of language refusal. Finally, the stage which each child's bilingual development had reached will be discussed.

2.5.1 Auditory comprehension test

The results of the translated version of Zimmermann's et al. (1979) *Auditory Comprehension Test* are shown in Table 2.5. The figures depict the children's comprehension level in relation to their age. The quotient of 100 indicated the 50% mark at the time and place of standardization. The function of the test for the present sample lies solely in determining that all six children understood

German appropriately for their age and that their comprehension was not just due to the familiar interlocutor, verbal routines or situational clues.

Table 2.5: Auditory comprehension quotient

	Keith	Alice	Jacob	Agnes	Fiona	Trudy
1st recording	131	131	169	108	139	129
2nd recording	114	126	142	107	137	141

2.5.2 Language choice

Each child-utterance was classified as to whether it was uttered in German, English, in a mixture between German and English or in neither one nor the other language. The last category consisted mainly of names, non-words and words which can be equally well attributed to German as to English. A German word plus a "neither" element was automatically categorized as German, as was an English word plus a "neither" element categorized as English. Table 2.6 shows the children's language choice towards their German-speaking parents during the first recording. The calculation was based on the total of each child's codable utterances towards his/her German-speaking parent during that particular recording. Table 2.6 indicates that Keith, Fiona and Trudy used German in interaction with their German-speaking parents in about 50% of all their utterances. Alice and Agnes used German in about 20% and Jacob in only 8% of the utterances directed towards their German-speaking parents. Correspondingly, Alice and Agnes addressed their German-speaking mothers in English in nearly 60% and Jacob in nearly 80%. All children mixed German and English at times.

Table 2.6: Children's language choice towards German-speaking parents during the first recording

	Keith	Fiona	Alice	Jacob	Agnes	Trudy
German	48.4%	55.8%	20.3%	8.3%	19.1%	55.3%
English	40.8%	21.8%	159.7%	78.1%	57.5%	23.1%
Mixed	8.5%	16.1%	10.8%	8.2%	8.5%	10.5%
Neither	2.3%	6.3%	9.2%	5.4%	14.9%	11.1%

Six months later, the children's language choice polarized the sample even more strongly (see Table 2.7). Alice and Agnes had cut down their use of German to the level of Jacob. Keith and Fiona had increased their German considerably. However, Trudy, who had spoken as much German as Fiona during the first recording, spoke only about half as much German during the second recording as she did during the first recording. The children's relative use of English changed accordingly: Alice, Agnes and Trudy used more English during the second recording than they did during the first recording, and Keith and Fiona used less. The distribution of English and German in Jacob's speech remained stable. The relative amount of mixed utterances decreased substantially in Keith's and Fiona's speech, slightly in Alice's and Trudy's speech, they stayed the same in Jacob's speech, but increased a little in Agnes's speech.

Table 2.7: Children's language choice towards German-speaking parents during the second recording

	Keith	Fiona	Alice	Jacob	Agnes	Trudy
German	83.3%	68.8%	6.1%	8.3%	10.9%	30.9%
English	10.2%	12.0%	82.7%	79.5%	69.4%	55.7%
Mixed	3.8%	7.6%	7.2%	8.0%	10.2%	9.4%
Neither	2.7%	11.6%	4.0%	4.2%	9.5%	4.0%

Tables 2.8 and 2.9 show the children's language choice in interaction with their English-speaking parents. All children used English in interaction with their English-speaking parents more consistently than they used German with their German-speaking parents. The two younger children, Fiona and Trudy, showed stronger inconsistencies with their English-speaking parents than did the older children during the first recording, but not any more so during the second recording. Mixed utterances were also rarer in interaction with the English-speaking parents than with the German-speaking parents.

The children's utterances in each of the three language varieties, *i.e.* German, English and mixed, could be further identified as belonging to one of six modes: original, imitated, reiterated or translated utterances, polar responses or games. The mode "games" was used extremely rarely and in only

Table 2.8: Children's language choice towards English-speaking parents during the first recording

	Keith	Fiona	Alice	Jacob	Agnes	Trudy
German	——	8.2%	5.1%	0.9%	1.9%	13.5%
English	99.2%	68.5%	84.8%	92.6%	77.1%	66.8%
Mixed	——	4.1%	6.0%	1.3%	3.8%	10.9%
Neither	0.8%	19.2%	4.1%	5.2%	17.2%	8.8%

Table 2.9.: Children's language choice towards English-speaking parents during the second recording

	Keith	Fiona	Alice	Jacob	Agnes	Trudy
German	1.9%	3.1%	3.9%	1.9%	1.6%	3.4%
English	94.3%	87.2%	92.1%	86.2%	83.6%	85.3%
Mixed	2.4%	4.6%	3.0%	8.8%	3.3%	5.4%
Neither	1.4%	5.1%	1.0%	3.1%	11.5%	5.9%

one parent-child dyad. It will therefore not be discussed any further. *Polar responses* included accepting and rejecting moves in general, not just reactions to polar questions. Utterances in this class were characteristically very short. Table 2.10 shows their realization in the three language varieties in interaction with each of the German- and English-speaking parents at both times of recording.

Table 2.10: Polar responses

	rec.	Keith	Fiona	Alice	Jacob	Agnes	Trudy
I	1st	4.3%	8.1%	3.0%	2.5%	——	6.9%
t	2nd	1.5%	6.7%	0.8%	1.8%	0.7%	4.7%
II	1st	6.1%	——	10.3%	6.8%	10.6%	6.9%
	2nd	0.1%	2.7%	8.2%	8.3%	17.0%	2.7%
III	1st	——	——	——	——	——	——
	2nd	——	——	0.4%	0.3%	——	——
IV	1st	——	1.4%	1.6%	——	0.6%	2.6%
	2nd	——	——	——	——	——	0.4%
V	1st	9.2%	15.1%	18.6%	17.8%	9.6%	9.6%
	2nd	1.9%	18.3%	26.9%	14.5%	16.4%	8.0%
VI	1st	——	——	——	——	——	——
	2nd	——	——	——	——	——	——

I = German to German-speaking parent; II = English to German-speaking parent; III = Mixed to German-speaking parent; IV = German to English-speaking parent; V = English to English-speaking parent; VI = Mixed to English-speaking parent.

Some interesting trends can be noted from the language distribution over polar responses. Only Keith, Fiona and Trudy used "ja" and "nein" regularly, although alongside "yes" and "no", in interaction with their German-speaking parents during both times of recording. Alice, Jacob and Agnes clearly preferred English over German. This trend was even stronger during the second recording than during the first recording, and led to isolated mixed polar responses in the cases of Alice and Jacob:

(1)   [Al II, 975 - 976]
     M: *wirst du gut schlafen?*
           'will you sleep well?'
     C: *ja I WILL*
           'yes I WILL'

(2)   [Ja II, 254 - 255]
     M: *die Katrin kann mit der Farm spielen.*
           'Katrin can play with the farm.'
     C: *ja. .. sure.*
           'yes. .. sure.'

In both cases, the child had seemingly tried to repair the initial German reaction. German polar responses were rarely addressed to the English-speaking parents during the first recording and, except for one instance, never during the second recording.

Child *reiterations* have been shown to be progressive (cf. Käsermann 1980). Children realize a break in the communication or are queried, and therefore modify their utterance on the grammatical, phonological or semantic level. Bilingual children have the added option of repairing a difficulty in the communication through a re-evaluation of their language choice. If the two languages were well established and balanced, the child would be unlikely to reiterate in the "wrong" language. Inappropriate language choice for reiterations indicates that the child cannot yet differentiate the two languages properly, lacks

Table 2.11: Reiterations

	rec.	Keith	Fiona	Alice	Jacob	Agnes	Trudy
I	1st	6.4%	8.8%	3.6%	1.0%	4.3%	3.9%
	2nd	20.2%	8.5%	———	0.5%	0.7%	4.0%
II	1st	8.5%	9.8%	11.9%	23.3%	17.0%	3.6%
	2nd	2.3%	1.8%	15.0%	20.0%	15.0%	12.1%
III	1st	0.7%	6.7%	3.0%	2.0%	2.1%	2.1%
t	2nd	0.8%	0.5%	1.1%	1.3%	1.4%	2.0%
IV	1st	———	1.4%	0.8%	0.4%	———	1.8%
	2nd	1.0%	1.6%	———	1.3%	———	———
V	1st	20.0%	6.9%	10.4%	18.2%	15.9%	14.0%
	2nd	22.5%	11.7%	4.1%	17.0%	24.6%	18.1%
VI	1st	———	———	2.5%	0.4%	1.3%	1.3%
	2nd	———	2.0%	———	———	———	0.8%

I = German to German-speaking parent; II = English to German-speaking parent; III = Mixed to German-speaking parent; IV = German to English-speaking parent; V = English to English-speaking parent; VI = Mixed to English-speaking parent.

the necessary equivalents in the other language, or puts up a resistance to speaking one of the languages. Table 2.11 shows the use of reiterations in German, English or mixed German-English by the six children of the present sample.

In interaction with his German-speaking father, <u>Keith</u> used only slightly more reiterations in English than in German during the first recording. He increased the relative frequency of German reiterations drastically from the first to the second recording, and, at the same time, used less reiterations in English. <u>Fiona's</u> use of German and English reiterations towards her German-speaking mother was similar during the first recording. During the second recording, she had decreased the relative amount of English reiterations. Likewise, <u>Trudy</u> used reiterations in German about as often as reiterations in English when interacting with her German-speaking mother during the first recording. However, during the second recording, reiterations in English had increased considerably in her speech to her mother. <u>Alice, Jacob</u> and <u>Agnes</u> reiterated their utterances mainly in English at both times of recording.

In interaction with the English-speaking parents, reiterations in German were rare at both times of recording for all children. Mixed German-English reiterations were generally limited. However, they clearly occurred more often in interaction with the German-speaking parents than in interaction with the English-speaking parents, and more often at the younger age than at the older age. They can, therefore, be taken as a sign of the children's struggle to speak German on the one hand, and a sign of insufficient language differentiation on the other hand. Given the children's use of mixed German-English reiterations during the second recording compared with that of the first recording, Fiona had struggled to use German more consistently with her German-speaking mother at 2;4 years of age and succeeded to do so at 2;10 years of age. Alice, Jacob and Agnes did not seem to have made any strong attempts to speak German, but had clearly improved their differentiation between the two languages at the time of the second recording when they produced fewer mixed German-English reiterations with their German-speaking parents and none with their English-speaking parents. Only the two younger children, Trudy and Fiona, mixed German and English in reiterations addressed to their English-speaking fathers during the second recording.

The relevance of *imitating* adults' speech for children's language acquisition has been widely debated (For a discussion of this issue see Chapter 5). The amount of speech that is imitated from an adult model varies greatly from child to child, and it generally decreases as the child grows older. Table 2.12

presents the relative frequencies with which the children imitated their parents' linguistic models in English and German immediately, *i.e.* within the next three turns. Mixed German-English imitations involved a German element which was imitated and incorporated into the child's otherwise English utterance.

Table 2.12: Imitations

	rec.	Keith	Fiona	Alice	Jacob	Agnes	Trudy
I	1st	14.8%	7.7%	4.4%	1.7%	——	15.0%
	2nd	13.4%	11.7%	3.0%	2.9%	1.4%	7.4%
II	1st	——	0.4%	——	0.1%	1.4%	0.9%
	2nd	——	——	——	——	1.4%	——
III	1st	0.7%	——	2.6%	1.7%	——	0.3%
	2nd	——	——	3.0%	1.8%	2.0%	1.3%
IV	1st	——	——	1.1%	——	——	2.2%
	2nd	——	——	0.5%	——	——	0.8%
V	1st	10.0%	13.7%	6.9%	2.2%	4.6%	10.9%
	2nd	8.1%	8.2%	3.1%	4.4%	——	1.7%
VI	1st	——	——	1.4%	——	——	2.2%
	2nd	——	——	2.0%	5.0%	——	0.4%

I = German to German-speaking parent; II = English to German-speaking parent; III = Mixed to German-speaking parent; IV = German to English-speaking parent; V = English to English-speaking parent; VI = Mixed to English-speaking parent.

Keith and Fiona imitated both their parents' linguistic models more readily at both times of recording than did any of the other children. Mixed German-English imitations were nearly non-existent in their speech. Once, during the first recording, Fiona said something to her mother which was, in fact, an immediate imitation of her father; hence the English imitation towards her German-speaking mother. Alice imitated both her parents less than did Keith and Fiona. Her imitative behaviour did not differ much in frequency from one parent to the other. A substantial part of Alice's imitations of her mother's German resulted in mixed German-English utterances. She was also able to copy some German from her father (see 3.4.2.1 for discussion of the parents' language choice). Jacob rarely imitated his mother's German, but did so slightly more during the second recording than during the first recording. He was slightly more willing to copy his father's linguistic model. The mixed German-English imitations in interaction with his father during the second recording were the result of him not knowing a word in English which he had just heard from his mother. They all happened in close succession. Agnes displayed the least imitative behaviour of all the children in the sample, and only few of her imitations were straight German. During the first recording, she only copied from her father's linguistic model, whereas during the second recording she only imitated her mother's speech. Trudy imitated her mother's German frequently during the first recording, and although less during the second recording, still more often than did Alice, Jacob and Agnes. Mixed German-English imitations increased from the first to the second recording. In interaction with her father, Trudy imitated freely during the first recording. She also had the chance to imitate some German from him, as well as mixed German-English utterances. During the second recording, Trudy imitated her father's linguistic model only infrequently.

Translations are a diverse mode in bilingual children's speech. They could entail a translation of the child's own or someone else's English word or phrase into German for the benefit of the German-speaking parent. Or they could mean a translation of the child's own or someone else's German phrase or word into English for the benefit of the English-speaking parent. However, the children also translated German elements into English or mixed German-English utterances while still interacting with the German-speaking parent. Table 2.13 shows in more detail how the children made use of translations.

Table 2.13: Translations

	rec.	Keith	Fiona	Alice	Jacob	Agnes	Trudy
I	1st	1.4%	0.4%	0.6%	0.2%	———	———
	2nd	2.3%	1.8%	———	0.5%	———	1.3%
II	1st	3.2%	0.4%	1.6%	5.0%	———	1.8%
	2nd	1.5%	0.5%	1.1%	3.4%	0.7%	1.4%
III	1st	0.5%	0.4%	0.2%	0.1%	———	0.3%
	2nd	———	0.9%	———	0.8%	0.7%	———
IV	1st	———	1.4%	———	———	———	———
	2nd	———	———	———	———	———	———
V	1st	———	———	1.1%	———	———	0.9%
	2nd	1.4%	0.4%	———	———	———	0.4%
VI	1st	———	———	———	———	———	———
	2nd	———	———	———	———	———	———

I = German to German-speaking parent; II = English to German-speaking parent; III = Mixed to German-speaking parent; IV = German to English-speaking parent; V = English to English-speaking parent; VI = Mixed to English-speaking parent.

Keith, Fiona, Jacob and Trudy all increased the frequency with which they translated from English to German from the first to the second recording while interacting with their German-speaking parents. Alice translated into German for her mother a few times during the first recording, but not at all during the second recording. Agnes did not translate into German at either recording. Translations from German to English were generally more frequent than translations from English to German. However, the former decreased from the first to the second recording in the interactions between Keith, Alice, Jacob, Trudy and their respective German-speaking parents. The frequency of translations by Fiona did not change from the first to the second recording, and Agnes, who had not translated at all during the first recording, translated into English a few times during the second recording. Partial translations into English were dropped altogether by Keith, Alice and Trudy during the second recording, but increased from the first to the second recording in Fiona's and Jacob's speech. Agnes took up partial translations alongside complete translations into English in interaction with her mother during the second recording.

Both the increase of translations into German as well as the decrease of translations into English in interaction with the German-speaking parents are signs of the children's growing ability to differentiate between the two languages. Partial translations indicate a lack in linguistic knowledge of the target language.

The children rarely translated in interaction with their English-speaking parents. Keith's and Fiona's translations into English during the second recording were interactionally appropriate language choices. Fiona's translations into German during the first recording were due to her not having known the English equivalent before her father taught her. They were therefore a form of linguistic practice. Alice's and Trudy's translations into English were results of their fathers' inconsistent language choices (cf. 3.4.2.1).

Finally, but most importantly, the frequencies of *original* utterances in the three language varieties of the children's speech will be discussed. Original utterances were defined as all those utterances which were not immediate imitations, reiterations, translations or polar responses, but which were examples of the children's independent and creative language use. In contrast to imitations, which are often the easiest way for a child to express something, or reiterations, which are somewhat forced onto the child, original utterances represent most clearly the children's *intentional* language choice. (Translations would do that too, if they were used more frequently by all the children).

Mixed German-English utterances in the mode "original" refer to the German elements as being original. The English elements could belong to any of the other modes. Table 2.14 shows the children's distribution of original utterances over the three language varieties.

During the first recording, <u>Keith</u>, <u>Fiona</u> and <u>Trudy</u> addressed their German-speaking parents with original German utterances between 21% and 31% of the time, which was more often than for <u>Alice</u>, <u>Jacob</u> or <u>Agnes</u>. At the time of the second recording, the relative frequency of original German utterances had increased to 46% and 40% in the speech of Keith and Fiona respectively, but it had decreased to about 9% in Trudy's speech. Now Trudy used German "originally and intentionally" as little as did Alice, Jacob and Agnes.

The "original and intentional" use of English by these three children developed correspondingly. Whereas <u>Keith</u>, <u>Fiona</u> and <u>Trudy</u> addressed their German-speaking parents with original English utterances between 10% and 23% of the time, <u>Alice</u>, <u>Jacob</u> and <u>Agnes</u> did so between 30% and 43% during the first recording. During the second recording, Keith's and Fiona's original English utterances had reduced to 6% and 7% respectively, whereas Trudy's original English utterances had increased to 40%. Therefore, Trudy spoke as much English with her German-speaking mother during the second recording as did Alice, Jacob and Agnes with their German-speaking mothers. Mixed German-English utterances decreased in all children's speech from the first to the second recording.

Table 2.14: Original utterances

	rec.	Keith	Fiona	Alice	Jacob	Agnes	Trudy
I	1st	21.0%	30.9%	8.7%	2.9%	14.9%	29.4%
	2nd	45.8%	39.9%	2.6%	2.6%	8.2%	8.7%
II	1st	23.0%	11.2%	35.8%	43.0%	29.8%	9.9%
	2nd	6.1%	7.2%	57.7%	47.9%	35.4%	39.6%
III	1st	6.9%	9.1%	5.1%	4.4%	6.4%	7.8%
	2nd	3.1%	6.3%	3.0%	3.9%	6.1%	6.0%
IV	1st	——	4.1%	1.4%	0.4%	1.3%	7.0%
	2nd	1.0%	1.6%	3.6%	0.6%	1.6%	2.1%
V	1st	60.0%	32.9%	47.7%	54.6%	44.0%	31.4%
	2nd	60.3%	48.6%	57.9%	50.3%	42.6%	56.3%
VI	1st	——	4.1%	2.2%	0.9%	2.6%	7.4%
	2nd	2.3%	2.7%	1.0%	3.8%	3.3%	5.0%

I = German to German-speaking parent; II = English to German-speaking parent; III = Mixed to German-speaking parent; IV = German to English-speaking parent; V = English to English-speaking parent; VI = Mixed to English-speaking parent.

In interaction with their English-speaking parents, original German utterances were few. They were the result of a failure to switch to English in time, as in the case of Keith during the second recording, linguistic insecurity in the cases of Fiona, Jacob and Agnes, or due to the English-speaking father's German initiations in the case of Alice. The relatively high proportion of original German or mixed German-English utterances in Trudy's speech to her father during the first recording was related to her father's use of German and mixed German-English utterances when he was talking to her (cf. 3.4.2.1).

So far, we have established a basic difference in these children's bilingual language development as far as the balance of the two languages in the children's speech was concerned: although English was the dominant language for all children at both times of recording, Keith and Fiona used German more often and more freely than did Alice, Jacob and Agnes. Moreover, Keith and Fiona used German more often and more appropriately during the second recording than during the first recording, whereas Alice, Jacob and Agnes spoke even less German with their German-speaking parents when their speech was recorded again six months later. Trudy started out speaking German as frequently as did Keith and Fiona, that is, she used German regularly and freely during the first recording, but at the time of the second recording, Trudy spoke as little German as did Alice, Jacob and Agnes.

2.5.3 Language progression

It is now time to determine whether the children's language proficiency in German developed parallel to their proficiency in English from the first to the second recording. The complexity of the children's language was measured in terms of their mean length of utterance (MLU) in words. Table 2.15 presents the children's MLU in general, distinguishing only between their speech to their German- and English-speaking parents.

Table 2.15: Children's MLU in general

	rec.	Keith	Fiona	Alice	Jacob	Agnes	Trudy
I	1st	2.47	3.24	2.91	2.60	2.34	1.86
	2nd	2.94	2.92	3.56	3.87	2.50	3.30
II	1st	2.67	2.12	3.38	2.32	2.49	2.04
	2nd	3.61	2.99	2.78	3.06	2.97	3.02

I = with German-speaking parent; II = with English-speaking parent.

Table 2.15 indicates that Keith's, Jacob's, Agnes's and Trudy's speech gained in complexity from the first to the second recording independently of whether they interacted with their fathers or with their mothers. Alice's speech seemed to have decreased in complexity in interaction with her English-speaking father, and Fiona's language complexity seemed to have decreased in interaction with her German-speaking mother.

Table 2.16: Children's MLU in the three language varieties

	rec.	Keith	Fiona	Alice	Jacob	Agnes	Trudy
I	1st	2.33	2.62	2.35	1.57	3.00	1.71
	2nd	3.00	3.14	2.24	1.91	1.67	3.09
II	1st	2.52	4.52	3.21	2.77	2.30	1.88
	2nd	2.70	2.30	3.76	3.17	2.63	3.37
III	1st	3.35	4.547	3.83	3.06	3.25	3.31
	2nd	4.10	4.77	3.90	4.36	3.87	4.57
IV	1st	———	3.00	1.42	1.00	1.67	1.94
	2nd	3.00	1.43	1.00	1.00	3.00	1.25
V	1st	2.69	2.28	3.56	2.39	2.73	2.00
	2nd	3.62	3.13	2.84	3.02	3.26	3.15
VI	1st	———	2.6	4.00	3.33	4.50	3.16
	2nd	5.00	3.42	3.83	4.57	2.50	4.13

I = German to German-speaking parent; II = English to German-speaking parent; III = Mixed to German-speaking parent; IV = German to English-speaking parent; V = English to English-speaking parent; VI = Mixed to English-speaking parent.

Table 2.16 separates the children's linguistic progression into the three possible language varieties. One can see from Table 2.16 that the complexity of Keith's language increased in all three varieties in interaction with both his parents. However, his German was more complex than his English in interaction with his German-speaking father. The linguistic complexity of Fiona's German towards her German-speaking mother increased from the first to the second recording. However, the complexity of her English decreased drastically during the same interval; hence the overall decrease of MLU in Fiona's speech to her mother. In interaction with her father the trend was reversed: Fiona used more complex English utterances but less complex German utterances during the second recording than she did during the first recording. Keith and Fiona produced more complex German than English utterances in interaction with their German-speaking parents by the time of the second recording. Alice's German decreased in complexity in interaction with both her German-speak-

ing mother and her English-speaking father from the first to the second recording. Surprisingly, she also used less complex English utterances in interaction with her father during the second recording than during the first recording. The English she used in interaction with her mother, however, had
progressed past her former level of complexity in interaction with her father
by the time of the second recording. Jacob's linguistic ability developed towards longer MLU in both German and English while interacting with his
mother, but his development in German lagged way behind his development
in English. He spoke in slightly more complex English to his father than he
did to his mother. Agnes's German decreased drastically in complexity in interaction with her German-speaking mother from the first to the second recording. At the same time, her English increased slightly in complexity. Due
to only one utterance during the second recording, the complexity of Agnes's
German increased by the same drastic rate in interaction with her father as it
decreased in interaction with her mother. This result can be disregarded.
Agnes's English utterances addressed to her father were more complex during the second recording than during the first recording. They were also more
complex than her English utterances addressed to her mother. Both Trudy's
German and English became more advanced in interaction with her German-
speaking mother from the first to the second recording. In interaction with her
English-speaking father, however, only her English progressed, whereas her
German regressed. Although Trudy's German gained in complexity from the
first to the second recording comparable to Keith's and Fiona's, Trudy used
more complex English than German when addressing her German-speaking
mother. In that respect, she behaved more like Alice, Jacob and Agnes than
like Keith and Fiona.

Mixed German-English utterances increased in complexity from the first
to the second recording in most cases as well. At the same time, they tended
to be longer than utterances in either German or English. Alice and Agnes,
however, constituted exceptions to this rule. In interaction with their English-
speaking fathers, mixed utterances in their speech decreased in complexity from
the first to the second recording. In Agnes's case, the mixed utterances were
also shorter than the English utterances during the second recording.

In sum, the analysis of the children's mean length of utterances in words
parallels the analysis of the children's language choice in that it separates them
into two groups: on the one hand, Keith and Fiona, who were willing to speak
German and who progressed in German, and on the other hand, Alice, Jacob
and Agnes, who did not want to speak German and who did not progress.

Trudy's German had progressed although she did not want to speak German any more during the second recording.

2.5.4 Refusal to speak German

Keith and Fiona took the path which would have been expected by theoreticians, that is, of acquiring both languages parallely, one language from each of their parents. In contrast to them, Alice and Agnes never really developed German to the same extent as they did English. However, only Jacob and Trudy showed signs of active rejection of German.

As compared with the other children in the sample, Jacob translated most frequently from German into English at both times of recording. At the same time, Jacob repeated less of his mother's German model than did any of the other children (except for Agnes during the first recording). This often involved a special effort by Jacob, as shown in the following example from the transcript:

(3)   [Ja I, 185 - 191]
    C: *I want to piss*
         'I want to wee'
    M: *geh schnell*
         'go quickly'
    C: *yeah. I geh schnell*
         'yeah. I go quickly'
         quick run quick run
    M: *jetzt geh schnell Jacob*
         'now go quickly Jacob'
    C: <p *quick run quick run* p>

Such incidences were numerous, usually without the accidental imitation. That these translations meant a special effort on Jacob's part was also indicated by the fact that they were often delayed by several turns, therefore being interactionally somewhat out of line. In comparison, Alice and Trudy, and even Agnes during the second recording, would have been quite content with integrating part of their mother's German phrase into their otherwise English sentence. After all, that is the easiest way to go. The argument of language rejection via the amount of imitations from his mother's linguistic model is further strengthened by the fact that Jacob was more prepared to imitate what his father had said to him than what his mother had said to him. The combination of high levels of German to English translations and low levels of German imitations indicate that Jacob refused to speak German consciously. Incidentally, Jacob was the only child who rated difficult on the Toddler Temperamental Scale (cf. 2.2). Arnberg (1987) cited a study by Metraux (1965) who found a relationship between children's personality factors and their degree of bilingualism. Metraux's "results showed that extroverted children who easily adapted to new situations had an easier time learning a second language than those who were introverted or slow in adapting to new situations" (Arnberg 1987:33).

The drop of translations and the increase of imitations from the first to the second recording, displayed a more relaxed attitude towards German at the time of the second recording. It gave the parents the impression that he talked more German during the second recording, although objectively he did not. Since Jacob imitated his father's English more frequently as well, he was probably more receptive of what had been said to him in general.

Trudy appeared to acquire German at much the same rate as did Keith and Fiona at the time of the first recording. At the time of the second recording, however, the amount of German she used in interaction with her German-speaking mother had dropped from 55.3% to 30.9%, and the amount of English had increased from 23.1% to 55.7%. Trudy reduced the frequency of her original German utterances most drastically. She also imitated less of her mother's model. Moreover, Trudy was equally likely to repair a communication problem in German or in English when talking to her mother during the first recording, but was three times as likely to reiterate in English than in German during the second recording. At the same time, she had started to call her father "Dad" instead of "Papa", although both parents used the German label exclusively. The mother reported that Trudy did not want to sing German songs any more and that she refused to translate well-known concepts into German when asked to do so by the baby-sitter. A metalinguistic incidence from the second recording illustrates her changed attitude to German:

(4)   [Tr II, 547 - 548]
        F: ((to M)) *ich möchte eine Tasse Kaffee bitte Mama,*
                'I would like a cup of coffee please Mum,'
                        (8.8)
        C: *Papa talk that funny language.*

2.5.5 Evaluation

The children of the present investigation all went through the first developmental stage as described by Taeschner (1983; cf. 1.2.5). By the time of the first recording, <u>Keith</u> and <u>Fiona</u> had entered the second stage. They had developed equivalents for part of their lexicon and addressed their parents in the appropriate language with higher-than-chance frequency. However, lexical interferences were frequent. Both children acquired the syntactic and morphological systems of German and English parallely. At the time of the second recording, Keith's and Fiona's bilingual development had reached the beginning of the third stage. They rigidly followed the 'one parent–one language' principle, but interferences from English to German still occurred. Most interferences were lexical interferences and word order interferences. All grammatical overextensions were intralinguistic; morphosyntactic interferences were not encountered during the recordings.

<u>Alice</u>, <u>Jacob</u> and <u>Agnes</u> had also entered the second developmental stage at the time of the first recording. They had realized that their mothers and fathers spoke different languages to them, and they had acquired equivalents in both languages for part of their vocabulary. However, according to their parents, Alice and Jacob used this new knowledge in order to avoid speaking German, and Agnes did not talk much to her mother at all. German sentence structure and morphosyntactic markers were virtually non-existent. Their English, on the other hand, developed appropriately for their age. At the time of the second recording, their German lagged behind their English even further.

<u>Trudy</u> had only just entered the second developmental stage at the time of the first recording. While during the first stage she spoke nearly only German to both her parents, she now acquired more and more English words as well as English equivalents for German words, and consequently spoke more English every day. She addressed each of her parents in the appropriate language with higher-than-chance frequency. However, her sentence structure was still rudimentary in both languages, and morphosyntactic markers had not appeared yet. By the time Trudy's family was recorded for the second time, Trudy had started to refuse to speak German. She now knew that her father did not understand much German and consequently avoided speaking German to him even if he addressed a few German words or sentences to her. She also preferred to speak English to her mother and approached her in English with higher-than-chance frequency. English word order had been established and was used in all utterances. Morphosyntactic markers appeared in English, but not in German. In sum, Trudy did not continue to develop towards balanced bilingualism.

As Taeschner (1983) had already indicated, children's bilingual development enters into a critical phase some time during the second stage. Once children become conscious of the fact that one of their parents speaks a language which is more or less exclusive to the interaction between that parent and the child, and once children have acquired the ability to express themselves in either of the two languages, they are also able to consciously choose to speak one or the other of the two languages. Two of the children in the present investigation took the path described by Taeschner: they continued to use both languages in interaction with their respective parents and developed both linguistic systems parallely; they had entered the third stage at the ages of 3;2 and 2;10 respectively and were on the way to becoming truly bilingual. The other four children, however, did not develop their bilingualism past realizing that each of their parents spoke a different language. In addition, although their comprehension of German increased, their reluctance to use German actively resulted in an ever widening gap between their ability to express themselves in English and in German.

2.6 Analysis of the data

The analysis of the data centres around the following question: in what way did the language environment and the linguistic input differ for those children who acquired German as well as English as opposed to those children who failed to acquire the minority language actively?

The present sample has a number of advantages. The children had started to relate to their environment predominantly verbally, but they were still young enough to spend most of their time in the care of their parents. Thus influences from the community and especially peers were kept to a minimum. The 'one parent–one language' principle ensured parallel exposure to German and English by the two people who were most significant in these young children's lives. This setting allowed the tracing of the verbal sources for the children's language acquisition to either of two people. And since each of the two parents spoke a different language with the same child, it will be possible to get a step closer to differentiating between the parents' influences on the child and the child's influences on the parents.

Because of the complexity of the material and the time involved in collecting and processing the data, the limited sample size of only six families seemed optimal for an in-depth analysis with the opportunity of some cross-sectional comparisons. This investigation has to be looked at in terms of six case studies. No statistical significance can be expected.

The distortion of the naturalistic data due to the author's presence during the recordings is negligible. Graves and Glick (1978) reported that "middle class mothers who believe they are being observed in one-shot observation sessions change their speech patterns to their children apparently in an effort to display their children to best advantage" (cited from Furrow and Nelson 1986:169). However, the length of time for which these six families were observed, and the uncertainty as to which part of the recordings would be used for analysis, distinguish the present investigation strongly from those which use half-hour play sessions between mothers and children as their data base. The interactive demands of an unimpressed child let even the most self-conscious parent fall back into established behaviour patterns. All parents appeared as relaxed during the actual recordings as they were before and afterwards.

And finally a word about the reliability of the analysis. All transcripts were checked several times by myself, and the parents helped to verify the transcripts as best they could. Due to limitations in financial resources, it was impossible to have anybody trained to do reliability checks on the analysis. However, the relative stability of the parents' verbal behaviour from the first to the second recording displays intra-analytic consistency.

3. The Language Environment

3.1 Introduction

As we have seen from the description of the children's language development in the last chapter, the children reacted quite differently to the bilingual environments created by their parents. Traditionally, the success or failure of bilingual first language acquisition is related to sociolinguistic factors such as the amount of exposure to the minority language, the need to talk the minority language and the status of the minority language in the society at large. For that reason, and in order to provide general background information for the chapters to come, sociolinguistic factors in the children's language environments will be discussed in this chapter. I will first give a brief description of the situation in which German-speaking parents find themselves in Australia, and then present a number of studies on environmental features which are believed to promote bilingualism in the individual. Subsequently, the language environments of the six children will be compared. Finally, a look at each family individually will highlight particular characteristics in the children's immediate environments which may have influenced the children's reactions to the two languages in their homes.

3.2 Language maintenance among German-Australians

German-Australian parents often do not have extensive contact with their extended families. In the case of new immigrants, the parents' parents and siblings do not usually live in Australia, and in the case of second-generation German-speaking parents, the parents' brothers and sisters tend to speak English to the parent and their children because this is the language of their own peer group and they have always spoken English to one another. Clyne (1982) cited research on various languages in Australia which shows that "whatever language children may use to the parents, they employ English in communication with their peer group in the absence of parents or other members of the older generation" (Clyne 1982:27). Moreover, even the prospective bilingual child's grandparents tend to discontinue their use of German if their grandchild responds in English.

German-speaking parents who want to raise their children bilingually receive hardly any language support from within the community. German speakers do not usually concentrate in the same neighbourhoods, and because Germans, and especially mixed-ethnic German-Australian couples, are little organized in ethnic institutions, these families often do not know about one another and have only limited ways of finding out. For the same reasons, general community contact, such as in shops, banks, doctor's surgeries, churches etc., hardly ever takes place in German. Consequently, the children do not easily develop a sense of usefulness for German outside the home. For children under three years of age, parents cannot rely on the assistance of the media either; radio and television programs for children are rare and only address older children, and local libraries do not stock many books for very young children.

Those parents who decided against maintaining their ethnic language in the home, claim that they had to do so because the children refused to speak German. In fact, Clyne (1970) found that "while German-speaking parents used mainly German to their children, the children tended to answer principally in English" (Clyne 1982:27).

It is widely believed in Australia that raising one's children bilingually is doomed to failure. This failure often seems to be anticipated and feared by young parents, and they are likely to give up speaking German to their children if success is not immediate.

3.3 Factors promoting individual bilingualism

Ben-Zeev (1977b) pointed out the importance of the status of the minority language. She argued that it is "only when the status of the two languages is both high and relatively equal, and when both languages are spoken by individuals important to the child that the child rises to the challenge of becoming bilingual" (Ben-Zeev 1977b:39). Clyne (1982) stated as important factors of language maintenance "the presence of grandparents, either permanent or visiting from overseas; trips to the parents' homeland; availability of the language as a school or examination subject; its regular (or uncompromising) use by the parents; and the presence of older (overseas-born) siblings living at home" (Clyne 1982:28). Thus, Clyne and Ben-Zeev agree that a child must perceive both languages as being useful outside the home, and have a variety of contacts with the minority language. Saunders (1982b) suggested ways in which the parents could increase the children's contact with the minority language and thereby raise its status in the eyes of the children. He listed books, records, cassettes, radio and television as useful aids, and encouraged parents to take the children to ethnic schools and playgroups, or "locate shops, banks, restaurants etc., where someone knows that language and is prepared to speak it to the customers" (Saunders 1982b:239).

However, the child's immediate family, and especially the parents, play a determining role in the acquisition of the minority language. The importance of the parents' consistency in their language choice has generally been acknowledged (Ronjat 1913; Leopold 1949; McLaughlin 1978; Clyne 1982, cf. quote above; Saunders 1982b; Kielhöfer and Jonekeit 1983; Taeschner 1983). Strict separation of the two languages allows the child to process both languages separately. This is believed to be a prerequisite for the acquisition of two independent language systems. Ben-Zeev (1977b) and Porsché (1983) suggested that "children who become bilingual early do so in response to environmental demands" (Ben-Zeev 1977b:39); thus they will learn to understand the minority language if they have a need to understand it, *i.e.* if one or more people who are important to the children will consistently use the minority language in interaction with them.

A large number of receptive bilinguals, however, prove that the need to understand a language does not automatically create a need to talk the language. For young children whose exposure to a minority language is limited to a few bilingual adults, the necessity to talk the second language needs to be installed by those adults. Both Taeschner (1983) and Saunders (1982b) acknowledged that and proposed strategies: parents must learn to differentiate between the children's inability to express themselves in the minority language and the children's reluctance to do so. To overcome linguistic shortcomings, the parent would have to be sensitive to the child's momentary linguistic needs and supply missing vocabulary and missing structures. Such translations function as gentle reminders as to which language should appropriately be spoken and will eventually be accepted by the child (Saunders 1982b:141). If the children, however, use the majority language instead of the minority language in spite of their ability to do otherwise, a more coercive approach is recommended.

Taeschner and Saunders both successfully employed the "what"–strategy with their own children, thereby indicating that they were not going to continue the interaction unless the child switched to the appropriate language. Variations of this strategy are "wie bitte?" (I beg your pardon?), "wie heißt das?" (what do you say, what is that called?), "was hast du gesagt?" (what did you say?), "was willst du?" (what do you want?), or even "Mami versteht nicht" (Mummy doesn't understand). Taeschner acknowledged, however, that "the *wie* tactic is less likely to succeed in interactions where it is primarily the adult who is interested in the conversation. But when the child is the more interested participant, this strategy is at its best" (Taeschner 1983:205). Saunders emphasized the superiority of the "what"-strategy over simply translating the child's utterance. He stated that "it is (...) the father's impression that (...) if he had continued to speak German to Frank and Thomas but had not persisted in eliciting German responses from them, they would have become receiving bilinguals only, with their knowledge of German confined to comprehension and their ability to speak the language limited" (Saunders 1982b:140).

Both translations and the "what"–strategy are paralleled in the interaction of monolingual adults and children. Corsaro (1977) considered expansions and paraphrases one possible form of clarification request. Käsermann (1980) suggested that the interactive virtue of expansions rested with their function to signal understanding or misunderstanding to the child. In that way, translations are, indeed, likely to function as insistence on the appropriate language in interactions of bilingual adult-child dyads. The general, or non-specific, clarification request can, however, be expected to have a more powerful effect on the subsequent language choice of the child. It has been found that children tended to revise rather than repeat the utterance in question, obviously assuming that the problem was lying in their own linguistic performance. The revisions incorporated phonological changes, lexical substitutions and increased syntactic complexity (Gallagher 1977; Käsermann 1980; Langford 1981). By the same token, the non-specific clarification request can be expected to motivate a language switch in the bilingual child.

One further factor in the promotion of individual bilingualism was pointed out by Saunders (1982b) and Kielhöfer and Jonekeit (1983). In both books the detrimental effect of external negative attitudes towards bilingualism on the bilingual development of the language learning child was discussed. These negative attitudes usually take the form of disapproval of the minority language being spoken in the presence of monolingual speakers, or they are disguised as advice from, for example, health workers and teachers. Parents are easily made self-conscious about, and insecure of, their educational principle and tend to dismiss the project in the light of such unfavourable reactions from the environment (Saunders 1982b).

3.4 The children's language environments

Although the sociolinguistic situation in the society at large was the same for all six children of the sample, considerable differences were encountered from one family to the next. The children's language environments will be compared with respect to the extent of contact the children had with German, the consistency with which the parents adhered to the 'one parent-one language' principle, the need to talk German as created by the parents for the children, and the parents' attitudes towards bilingualism in general and their children's chances to succeed in particular.

The analysis of the sociolinguistic situation was mainly based on the initial interviews and the information gathered during the recording sessions. However, the transcribed material was called on for determining the parents' consistency in language choice and the methods employed by them for insisting on the children's use of German in interaction with their German-speaking parents.

It was hypothesized that a child would be more likely to acquire German actively in a home where both languages were used consistently by the respective parents and thereby kept well separated for the child's processing. This consistency, coupled with the German-speaking parent's insistence that the child spoke German as well, was seen as creating the necessity for the child to become a productive bilingual. The amount of time for which the child usually heard German in the course of a day, the number of German-speaking people with whom the child had contact as well as the regular exposure to German books were also expected to influence the child's active acquisition of the minority language. Finally, the parents' confidence in their child's intellectual capacities, and an environment that supported the family's decision to take this educational path, were believed to foster the child's active participation in acquiring German.

3.4.1 Contact with German

It has already been mentioned in Chapter 2 that five of the six children were exposed to German through their mothers, but that Keith heard German from his father (see Table 3.1 for presentation of data relevant to this section). Since Keith's father was a foreign-language learner, Keith did not have any other German-speaking relatives. The only other people who ever spoke German to Keith were friends of his father, who were foreign-language speakers themselves. Keith saw them once or twice a month for about an hour or two. Once a week, the mother took Keith to a woman in the neighbourhood who tried to teach German to a few children in her home. With respect to German-speaking relatives, Jacob and Agnes were in the same situation as Keith: their mothers had only recently come to Australia and all of their mothers' relatives lived in Germany. The children had therefore no contact with them. Both Agnes's and Jacob's parents had only a few German-speaking friends, and the children's contact with them was minimal. However, Jacob's mother knew an elderly lady in their neighbourhood, and she looked after Jacob for a couple of hours each week. Alice and Trudy saw their maternal grandparents as well as their mothers' brothers regularly. However, their uncles never spoke German to either them or to their mothers (cf. 3.2), and in the case of Alice, neither did her grandparents. The grandparents found it too difficult to continue to speak German while Alice addressed them in English. Much of the interaction between Alice's mother and grandmother took place in English as well. Trudy's grandparents spoke German with her all the time, but Trudy only saw them once a fortnight for a couple of hours. The parents had only a few German-speaking friends, but those friends had hardly any contact with Trudy and usually spoke English anyway in order not to exclude her English-speaking father. Fiona was the only child in the sample whose exposure to German-speaking people was extensive. Although none of her mother's relatives lived in Australia, they came to visit frequently and stayed for several weeks at a time. The family had many German-speaking friends who spoke German exclusively

Table 3.1: Contact with German

	Keith	Fiona	Alice	Jacob	Agnes	Trudy
German-speaking parent	F	M	M	M	M	M
other German-speaking adults	few	many	none	few	none	few
German-speaking peers	(class) peers	none	(play-	(friends) group)	none	none
German media	songs,	songs, books, films	songs books	books,	none songs	books, songs
time hearing German compared to English	less	more	less	more	less	more

to Fiona and her mother. Fiona's paternal grandparents were Hungarian, but had an extensive knowledge of German. They always spoke German to Fiona's mother and either German or Hungarian to Fiona.

Although all of the children had some English-speaking friends, the children's contact with German-speaking children was scarce and its impact on their language development questionable. Fiona, Trudy and Agnes did not know any other children whose parents spoke German to them. Alice used to go to a German playgroup prior to the first recording. However, the children in this playgroup never spoke German to one another, and since the mothers did not provide any structured activities, Alice did not hear the other children speak German. Jacob's mother held a kindergarten class in her home two mornings a week, and one of the children in the group was also spoken to in German by her mother. However, like Jacob, she usually responded in English. Jacob also accompanied his mother to a local Saturday school where the mother taught children with German family background. Some of the children attending the school used German actively, but since they were older, Jacob did not interact with them. Keith, who attended a private language class, cannot be said to have had German-speaking peers either, since he was the only child in the group who heard German at home and who could carry on a conversation in German. All the other children in that group spoke German at a very elementary level only.

Fiona's, Jacob's and Trudy's language environments were regularly enriched with German picture books and German songs. Alice's mother sang German songs with her daughter as well, but the family did not have any German picture books at the time of the first recording. By the time of the second recording, a few German picture books had been acquired; however, they were still too advanced for Alice. <u>Agnes's</u> mother did not spend much time singing or reading to her daughter. There were a number of German picture books on the shelf in the child's room, but most of them were above Agnes's level of understanding. Like Fiona, Jacob and Trudy, <u>Keith</u> read many picture books with his father and regularly sang German songs. Moreover, the parents video-taped German children's programs from television, which Keith watched repeatedly. At the time of the first recording, a German language lesson produced for adults was his favourite program. Keith had incorporated a number of phrases and words into his active vocabulary which stemmed quite clearly from that program.

The parents were asked to estimate the amount of time which their child spent in contact with German as compared to the amount of time the child spent in contact with English in the course of a normal day. Although the parents found it difficult to indicate the number of hours spent with either German or English, they were very certain about the balance of the two languages. Keith's, Alice's and Agnes's parents reported that English outweighed German. In Keith's case that was due to his German-speaking father being away at work during most of the day. Alice's and Agnes's parents found that the time the children spent with their fathers, their friends, in listening to the mother speaking English to other people, and while they were being minded (although neither of them was in full-time care), exceeded the time they heard their mothers speak German to them. Fiona's, Jacob's and Trudy's parents stated that their children heard more German than English in the course of a day.

3.4.2 Necessity to become bilingual

The two main factors in the home which create a necessity for the child to become bilingual are the parents' consistency in their language choice and their insistence that the child respects the 'one parent-one language' principle.

3.4.2.1 Consistency of parents' language choice. The parents' language choice was analysed parallel to that of the children. Every parent utterance addressed to the child was identified as either German, English, mixed German-English, or neither German nor English. For the German-speaking parent, utterances which were completely in German or which could have been ascribed to either German or English equally well were considered consistent language choice; mixed German-English and English utterances were considered to be inconsistent language choices. Likewise, utterances by the English-speaking parent were counted as consistent in terms of language choice if they were completely in English or in neither German nor English; mixed German-English utterances and solely German utterances were counted as inconsistent language choices. For the consistency of the parents' language choice to each other I had to rely on the parents' information as elicited in the initial interview. Table 3.2 shows each parent's consistency with regard to language choice in interaction with the child as well as the parents' consistency in language choice to each other.

Table 3.2: Parents' consistency in language choice

	rec.	Keith	Fiona	Alice	Jacob	Agnes	Trudy
I	1st	99.6%	99.5%	97.8%	98.9%	94.9%	95.7%
	2nd	99.5%	100.0%	98.6%	97.5%	97.0%	95.6%
	mean	99.6%	99.8%	98.2%	98.2%	95.9%	95.6%
II	1st	100.0%	100.0%	94.9%	99.7%	99.5%	73.7%
	2nd	100.0%	98.8%	91.1%	99.5%	92.9%	79.0%
	mean	100.0%	99.4%	93.0%	99.4%	96.2%	76.4%
III	99.8%	99.6%	95.6%	98.9%	96.1%	86.0%	
IV	+3.8% of 96%	+3.6%	-0.4%	+2.9%	+0.1%	-10.0%	
V		English	English	English	60% English	English	English

I = German-speaking parent; II = English-speaking parent; III = mean for both parents at both times of recording; IV = sample mean; V = parents to each other,

Table 3.2 indicates that <u>Keith's</u> and <u>Fiona's</u> parents were the most consistent in their language choice. The scores for both their German- and English-speaking parents were well above the sample mean of 96% at both times of recording. The scores for <u>Alice's</u> and <u>Agnes's</u> parents were closest to the sample mean. In Alice's case, the father was more consistent than was the mother. <u>Trudy's</u> parents were least consistent in their language choice. Their mean consistency remained 10% below the sample mean and nearly 14% below the level of consistency displayed by Keith's and Fiona's parents. The scores for <u>Jacob's</u> parents were above the sample mean; the scores for the mother were comparable with those for Alice's and Agnes's mothers, and the scores for the father resembled those for Keith's and Fiona's parents. However, whereas all of the other parents reported to be using English exclusively to one another, Jacob's parents stated that they spoke English to each other for about 60% of the time only. The overall level of consistency experienced by Jacob was therefore similar to the level of consistency Trudy experienced.

The English-speaking parents' consistency in language choice needs to be seen in the light of their proficiency in German. Table 3.3 differentiates three levels of proficiency: little, some and good knowledge of German. The parents were not tested, however. Their grouping into one of the three levels was made on the basis of their own reports regarding how well they could understand and speak German, their spouses' reports, information gathered about their exposure to German, *e.g.* schooling, time spent in German-speaking countries etc., and the language proficiency they displayed during the days of recording, *i.e.* their reactions to completely German conversations between German-speaking parent and child as well as between German-speaking parent and researcher, and their own active use of German, where this was the case.

Table 3.3: English-speaking parents' knowledge of German

Keith	Fiona	Alice	Jacob	Agnes	Trudy
little	good	little	good	some	little

Only <u>Fiona's</u> and <u>Jacob's</u> English-speaking parents had a good grasp of German. They had both lived in a German-speaking country for some time and could follow any type of conversation. Fiona's father, however, never spoke German to any of his family's German-speaking visitors, whereas Jacob's father did. <u>Agnes's</u> father could follow easy conversations. He had some schooling in German and used to travel to Germany frequently when the couple still lived in England. Yet he never talked German to German-speaking visitors. <u>Keith's</u>, <u>Alice's</u> and <u>Trudy's</u> English-speaking parents all had very little knowledge of German. They could hardly follow easy conversations and at times did not even comprehend the exchanges between their children and their spouses. All three of them started being interested in German only after the children's birth. Alice's and Trudy's fathers picked up the German they knew from their wives and their wives' families, and Keith's mother attended a private language school for a while.

Although Table 3.2 showed some diversion from the 'one parent-one language' principle in the case of Trudy's father, the fact that he was actually not capable of speaking German on anything but a very restricted level, made the 'one parent-one language' principle a necessity rather than a conscious choice. The original choice in Trudy's family was, in fact, that both parents speak German to Trudy. However, by the time of the first recording, Trudy had already outgrown her father's linguistic ability in German and the father resorted more and more to English (cf. 3.5.6).

3.4.2.2 Parents' insistence on the 'one parent-one language' principle. In the majority of cases the children's inappropriate language choice was ignored by the parents but their speech act was acknowledged. Nevertheless, six strategies could be identified which the German-speaking parents used in dealing actively with inappropriate language choice. These strategies could be divided into response-eliciting strategies and non-response-eliciting strategies. The two non-response-eliciting strategies were *translation* and *incorporated translation.*

(1)   Translation
       [Ke I, 615 - 618]
       ((F and C are reading a book))
       C: *the cat !*
       F: *das ist eine Katze ,*
            'that is a cat ,'
       C: *and got amals .*
       F: *VIEle Tiere .*
            'many animals .'

Translations were coded for utterances which converted a message from English into German in a sequence-ending manner (cf. *translation plus question* for sequence-initiating translations). Due to interactional demands translations often featured a change in person from first to second or vice versa.

(2)   Translation
       [Al I, 659 - 660]
       C: *did you have dinner ?*
       M: *ja wir haben gegessen ,*
            'yes we have eaten ,'

Incorporated translations were coded when the parent translated only part of the child's utterance, but incorporated that into his/her own utterance.

(3)   Incorporated Translation
       [Ja I, 384 - 385]
       ((M and C are painting pictures))
       C: *I make mouth for you*
       M: *jawohl + ist der + ist der Mund auf der Stirn ?*
             'yes + is the + is the mouth on the forehead ?'

Translations and *incorporated translations* are very low constraint strategies, since they do not require the child to acknowledge the translation in any
way. However, *incorporated translations* can be expected to be even less effective as a means of introducing a language switch than are *translations*. They
are an unavoidable feature of verbal exchanges between an English-speaking
child and a German-speaking parent. *Translations*, on the other hand, are much
more marked in that they stand out as redundant when a simple "yes" or the
like would have been sufficient in a monolingual context.

The four response-eliciting strategies could be further sub-classified into
strategies which required polar responses and strategies which required content responses. The two strategies which required polar responses were
translation plus question and *challenging question*.

(4)   Translation plus Question
       [Ja I, 840 - 841]
       C: *this hurts me a bit*
       M: *tut ein bißchen weh ?*
             'does it hurt a bit ?'
       C: *yeah + hurts.*

In contrast to a *translation*, the *translation plus question* requires the child
to verify the translation and implicitly states that a message can only be received
successfully when it is encoded in German. In that way, this strategy exerts
somewhat more pressure on the child than does a simple translation.

Challenging questions as a means of switching from English to German
were limited to one parent-child dyad. They constituted a well-established game
for Keith and his father, in the course of which Keith usually forgot his resistance to speaking German.

(5)   Challenging Question
       [Ke I, 139 - 149]
       F: *du bist ein böses Kind , ja ,*
             'you are a naughty child , yes ,'
       C: *no: !*

F: *bist du böse ?*
        'are you naughty ?'
C: *no: !*
F: *bist du gut ?*
        'are you good ?'
C: *gut .*
        'good .'
F: *bist du schön ?*
        'are you beautiful ?'
C: *gut .*
        'good .'
F: *bist du häßlich ?*
        'are you ugly ?'
C: *neihein .*
        'noho .'

The two strategies which called for content responses were display or
pretence of *not-understanding* and the *request for translation*.

(6)   Not-Understanding
        [Ke I, 841 - 845]
        C: *nein + go + a + way*
        F: *das versteh ich nicht*
                'I don't understand that'
        C: *go away !*
        F: *verSTEH ich nicht .*
                'don't underSTAND that'
        C: *GEH WEG !*
                'GO AWAY !'
        F: ((laughs)) *okay . das versteh ich .*
                'that I understand .'

The pretence of not-understanding often just took the form of "what?" or
"what did you say?". It was virtually indistinguishable from a genuine lack of
understanding, as shown in the following example.

(7)   Genuine Not-Understanding
        [Ke II, 219 - 227]
        ((C and F are looking at a book))
        C: *da . + das ist ein [gra=ft] Mensch . hat der [gra=ft] ?*
                'there . + that is a strong man .' is he strong ?
        F: *wo . was sagst du .*
                'where . what are you saying .'
        C: *hat der [gra=ft] ?*
                'is he strong ?'

F: *wo . was meinst du .*
        'where . what do you mean .'
        ich versteh nicht .
        'I don't understand .'

C: *hat der [gra=ft] + hat-*
        'is he strong + is-'

F: *das versteh ich nicht*
        'I do n't understand that '

C: *hat- hat- die (Bauch) Men- Mensch [gra-] [gra=ft] ?*
        'is the belly man strong ? '

F: *Kra=ft ! ja ! ist kräftig .*
        'strong ! yes ! is strong .'

However, only those sequences which were meant to elicit a translation into German from the child were counted as the insisting strategy *not-understanding*. Whether or not they did was judged by the course which the immediately following conversation took. Similar to other parental requesting behaviour, the parent would make his/her speech act more explicit if it failed to produce the intended effect. In the case of a genuine lack of understanding, the obstacle was resolved accordingly and the parent eventually accepted what the child had said, independently of the language used. However, the insisting strategy was likely to be followed up with a marked *translation* or a *request for translation*.

Whereas the strategy of *not-understanding* was interactively well integrated, the *request for translation* brought the ongoing conversation to a halt. It stated clearly that the parent understood, but was not prepared to continue unless the child switched to the appropriate language. Taeschner (1983) suggested that the *request for translation* might have a negative effect on the child's willingness to speak the minority language, since it invites open refusal. The following is an example of this type of insisting strategy.

(8)   <u>Request for Translation</u>
     [Ke I, 1226 - 1228]

     C: *make the bees + honey ?*
     F: *du sollst auf Deutsch sagen*
          'you are supposed to say in German'
     C: *Honig .*
          'honey .'

With regard to their level of constraint, insisting strategies which are meant to elicit a polar response exert less pressure on the child than insisting strategies which require a content response. The two strategies which elicit content responses display a further increase in constraint from *not-understanding* to *request for translation*. Since the *request for translation* is more explicit than a display of *not-understanding*, the latter can be followed up by the former.

(9) <u>Increasing Explicitness</u>
[Ke I, 1140 - 1149]

C:	*where is Mummy*
F:	*im Wohnzimmer glaub ich .*
	'in the livingroom I think .'
C:	*is talking to Susanna .*
F:	*was sagst du ?*
	'what do you say ?'
	(8.3)
C:	*is talking to Susanna . + SANna .*
F:	*ich versteh nicht , sag_*
	'I don't understand, say_'
C:	*_Sanna*
F:	*sag_*
	'say_'
C:	*_Sanna*
F:	*sollst auf Deutsch sagen .*
	"you're supposed to say in German .'

The six insisting strategies used by the parents of the sample can, therefore, be arranged on a continuum of increasing constraint on the ongoing conversation as well as on the child's linguistic ability in German (Fig. 3.1).

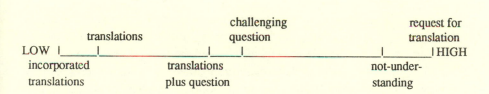

Fig. 3.1: Continuum of constraint exerted by insisting strategies

At the low-constraint end of this continuum we have *incorporated translations*, followed by *translations*. *Translations plus questions* and *challenging questions* place an intermediate level of constraint on the child's following response. The display of *not-understanding* must be considered a high-constraint strategy, the pressure from this strategy being surpassed only by the most explicit of all the insisting strategies, the *request for translation*. The degree of effectiveness of any strategy can be expected to parallel the level of constraint. We have seen above that *incorporated translations* are most likely to pass unnoticed whereas *translations* are more marked. All the response-eliciting strategies generate side-sequences (Jefferson 1972; Garvey 1977), which have precedence over the main topic. However, in the cases of *translations plus question* and *challenging questions* the child can get away with a yes/no-response. Only the high-constraint strategies *not-understanding* and *request for translation* force the child to apply his/her knowledge of German actively.

The absolute number of insisting strategies used by each of the German-speaking parents was calculated against the children's original English and mixed German-English contributions to the interaction. The children's original contributions in the "wrong" language were taken as the 100% base to which the parents could have reacted with insisting strategies. This procedure made it possible to determine the extent to which the parents applied these insisting strategies. Table 3.4 shows the overall level of insisting strategies used by the parents at both times of recording.

Table 3.4: Insisting strategies

	Keith	Fiona	Alice	Jacob	Agnes	Trudy
1st recording	44.2%	13.8%	7.8%	19.1%	5.9%	15.3%
2nd recording	12.5%	14.0%	3.7%	21.0%	26.3%	19.1%

Keith's father reacted with impressive consistency to his son's inappropriate language choice during the first recording, but less so during the second recording when Keith appeared to have accepted the 'one parent-one language' principle. Fiona, who addressed comparatively little English to her mother, gave the impression of naturally adhering to the 'one parent-one language' principle. The mother might therefore not have felt the need for constant reminders. Trudy's mother used insisting strategies with a frequency comparable with that of Fiona's mother during the first recording when Trudy's language choice was similar to that of Fiona's. Although Trudy spoke very little German during the second recording, the mother did not increase the frequency with which she used insisting strategies very much. Alice's mother reduced the frequency with which she employed insisting strategies by about half from the first to the second recording although there was no improvement in the appropriateness of

Alice's language choice. Jacob spoke as little German as did Alice, but this did not seem to have had a similarly discouraging effect on his mother as it did on Alice's mother. Jacob's mother employed insisting strategies for about a fifth of her son's original English utterances. While she did so only about half as frequently as did Keith's father during the first recording, she did it more consistently than any of the other German-speaking parents at both times of recording. Agnes's mother made only infrequent attempts at insisting on German during the first recording, but followed up about a quarter of Agnes's original English utterances with insisting strategies during the second recording.

A closer look at the type of insisting strategies which the German-speaking parents chose to employ, better revealed the relationship between insisting strategies and the children's willingness to speak German. Table 3.5 differentiates between non-sequential insisting strategies, *i.e. incorporated translations* and *translations*, insisting strategies which require a polar response, *i.e. translation plus question* and *challenging questions*, and insisting strategies which require a content response, *i.e. not-understanding* and *request for translation*. In addition, the percentages indicating the frequency with which sequential insisting strategies were employed, were totalled. This facilitates the comparison of sequential with non-sequential strategies.

Keith's father employed as many sequential as non-sequential insisting strategies during the first recording. At the time of the second recording, sequential strategies had increased to twice the frequency of non-sequential strategies. Content responses were required more often than polar responses at both times of recording. Fiona's mother used more non-sequential than sequential strategies during the first recording, but during the second recording the sequential strategies outweighed the non-sequential ones. Her sequential strategies required more polar responses during the first recording, but more content responses during the second recording. Alice's mother preferred non-sequential insisting strategies to sequential insisting strategies at both times of recording. The few sequential strategies she employed all required polar responses during the first recording. During the second recording they were equally divided into polar and content response requiring strategies. It must be kept in mind, however, that Alice's mother used insisting strategies far less frequently during the second recording than she did during the first recording. Jacob's mother employed non-sequential strategies about three times as frequently as she did sequential strategies at both times of recording. All of Agnes's mother's insisting strategies were non-sequential during the first recording. During the second recording, she employed some sequential strategies as well, the vast majority of which required polar responses. Apart from one *translation plus question* during the second recording, Trudy's mother used only non-sequential strategies.

The types of insisting strategies preferred by the German-speaking parents appeared to be related to the children's willingness and ability to speak German in the expected way: the two actively German-speaking children, Keith and Fiona, were reminded to speak German by means of high-constraint insisting strategies more often than were the other children. The proportions of high-constraint and low-constraint insisting strategies in their parents' speech changed in favour of even more high-constraint strategies once the children had entered the third developmental stage (cf. 2.5.5). The parents of the other four children preferred low-constraint insisting strategies to high-constraint insisting strategies throughout.

Table 3.5: Types of insisting strategies employed by the German-speaking parents

a) first recording

	Keith	Fiona	Alice	Jacob	Agnes	Trudy
non-sequential	21.5%	8.6%	5.4%	14.6%	5.9%	13.6%
sequential	22.7%	5.2%	2.4%	4.5%	——	1.7%
polar sequence	6.6%	3.5%	2.4%	4.0%	——	1.7%
content sequence	16.1%	1.7%	——	0.5%	——	——

b) second recording

	Keith	Fiona	Alice	Jacob	Agnes	Trudy
non-sequential	4.2%	5.0%	2.5%	16.0%	18.1%	19.1%
sequential	8.3%	9.0%	1.2%	5.0%	8.2%	——
polar sequence	——	3.3%	0.6%	5.0%	6.6%	——
content sequence	8.3%	5.7%	0.6%	——	1.6	——

3.4.3 Parents' attitudes

Towards the end of the initial interview, the parents were asked in what way they believed bilingualism effects children, how they felt about their children's linguistic development, and whether they had ever encountered any negative criticism of their educational approach. The reactions to these questions generally displayed very positive attitudes on the side of the parents as well as their relatives, friends and neighbours. The majority of parents reported that they could only envisage advantages from bilingualism for their children in terms of intellectual development, success in school and wider opportunities in the job market. Most of them were very pleased with their children's language development, seeing that the children developed adequately for their age in English and acquired some knowledge of German at the same time. Relatives, friends and neighbours reacted very favourably, encouraging the parents not to waste an opportunity like this and stressing the importance of being bi- or multilingual in today's world. Many of them took delight in questioning the children about equivalents in German, tried to pick up some German themselves or would have liked it if their own children were spoken to in German by the respective parent of the sample as well. Only two families in the sample were not quite as unreservedly positive in their attitudes. Agnes's parents were wondering whether the two languages could have been the cause for their daughter's late start in speaking (cf. 3.5.4). Consequently, they were not as pleased with their daughter's language development in English as were the other parents. Trudy's mother was very self-conscious about putting her daughter in a socially awkward position by speaking German to her in front of monolingual English friends. Therefore, she tended to speak very quietly to her when they were at playgroup, for example. The mother admitted, however, that her self-consciousness stemmed more from her own experience as a bilingual child in Australia than from reactions by her neighbours and friends today.

3.5 Discussion of each individual family

In spite of the cross-sectional comparison which I have attempted in the preceding section, it has already become evident that the circumstances were very special for each family. Many aspects had to be omitted because they had relevance for only one family at a time. These individual aspects will be presented in this section, alongside some more intuitive features of the language environments of the children, which are beyond the analytical means of this thesis. In this and the following chapters, the older children's families will always be discussed before the younger children's' families.

3.5.1 Alice

Alice's mother reported that she had spoken German to Alice with varying consistency during the first two and a half years of her daughter's life, which was, in turn, due to the varying support she received from friends and family. There was, in fact, a period of great consistency as well as insistence just after Alice's second birthday. During that period, the mother insisted that Alice uttered requests in proper German sentences before the mother complied with the request. Hence, Alice was able to produce requests like the following during the first recording.

e.g.   [Al I, 138]
     C: *ICH möchte Soße haben*
         'I want to have gravy'

This was the only incidence of that sort, however, and it produced the probably intended effect of catching the parents' complete attention for a moment.

Whereas the mother did not make very much use of conversational strategies to aid her insisting on Alice speaking German, particularly with regard to high-constraint strategies, she did not hesitate to put pressure on Alice to say "please" and "thank you". A few instances in which it was not possible to decide whether the particular speech act was a *request for more politeness* or a *request for translation* suggested that the more coercive insisting strategies had not been used because the mother was unsure where her priorities lay.

e.g.   [Al II, 85 - 90]
     C: *I don't want milk .*
         I want Wasser .
         'I want water'
     M: *wie heißt dis ? + wie heißt dis ?*
         'what do you say ?'
     C: *bitte* ((laughs))
         'please'
     M: *ich möchte Wasser trinken* bitte ._
         'I would like to drink some water please ._'
     C: *_ich möchte Wasser trinken bitte .*

The small amount of German which Alice actually spoke was difficult to understand, and even the mother understood Alice better when she spoke English. Thus Alice did not receive much encouragement to speak German, even if she tried to do so.

Both parents stated that the interaction between father and daughter was very intense, and that he was more patient with Alice and had a closer relationship with her than did the mother. For the last few months before the first recording and for a few more weeks afterwards, the father was unemployed and spent much time with Alice.

3.5.2 Keith

Until Keith was 2;4, he spoke English only, but the father persisted and never gave up speaking German to his son. At around the time of the first recording, when Keith was aged 2;8, the father started to insist on German being spoken by Keith as well. Then the father went through two months of constantly reminding the son to speak German, before Keith accepted German as the principle language in interaction with his father. By the time of the second recording, the father's insisting strategies had become very subtle: he often just did not react when Keith talked to him in English in the presence of both parents. This could be considered conversationally well integrated: the father operated under the assumption that utterances in English were meant for the mother. Keith then translated his English utterances into German or turned to the mother fully.

Keith showed a strong sense for order with respect to his two languages during the first recording. He never spoke German to the mother and refused to sing his German songs with her, although he loved them very much and often started to sing them on his own. This situation eased a little bit towards the second recording.

Both of Keith's parents were very quiet people. The mother felt that she should talk and play more with Keith and his baby brother. The father had much patience and was very imaginative and persistent in his play with Keith. He spoke rather slowly and clearly, and definitely more so than did the mother. The pace with which turns in speaking were taken in this family was slower than in most other families, allowing Keith plenty of time to formulate his sentences.

Keith's German was easy to understand, at times easier than his English, and Keith received much encouragement to speak German from the few other German-speaking people he met. Moreover, Keith appeared to be very ambitious. It was evident throughout the transcripts that he wanted to speak German and was frustrated when he could not live up to his father's expectations. The following is an example from the transcripts which illustrates this point particularly well.

e.g.   [Ke I, 470 - 485]
        ((F and C are reading a picture book))
        F: *ein Vogel + fliegt .*
               'a bird + flies .'
               ja , und was noch .
               'yes , and what else .'
               ein Schwein , + was macht das .
               'a pig , + what does that do .'
        C: *Schwanz !*
               'tail !'
        F: *läuft . ja ,*
               'runs . yes ,'
               (2.4)
               und ein Pferd ?
               'and a horse ?'
        C: *Schwanz !*
               'tail !'
        F: *läuft ,*
               'runs ,'
               (1.8)
               und das Hühnchen ?
               'and the chicken ?'
        C: *hhhh .*
        F: *hüpft .*
               'hops .'
        C: *(xxx xxx) ! too heavy .*
               is + stop heavy .
        F: *das ist zu {schwierig}1_*
               'that is too difficult_'
        C: *{ finish }1*
        F: *_meinst du ?*
               '_you mean ?'
        C: *finish*
        F: *ist das zu schwierig ?*
               'is that too difficult ?'
        C: *mh.*
               'uhuh .'
        F: *das hast du ge{ schafft }1 ! + gut !*
               'you did it ! + good !'
        C: *{ no }1*
               (2.2)
               ich hab + nicht + schafft . ich hab nicht ge + schafft .
               I did not do it.

3.5.3 Jacob

Jacob's mother reported that Jacob stopped using German expressions as soon as he had learned their English equivalents. There were only two instances of *requests for translation* to be found in the transcripts from Jacob's family, both of which took place during the first recording. The example below gives an indication as to how difficult it was to make Jacob translate into German:

e.g.　[Ja I, 1036 - 1052]

C:　*is my applejuice*

M:　*dein Apfelsaft*
　　'your applejuice'
　　(3.2)

C:　*my applejuice ? my Apfel- (1.2) applejuice*
　　'my applejuice ? my apple-'

M:　*ja wie heißt es in Deutsch ?*
　　'yes what is it called in German ?'

C:　*applejuice ?*

M:　*na , ist Englisch .*
　　'no , is English .'

C:　*English ,*

M:　*vorsichtig { du schmeißt den Becher }1 um*
　　'careful you are throwing the cup over'

C:　*{ englisch + englisch }1*
　　'{ English + English }1'

M:　*nein { das ist }2 English .*
　　'no { that is }2 English ._'
　　wie {heißt es}3 in Deutsch —
　　'what { is it called }3 in German —'

C:　*{ englisch }2 { applejuice }3*
　　'{ English }2'
　　in Deutsch ?
　　'in German ?'

M:　*ja .*
　　'yes .'

C:　*Ap- + Apfel + saps .*
　　'ap- + apple + juice .'

M:　*ja . Apfelsaft .*
　　'yes . applejuice .'

The mother always spoke very fast and was aware of this since people had often commented on it. It is possible, therefore, that Jacob had problems differentiating lexical and grammatical units in his mother's speech. Jacob tried to speak very fast as well, thereby often not pronouncing major parts of the sentence. His English was very difficult to understand for outsiders, and his German was nearly incomprehensible. Consequently, he did not get much encouragement from interactants for using German.

Both parents played with Jacob very often and with great intensity. The mother claimed that the father's playing was more imaginative than was her own.

3.5.4 Agnes

Agnes's mother found it difficult to understand her daughter's language. Therefore, all but one clarification request were genuine. This difficulty was shared by the researcher. Agnes's speech was defective in pronunciation and sentence structure. Her MLU count (cf. 2.5.3) was artificially boosted because of her habit to put vocatives at the end of many utterances. An indication of Agnes's immature language use for her age was the confusion of the "I" and "you" perspectives at age 2;8:

e.g.   [Ag I, 26]
         ((C wants to climb onto F's lap))
         C: *sit here my knee Papa ,*

In fact, Agnes had only started to speak at age 2;6 when her mother was in hospital giving birth to the second child and Agnes was cared for by a neighbour, an elderly English-speaking woman. Moreover, Agnes scored lowest in the Auditory Comprehension Test of all children in the sample. Overall, her language proficiency at age 2;8 was more comparable to that of the two younger children, *i.e.* to Fiona's and Trudy's, language proficiency than to that of the other children in her own age group. Both her parents felt that Agnes was behind in her language development, and they wondered if her exposure to two languages could have been responsible (cf. 3.4.3).

Agnes's parents were themselves very hard to understand. This was evident from a great number of clarification requests on Agnes's side. The researcher had the same difficulty, during the recording sessions as well as while listening to the tapes. Both parents spoke with relatively quiet voices and indistinct pronunciation.

According to the mother, Agnes spoke more when interacting with her father than when interacting with her mother. The mother also thought that the father understood Agnes's attempts at speaking better than she did herself. Both parents agreed that the relationship between father and daughter was closer than between mother and daughter. However, the father did not read or play much with Agnes either (cf. 2.4).

3.5.5 Fiona

The two languages had never been a problem in Fiona's family. Fiona's father was raised bilingually himself. He was very aware of the importance of strict separation of the two languages. The parents believed that their own consistency would eventually make Fiona differentiate the two languages properly.

Accordingly, the mother employed insisting strategies infrequently only. Like Alice's mother, she used requests for translation alongside requests for more politeness:

e.g.   [Fe I, 633 - 638]
      C: *I want nappi*
      M: *wie sagt man ?*
            'what do you say?'
      C: *bitte .*
            'please .'
      M: *darf ich eine Papierserviette haben ?*
            'may I have a paper napkin ?'
      F: *can you say it to me ?*
      C: *yes*
      ((end of topic))

It is not clear to whom the child's original request was addressed. At first, it appeared to be meant for the mother. Fiona took the mother's following request to mean a request for more politeness. Yet the mother was not satisfied and translated the child's request into an, albeit more polite, German request. The father's following move calls the original interpretation, *i.e.* that the mother was the addressee of Fiona's request, into question. Therefore, it is likely that the mother did, in fact, make a request for more politeness rather than for translation. The 'one parent–one language' principle, however, triggered "bitte" rather than "please". This principle also restricted the mother to changing the basic request in English into a more polite request in German, even though the request was addressed to the English-speaking father. The task of translating the more polite version of the original request back into English was left to the child or the English-speaking father. This is a typical illustration of the 'one parent–one language' principle. By the very nature of this principle, it is difficult to differentiate between requests for translation and requests for more politeness, unless parents are very clear about their priorities (cf. 3.5.1).

3.5.6 Trudy

For the first two years of Trudy's life both parents spoke German to her, in spite of the fact that the father did not know any German before Trudy was born. He learned from his wife what he needed in order to talk to his baby daughter. At the time of the first recording Trudy's communicative abilities had already outgrown her father's knowledge of German, and he spoke a mixture of English and German to Trudy. Towards the second recording, he only used the occasional German word in his otherwise English utterances to Trudy.

When Trudy first started to speak, she spoke German only. At the age of 2;4, Trudy tended to speak German with her mother and English with her father. Trudy's mother was by then already concerned about the constant decrease of German and increase of English in Trudy's speech to both her parents. Six months later, Trudy had practically stopped speaking German.

The mother did not want to put pressure on Trudy to speak German for fear of risking the good relationship with her daughter, which she believed to be already better between father and daughter. She therefore only used low-constraint insisting strategies.

On the other hand, the mother exerted considerable pressure on Trudy in order to make her say "please" and "thank you". First the mother used the *not-understanding* strategy and then increased the explicitness with a more direct *request for politeness*.

e.g.   [Tr I, 601 - 607]
      C: *Trudy want down*
      M: *das versteh ich NICHT + hey . hey Trudy + du ?*
            'I do NOT under-stand that + hey . hey Trudy + do n't !'[5]
      C: ((cries))
      M: *was sagst du denn .*
            'what do you say .'
            du- du hast zuerst mal nicht das Zauberwort gesagt ,
            'you- you have first of all not said the magic word ,'
      C: ((whining)) *bitte*
            'please'
      M: *hhha !*

The following example from the second recording suggests that Trudy might have been more tolerant of strategies insisting on the use of German than her mother gave her credit for.

e.g. [Tr II, 5-9]
     C: *you put that in [dom]* ,
     M: *was soll ich , was .*
            'what shall I do , what .'
     C: *das bitte [dom]*
            'that please [dom] ,'
     M: *ich soll den Deckel drauf tun*
            'I shall put the lid on'
     C: *machst du bitte Deckel [drom]* .
            'do you please put the lid [drom] .'

The mother genuinely did not understand what Trudy wanted. Her clarification request triggered both a translation and an increase in politeness. The word [dom] might have been a combination of "on" and "drauf".

3.6 Conclusions

Various factors in the children's family situations were expected to foster active bilingualism given the condition that the families lived in the same general sociolinguistic environment. These factors ranged from the extent and variety of exposure to the minority language, over the parents' consistency in their language use and insistence that the children adhered to the 'one parent–one language' principle, to the parent's attitudes to bilingualism and their children's language development.

No correlation was found between the extent and variety of contact with German on the one hand and the children's development of active bilingualism on the other hand. The two German-speaking children, Keith and Fiona, could not be distinguished from the other four children in this respect. According to traditional expectations, all the odds were against Keith and his non-native German-speaking father (Kielhöfer and Jonekeit 1983:15) and in favour of Fiona, Jacob and Agnes and their native German-speaking mothers. However, whereas Keith developed towards active bilingualism, Jacob and Agnes did not.

Keith's father compensated for the original disadvantage by arranging contact with other German-speaking people and exposing Keith to a variety of different language media. Fiona's language learning environment was naturally rich, and she developed as would have been expected. However, Jacob did not, although he was in much the same situation as Fiona. Trudy, Alice and Agnes all had less contact with German than did Fiona and Jacob, but more than did Keith.

In terms of necessity to become bilingual, however, Keith's and Fiona's parents created language environments for their children which were superior to those of the other children. Keith's and Fiona's parents were more consistent in their language use of both German and English than were any of the other parents. Jacob's and Trudy's parents were the least consistent. The children's bilingual language development correlated with the parents' consistency: the two children of the very consistent parents, Keith and Fiona, acquired an active command of German; the two children of the least consistent parents, Jacob and Trudy, showed signs of open refusal to speak German; Alice and Agnes, whose parents represented the sample's mean of 96% consistency, did not choose to speak German, but neither did they go out of their way to avoid it.

A correlation between types of insisting strategy used by the German-speaking parents, although not frequency of the same, and the children's degree of bilingualism was found as well. Keith's and Fiona's German-speaking parents employed more sequential insisting strategies than did the other children's German-speaking parents. Moreover, they changed the relation of high- to low-constraint insisting strategies in favour of more high-constraint strategies from the first to the second recording. The other children's German-speaking parents tended to decrease the level of constraint, which may have been a sign of resignation.

Attitudes towards bilingualism and the children's language development were generally positive. None of the parents felt criticized for raising their children in that way. However, Agnes's parents were not sure that the two languages did not have a delaying effect on their daughter's language development, and Trudy's mother had internalized rejections for speaking a community language other than English, which stemmed from her own childhood.

In summary, the difficulties in passing on German to ones' children as encountered in the Australian society at large were experienced in much the same way by the parents of the present sample. A first glance at the parents' actual verbal behaviour, however, indicated that parents *can* modify the quality of their children's language environments.

4. Discourse Structures

4.1 Introduction

A family's sociolinguistic situation may predict tendencies towards the success or failure of attempts to raise a child bilingually. However, viewed on its own, it does not give sufficient reasons for either positive or negative results of such an educational approach. The present study expects a relationship between features of the parents' language towards the children which have been found related to first language acquisition in general and the degree to which children acquire the minority language. It is therefore necessary to study the actual use of language in each of the six families more closely.

The discursive strategies used by each parent in interaction with his/her child will be examined first. For the purpose of this study, a model for analysing conversations between parents and young children has been developed. Any analytical model can only examine a limited aspect of what happens in natural conversation, and which aspects are highlighted by a particular analysis depends on the model used. The present model draws its categories from studies done on factors which promote language development of, and sustain conversations with, young children, as well as from studies which reflect the interactional intent of parents. Stubbs's (1983) and Keenan and Schieffelin's (1976) discourse models serve as the frame into which the categories derived from research on parent-child verbal interaction are integrated.

After a discussion of the relevant literature on parent-child verbal interaction, a modified version of Stubbs's (1983) discourse model will be introduced and extended in order include some features of the model by Keenan and Schieffelin (1976). The discourse model thus derived will then be sub-classified in order to capture features which are believed to sustain conversations with young children and/or promote their language development. Finally, moves with common interactional directions are combined into interactionally relevant clusters.

The application of the discourse model will be discussed in the second part of this chapter. After a brief comparison across the sample, which did not render the expected results, the children's communicative situation in the home will be described separately for each family. A modified way of cross-sectionally comparing the parents will yield the final results of this chapter.

4.2 The discourse model

4.2.1 Studies on parent-child verbal interaction

In the course of the "motherese" studies of the last twenty years, a number of features in the adult language directed towards children have been investigated. The earlier studies were mainly concerned with formal properties of speech, like length, complexity and type of sentences, and only marginally with semantic properties, like expansions; most of the results were contradictory. Increasingly, semantic properties were studied, like expansions (of grammatical forms), extensions (of content), repetitions, semantic relatedness of utterances, stock utterances and topic extensions. Others investigated adult strategies which were helpful in sustaining conversations with young children or, more generally, types of parental strategies in interacting with children. Although undertaken with differing perceptual goals, many of the studies point in the same direction.

McDonald and Pien (1982) were able to define two intentionally different interactional styles. The eleven mothers of 2;5 to 3;0 year old children fell into two opposing behavioural clusters. One was oriented towards conversing with the child, the other towards controlling the child. The interactional features which were found to constitute a conversation-oriented maternal speech style coincided with results from studies which suggested that certain structural features were influential regarding the speed of children's language development and with results from studies which investigated verbal features likely to sustain conversations with young children.

McDonald and Pien found that conversation-oriented mothers used a high amount of real questions and examination questions. Likewise, Cross (1978) reported that children who were aged between 1;7 and 2;8 and advanced in their language development were often asked wh-questions and polar questions. Barnes et al. (1983), Furrow et al. (1979), Howe (1981) and Lieven (1978) also suggested that polar questions correlate with faster language development, if the parents make use of them frequently. The children in the latter studies were aged 1;6 to 2;9. Wells et al. (1981) and Stella-Prorok (1983) looked more at the conversation sustaining aspects of certain language features and considered wh-questions, and, in the case of Wells et al., also polar questions important factors in the continuation of parent–child conversations. Wells et al. (1981) suggested that adjacency pairs in general have discourse sustaining functions because of the obligatory nature of the second move in an adjacency pair. They further argued that tag-questions fulfil a similar function, since they transform interactional moves which usually do not demand a response, like declaratives, into response demanding moves. Accordingly, Cross (1978) was able to show that advanced language learners were exposed to somewhat more tag-questions than normally developing children. One further question-like move formed part of McDonald and Pien's (1982) cluster of conversation orientation and was also proposed by Wells et al. (1981) as conversation sustaining. It is a move which acknowledges what the speaker has just said, but passes the turn straight back to the original speaker, as in the following exchange:

A: "I don't like beans".

B: "Don't you?"

A: "No. But I like peas".

McDonald and Pien (1982) called these moves verbal reflectives, whereas Wells et al. (1981) called them retroactive moves because of their reactive as well as initiative nature.

Moerk (1983a) re-analysed Brown's (1973) data on Eve, who was well advanced in her language development, and Adam, who acquired his linguistic skills more slowly. Moerk found that Eve's mother ended exchanges with her daughter with positive reinforcements of Eve's responses in more than 50% of the time, whereas few such conditioned positive reinforcements could be found in exchanges between Adam and his mother. Moerk's results correspond to findings by Cross (1978) and Lieven (1978) who were able to correlate higher numbers of expansions in the mothers' speech with children's faster language development. Nelson, Denninger, Bonvillan and Kaplan (1983) supported this, claiming that "moderate departures structurally from the child's utterances may enhance syntactic advance for the child if they are embedded in smoothly-continuing discourse" (Nelson et al. 1983:18). Hubbel (1977) and Stella-Prorok (1983) found expansions a means of sustaining conversations with young children. Adult repetitions and imitations, as studied by Cross (1978) and Stella-Prorok (1983), were also found to promote language development and sustain discourse with young children, but this view was not shared by others (for instance, Nelson et al. 1983).

Hubbel (1977) described parent-intervention programs which were aimed at helping language delayed children. The main advice given to parents in these programs was to follow the child's lead. Linguistic realizations of a child centred mode of interaction are, as just described, expansions, repetitions and retroactive moves, which all signal to children that the adult understood and accepted their last move. A more active approach is to semantically extend the child's utterance, as studied by Cross (1978), Lieven (1978), Barnes et al. (1983), Howe (1981) and Nelson et al. (1983), or to otherwise incorporate the child's topic (Brown, Cazden and Bellugi 1969; Hubbel 1977; Newport et al. 1977; Ellis and Wells 1980).

The features which McDonald and Pien (1982) found constituted a control-oriented style of interaction have been discussed by other researchers as being associated with less advanced language development and/or being inhibiting to the child's participation in the verbal interaction. Among the questions, repair questions were found to contribute to the behavioural cluster of parents' techniques of control. Similarly, Lieven (1978) reported a high number of queries directed to the less advanced child in her study. Furrow et al. (1979), Cross (1981) and Barnes et al. (1983) found wh-question, or, where this was studied more specifically, certain types of wh-question, disfavourable for children's rapid language development. Hubbel (1977) recommended minimal use of high-constraint questions, such as repair questions and some types of wh-questions, in the treatment of language delayed children.

Control-oriented mothers in McDonald and Pien's study used higher proportions of directives than did conversation-oriented mothers. In other studies (Newport et al. 1977; Cross 1978, 1981), directives were shown to be associated with slower language development. However, this opinion was not shared by Furrow et al. (1979) and Barnes et al. (1983), who suggested that there is a relation between imperative forms and faster language development because of the easily decodable structure of imperative forms. This discrepancy in results may possibly be due to differing experimental designs and interpretative procedures or the relatively younger age of subjects. However, indirect or direct directives do not demand verbal responses unless they are prods; and prods were shown to be associated with delayed language development by Cross (1981). Directives, therefore, do not enhance verbal interaction between parents and children.

Attentionals were found to be more a characteristic of control-oriented speech patterns than of conversation-oriented speech patterns by McDonald and Pien (1982). Likewise, Cross (1981) noted that high numbers of attentionals were a characteristic of the verbal environment encountered by language delayed children.

Rejections, which form part of McDonald and Pien's (1982) behavioural cluster of maternal control orientation, have received little attention elsewhere. Lieven (1978), however, noted that the slower developing child of her study was corrected more often than the faster developing child.

The control-oriented mothers studied by McDonald and Pien (1982) also used more spontaneous declaratives than did the conversation-oriented mothers. This is paralleled by Cross's (1978) work. Cross investigated the relationship between utterances which were semantically unrelated to the child's preceding move or which were related to third parties and non-immediate events and the children's speed of language development. Cross found that advanced language learners encountered less of these in their interaction with their mothers.

Both Cross (1978) and McDonald and Pien (1982) associated longer parental turns, *i.e.* more parental monologuing and greater parental dominance, with children's slower language development and control-oriented speech style of the parents respectively.

Lieven (1978) found that the mother of the more slowly developing subject ignored considerably more of her daughter's communicative attempts than did the mother of the faster developing subject. This mother also used ready-made responses more often. Similarly, Cross (1978) investigated stock utterances in the mothers' speech, which were also used more by mothers of slower developing children than by mothers of faster developing children. Moreover, Cross (1981) looked directly at the language environment of slow language learners. Their mothers seemed to have a greater need for self-repetitions and self-replies.

Although the question regarding whether the parents' verbal behaviour determines the children's contributions to conversations or whether the children influence the parents' speech styles has not been answered satisfactorily yet (Gleitman, Newport and Gleitman 1984; Furrow and Nelson 1986), some researchers, especially those who are associated with the Bristol longitudinal study on language acquisition, suggested that in spite of children having undeniable influences on their parents' verbal behaviour "it also seems that adults have characteristic preferences for particular styles of interaction" (Wells and Montgomery 1981:229). They claimed that "there is nothing necessary about the relationship between the type of contribution that children make and the strategies that their mothers adopt" (Wells, Montgomery and MacLure 1979:369). Wells (1980) stated that "adults vary in their ability, or at least their willingness to help the child sustain his conversational initiatives", and he hypothesized "that children who receive adult feedback of (the) sustaining and developing kind will, compared with children who receive less such feedback, be more highly motivated to engage in conversation and, as a result, will more rapidly develop skills in linguistic communication" (Wells 1980:73). Wells thereby indicated how closely the studies on the promotion of language development, the sustenance of conversation with young children and the variations in parental speech styles are related. What looks like a teaching strategy to one scholar, appears to be a discourse strategy for another, and means parental attention and affection to the child.

For children of bilingual families, differing interactive styles of their two parents are likely to influence the balanced or unbalanced acquisition of both languages:

> Without sufficient motivation and linguistic attention, the child's language acquisition is rendered more difficult and slowed down. This observation also applies to bilingualism: if, for instance, one of the parents does not have enough time (or interest) to speak his/her language with the child and the child's emotional bond to the other parent becomes stronger, then the child's language development will soon reflect this: one of the languages will develop faster, it will become the *strong language*, the other language will lag behind, it will become the *weak language*.
> (Kielhöfer and Jonekeit 1983:16; my translation)

It appears that a large number of features of parent-child verbal interaction have already been investigated, and that there is a considerable amount of overlap in results. Many of the results, however, did not reach statistical significance and some results were obtained with only a very limited number of subjects. Moreover, most researchers studied each of the more formal features of verbal interaction in isolation. Meanwhile, studies which investigated ways of sustaining verbal interaction with children suggest that certain interactional strategies either promote or inhibit the child's ongoing participation in conversation.

What is needed, then, is a model of conversational analysis which classifies each interactional move according to its more formal properties and immediate illocutionary forces as well as to its position in and relevance for the verbal interaction in progress. Moreover, the model should allow for the individual moves to be grouped into interactionally relevant clusters. In this way, individual differences between parents regarding the strategies they prefer in order to motivate their children's verbal participation can be outlined, and one would be able to see how much of the verbal interaction in the parent-child dyads is spent in strategies directed towards regulating the child's behaviour versus strategies directed towards conversing with the child.

4.2.2 The theoretical framework

The present analysis will demonstrate that those features which are believed to promote faster language development in children and which are likely to further engage children in verbal interaction are discourse structuring constituents of a similar type. The analysis will use categories from Stubbs' (1983) adaptation of the Birmingham model of discourse analysis.

According to Stubbs, interactional moves are either *initiating* or *reacting*. However, there are moves which are not only conditioned by the preceding move but at the same time condition a reactive move. These moves are both initiating *and* reacting.

Initiating moves either *introduce* a *new topic* or *re-introduce* an already *established topic*. At the same time, they either form the first part of an adjacency pair, and therefore *demand* some sort of a *response*, or they leave the hearer with the *option* of whether or not *to react*. Those initiating moves which introduce adjacency pairs (Sacks 1967-72) are oriented towards eliciting either a *verbal* or a *non-verbal* response.

Reacting moves either constitute the second part of an adjacency pair and are therefore *obligatory*, or are provided *optionally*. A speaker may also *fail* to provide a reactive move within an adjacency pair. Reacting moves, whether obligatory or not, can be *accepting* or *rejecting*.

There are also moves, especially in the interaction between parents and children, the function of which is to *announce* that an initiating move is about to come and to direct the hearer's attention towards it. And finally, there are occasional moves which indicate that a speaker considers an exchange to be *finished*.

The aim is to develop an analytical model which reflects the multifactorial function of each interactional move. It will show whether a move is:

> initiating or reacting or both,
> topic incorporating or unrelated,
> predicting or predicted or both,
> eliciting a verbal or a non-verbal response,
> accepting or rejecting.

Also, the model has to employ only a limited number of symbols so that it can be applied readily to naturalistic data and is visually appealing. In order to achieve these aims, the discourse models of Stubbs (1983) and Keenan and Schieffelin (1976) have been adapted and combined to serve as the basis for an integrated model of parent-child interaction.

4.2.3 Adaptation of the discourse model by Stubbs

In Stubbs' adaptation of Sinclair and Coulthard's (1975) model for the analysis of classroom interaction, the basic category is the *move*. Moves generally coincide with utterances, but the beginning or the end of a move can also be marked by a change in interactive quality. Stubbs assigns each move to one of eight clearly defined interactional categories: initiation (I), response (R), response/initiation (R/I), follow-up (F), re-initiation (Ir), information (Inf), opening markers (O) and closing markers (C). These categories differ according to whether they are predicting or predicted, initial or terminal.

Verbal interaction consists of chains of moves which are related to each other. These chains are called *exchanges*. An exchange is a series of subsequent moves, each of which is conditioned by the move which immediately precedes it. Intended exchanges are sometimes left in the rudimentary one-move stage, since the hearer can elect not to react to an initial move of the speaker. A minimal exchange consists of an initiation and a response [I R] or an initiation and a follow-up [I F].

The difference between a response (R) and a follow-up (F) is their predictability. An [I R] is implying an adjacency pair (Sacks 1967-72), *i.e.* an exchange structure in which the first move predicts and demands the second move. The most popular of these sorts of exchanges are question-answer sequences, offer-accept/reject sequences and greeting-greeting sequences. An [I F] structure, on the other hand, differs basically from an adjacency pair in that the second move may be socially desirable, but is not obligatory, *i.e.* it cannot be demanded, and the interactive partner cannot be reprimanded for not supplying the follow-up.

The category information (Inf) in the Stubbs' model is not used here. Instead, the present model differentiates between initiations which are the first part of an adjacency pair and thus predict a response [I R], and initiations which are not predictive of a response [I F]. In addition, an optional retroactive move (F/I) was included into the model for cases where the retroactive move does not follow the first part of an adjacency pair. Table 4.1 is an adaptation from Stubbs (1983:136–137 and 143–144) and incorporates the so far discussed changes:

Table 4.1: Adapted categories from Stubbs (1983)

	predicting	predicted	initial	terminal
I	can be	–	+	can be
R	–	+	–	can be
F	–	–	–	can be
R/I	+	+	–	–
F/I	+	–	–	–
Ir	can be	–	–	–
O	–	–	+	–
C	–	–	–	+

This revised model forms the basis of the my model for analysing natural interaction between parents and children.

4.2.4 Adaptation of the discourse model by Keenan and Schieffelin

Keenan and Schieffelin (1976) defined discourse as "any sequence of two or more utterances produced by a single speaker or by two or more speakers who are interacting with each other" (Keenan and Schieffelin 1976:340). In their model, continuous discourse is established by topic-collaborating moves, *i.e.* responses and follow-ups in Stubbs's terminology, and by topic-incorporating moves, *i.e.* initial moves which draw upon the same "propositional pool" as the preceding move (Keenan and Schieffelin 1976:342). Keenan and Schieffelin grouped topic-incorporating and topic-collaborating discourse moves under the heading "continuous discourse", and topic-introducing and topic-re-introducing moves under "discontinuous discourse".

In the present model, exchanges are considered as being part of the same topic as long as they are semantically related and/or pursue the same illocutionary directions. The decision as to whether an exchange still belongs to the same topic or whether it introduces a new topic is made on the basis of formal semantic relatedness, *i.e.* the use of the same nouns or pronouns, and actual discourse continuation, thereby taking the interactants' own interpretation into account. Topic-incorporating initiating moves are symbolized (T/Ir) and called *topic re-initiation*. A topic-re-initiation (T/Ir) will also be assigned if an interruption consists of only a short diversion of not more than a couple of moves or a longer pause. Usually such a diversion is directed at a third person. The notion of extension also falls into the category of topic re-initiations (T/Ir). By definition, extensions introduce some new content material, but stay within the same topic.

4.2.5 The integrated model

For the purpose of analysing long stretches of parent-child verbal interaction, each of the discourse constituting categories have been sub-classified further. The sub-classifications correspond to the features associated with accelerated language development and sustenance of conversation, as discussed in section 4.2.1.

All new topic initiations (I) and topic re-initiations (T/Ir) are sub-classified on the basis of whether or not they initiate adjacency pairs, *i.e.* whether or not they are response-demanding. The most common sub-classification of initiations are questions (qu) and behaviour modifying moves (bm). A question is responded to by an answer (ans) or by a minimal response (m) in the case of the answer consisting of only one word:

(1)   [Ke I, 540 - 541]
        F: *wo ist das Reh.*   (I-qu)
               'where is the deer.'
        C: *it got no Reh.*   (R-ans)
               'it got no deer.'

Behaviour modifying moves differ from questions basically in that they are ultimately responded to non-verbally. When the hearer complies with a directive non-verbally, this is usually indicated in the ongoing interaction by the speaker's signs of approval or simply by the speaker not re-initiating his/ her request. This being the case, the obligatory response to the behaviour modifying initiation is sub-classified as being non-verbal (nv):

(2)   [Tr I, 345 - 349]
    F: *let Papa break it up a bit - like this.*   (T/Ir-bm)
        (3.2)
    C: ((sighs))   (R-nv)
    F: *yeah.*

If behaviour modifying moves are responded to verbally, the response indicates that the hearer either accepts (ac) or rejects (rej) the request:

(3)   [Ke I, 85 - 88]
    F: *setz dich wieder.*   (T/Ir-bm)
        'sit down again.'
        bleib still!   (Ir-bm)
        'stay quiet!'
    C: ((crying)) *no:o.*   (R-rej)

Another common adjacency pair in adult-child interaction is the summons-answer sequence. As previously discussed, it is initiated with a summons and is usually responded to with a minimal response, which indicates that the hearer is prepared to listen:

(4)   [Ja I, 1599 - 1600]
    C: *Eddie!*   (I-sm)
        (1.6)
    F: *ja,*   (R-m)

Although requiring a minimal response, summonses do not constitute conversation *per se*. Rather, they secure the hearer's attention by interrupting the hearer's current activity. Moreover, summonses are usually followed by a new topic initiation (I). In that way, summonses have a strong directing function for the interaction.

Two further types of adjacency pairs are used by parents with varying frequency. Greeting-greeting sequences are predictable for certain daily routines, such as going to bed, but some parents and children make use of them at any time of the day in order to establish verbal contact:

(5)   [Fi I, 416 - 420]
    C: *hi: Papi!*   (I-greet)
    F: *yes Fiona*   (R-m)
    C: *hi:!*   (Ir-greet)
    F: *hello,*   (R-greet)
    C: *hello=*   (F-rep)

Likewise, slot-insertion sequences are predominantly used during picture-book reading time and the singing of songs. They can, however, be part of everyday conversations between parents and children as well:

(6)   [Tr I, 102 - 107]
    M: *was sagt 'n die Oma immer.*   (T/Ir-qu)
           'what does grandma always say.'
           hallo,   (Ir-slot)
           'hello,'
    C: *Trudy.*   (R-ins)

Slot-insertion sequences are unique to the interaction between parents and young children. For the child they are steps in learning how to encode messages spontaneously (Moerk 1974).

Any of the sequence-initiating moves can be responded to by an inappropriate reaction (inap), for instance when a follow-up is supplied instead of the appropriate response. An inappropriate reaction is usually followed by a re-initiation of the original move. In the present corpus, inappropriate moves (inap) were rarely encountered.

One move was used only by the children: the initial rejection (I-rej). A child's initial rejection starts an adjacency pair, and the appropriate response to it is an acceptance (ac) or rejection (rej) from the parent. If the parent fails to respond in that way, the child is likely to re-initiate the initial rejection until the expected response is supplied (preferably an accepting one):

(7)   [Al I, 209 - 211]
    C: *I don't want them*   (I-rej)
           (2.7)
           nein I don't want them   (Ir-rej)
           'no I don't want them.'
           + .hh I don't want them.   (Ir-rej)
    M: *dann Schnucki wird das essen.* (R-ac)
           'then Schnucki will eat it.'

If a parent uttered a similar move, the expected reaction from the child would be a non-verbal compliance. For parents, they were, therefore, classified as behaviour modifying moves (bm). This difference in expected reactions is due to the unequal relationship between parents and children.

Not all initiations introduce adjacency pairs. If they do not, they are sub-classified as non-sequential moves (nsqu). Non-sequential moves are statements and informatives. The hearer has the option of reacting to them with a follow-up:

(8) [Ke I, 541 - 542]
    C: *das ist sehr bunt.*   (I-nsqu)
           'this is very colourful'
    F: *ja!*   (F-ac)
           'yes!'

The father in the above example registers the child's statement with an accepting follow-up (ac). Accepting follow-ups can also have the form of exact or reduced repetitions (rep); they can be grammatical expansions (exp), stock expressions (st) like "good girl", or, in the case of bilingual families, translations (trans). However, as already mentioned, a semantic extension has to be classified as a topic re-initiation (T/Ir) in the frame of this model. The following example illustrates a stock expression (st) as being a follow-up to a non-verbal initiating move. The classification *non-verbal initiation* (I-nv) is unavoidable since interactive moves like the child's move in (9) are solely triggered by the adult's preceding non-verbal move, which, in turn, is not triggered by any preceding move of the child.

(9) [Tr I, 326]
    F: ((serving C dinner))   (I-nv)
    C: *thank you Daddy,*   (F-st)

Follow-ups can be negative at times. The hearer can reject (rej) what the speaker has just said or correct (cor) the speaker formally:

(10) [Ke I, 282 - 283]
    F: *Steven spricht DEUTSCH.*   (I-nsqu)
           'Steven speaks GERMAN.'
    C: *no!*   (F-rej)

(11) [Tr I, 1706 - 1711]
    M: *eins, - zwei*   (T/Ir-slot)
           'one, - two'
    C: *zwei*   (F-rep)
           'two'
    M: *drei*   (T/Ir-slot)
           'three'
    C: *fünf*   (R-ins)
           'five'
    M: *vier*   (F-cor)
           'four'
    C: *vier*   (F-rep)
           'four'

Overtly correcting follow-ups (cor) (cf. Jefferson 1974; Schegloff, Jefferson and Sacks 1977) were rare in the corpus and independent of the use of the two languages in the dyads. Translations (trans), which are typical for bilingual families, tended to have a generally accepting connotation of the child's preceding move.

(12)   [Fi I, 319 - 320]
      C: *das ist mein Milchi plate.*   (I-nsqu)
           'this is my milky plate.'
      M: *das ist dein Teller.*   (F-trans)
           'this is your plate.'

Only translations which were clearly meant as "no that's wrong; say it this way" were classified as corrections (cor).

Not all follow-ups relate clearly either positively or negatively to the preceding move. Minimal follow-ups (m), such as "uhuh", or particles (par), such as "oh", are quite neutral. Two further follow-ups need to be mentioned, although they are used rarely. They are inserts (ins), which are not triggered by an intentional slot, and inappropriate follow-ups (inap).

All follow-up moves can be used as follow-ups of other reactive moves. The number of successive follow-up moves is nòt formally limited:

(13)   [Ke I, 602 - 609]
      F: *ein Vogel - { fliegt 1}*   (I-nsqu)
           'a bird - flies'
      C: *{ fly 1}*   (F-ins)
      F: *nein auf Deutsch.*   (F/I-bm)
           'no in German.'
      C: *fly. - fly.*   (R-rej)
      F: *fliegt*   (F-trans)
           'fly.
      C: *fliegt.*   (F-rep)
           'fly.'
      F: *fliegt.*   (F-rep)
           'fly.'
      C: *fliegt.*   (F-rep)
           'fly.'

As one can see from example (13), similar looking moves can have very different values for the interaction. Some parents tend to utter multiple follow-ups on their own accord, as in example (14):

(14)   [Ke I, 204 - 206]
    F: (*and what 's that*)   (I-qu)
    C: *Bäumen*   (R-m)
            'trees'
    F: *Bäume* ,   (F-cor)
            'trees' ,
            ja ,   (F-ac)
            viele Bäume .   (F-exp)

Response-initiations and follow-up-initiations can be used instead of responses and follow-ups. One of their sub-classifications is the question (qu)
as in the following example:

(15)   [Tr I, 1654-1656]
    C: *des !*   (I-bm)
            'this !'
    M: *soll die Mama noch das vom kleinen Löwen lesen ?*   (R/I-qu)
            'should Mummy read the one of the little lion ?'
    C: *les Trudy Löwe*   (R-ans)
            'read Trudy lion'

Retroactive questions (R/I-qu) usually have the form of an expansion of
the child's original move with the added feature of questioning its correctness.
It is, then, up to the child to confirm or reject the proposed expansion. In bilingual families, this move is also used when the child does not use the expected
language.

(16)   [Ja I, 1191 - 1193]
    C: *do it again*   (I-bm)
    M: *noch mal ?*   (R/I-qu)
            'again ?'
    C: *yeah* .   (R-m)

In contrast to uttering a question, a speaker who utters a query (query) has
not understood all or part of the other person's move:

(17)   [Tr I, 1850 - 1852]
    C: *[babab] !*   (I-bm)
    M: *bitte ?*   (R/I-query)
            'pardon ?'
    C: ((sings)) *ba ba*   (R-ans)
            black sheep

The third and final possibility for sub-classifying response-initiations is the behaviour modifying move (bm), which directs the activity back to the original speaker:

(18)   [Tr I, 322 - 323]
      C: *Latz ON ,*   (I/bm)
           'bib ON ,'
      M: *na geh zu Susanne ,*   (R/I-bm)
           'well go to Susanne ,'
      C: ((goes))   (R-nv)

All three of these sub-classifications of response-initiations sub-classify follow-up-initiations as well.

Any of the initial moves can be re-initiated for one of several reasons. Speakers may want to either enforce or weaken their original move, or the hearer did not react appropriately, or the hearer may have failed to react at all. In the latter case, a post-positioned attentional (at) can be used instead of the repetition of the original move:

(19)   [Fi I, 607]
      ((M is feeding C))
      M: *noch ein Löffel ?*   (T/Ir-qu)
           'another spoonful ?'
           – Fiona?   (Ir-at)

If a reactive move, such as an answer (ans), an accepting (ac) move or a rejecting (rej) move, is repeated or paraphrased by the speaker, it is counted as a re-initiation as well:

(20)   [Tr I, 531 - 532]
      ((C was enquiring about the where-abouts of a doll))
      C: *where!*   (T/Ir-qu)
      M: *wo die Susanne – wohnt .*   (R-ans)
           'where Susanne – lives .'
           in Susannes Heim .   (Ir-ans)
           'at Susanne's place .'

Tag-questions (tag) are classified as re-initiations, since their function is to enhance the motivation to react to non-sequential initiating moves or to answers. They call for a reaction similar to polar questions (Wells, MacLure and Montgomery 1981).

(21)   [Tr I, 590]
    M: *Emma hat doch eine Nadel im Arm gekriegt .*   (T/Ir-nsqu)
           'Emma got a needle into her arm . '
           gell?   (Ir-tag)
           'didn't she ?'

It is interesting to note that tag-questions have often been grouped among questions in child language research (Snow 1977, 1978; Kavanaugh and Jen 1981; Wells and Robinson, 1982). In this analysis, the discourse function of tag-question is seen as somewhat different from the discourse function of questions. However, tag-questions are also to be differentiated from post-completers (Sacks, Schegloff and Jefferson 1974). Post-completers are not necessarily preceded by non-sequential moves, and they are only uttered if the hearer failed to react to the main move. In contrast to tag-questions, post-completers must be attributed less to the speaker's style of speech than to the hearer's non-compliance. Post-completers are, therefore, classified as re-initiated questions (Ir-qu).

(22)   [Al I, 219 - 220]
    M: *Alice wird bald baden, - und dann in die Heia gehen .*   (I-nsqu)
           'Alice will have a bath soon, - and then go to bed .'
           (2.5)
           mh ?   (Ir-qu)
           'huh ?'

The hearer's attention can be directed towards an oncoming initial move by an opening marker. The most common forms of opening markers in adult-child interaction are attentionals (at), such as "Mummy", behaviour modifying moves (bm), like "listen", and particles (par), like "oh". Occasionally, they have a more question like form:

(23)   [Fi I, 3 - 4]
    M: *na Fiona*   (O-at)
           'well Fiona'
           weißt du was ,   (O-qu)
           'you know what ,'
           jetzt werden wir baden .   (I-nsqu)
           'we'll have a bath now .'

There was one instance of an (O-nsqu) in the corpus:

(24)   [Ja I, 256 - 258]
      M: *ich hab eine andere Idee .*   (O-nsqu)
              'I've got another idea .'
              wie wär's wenn wir das deutsche Liederbuch   (I-qu)
              holen und ein paar Lieder singen .
              'how about if we get the German song book
              and sing a few songs .'
      C: ((crying)) *nein nein nein*   (R-m)
              'no no no'

Closing markers indicate a speaker's intention to close a topic and are always realized as stock expressions (st), such as "OK then", "good", "there you go", and the like.

In order to account for the interactants' lack of response, every occurrence of failure to respond to an initial move of an adjacency pair is counted, including tag-questions. In the case of strings of re-initiations, the failure to respond is only counted once, and it is assigned to the move with the strongest illocutionary force.

4.2.6 Interactionally relevant clusters of moves

Detailed categorization of each interactional move shows the multi-layered function of most moves, thus accounting for the complexity of verbal interaction. According to the demands and aims of the individual analysis, the analytic categories can be combined into clusters of moves with common interactional features. Because of the complexity of verbal interaction, as is evident from the fact that similar interactive functions can be fulfilled by quite different moves, establishing clusters consisting of moves which are comparable in their interactive function was seen as an alternative to studying each type of move in isolation. Whereas two adults may be comparable in the extent to which they use behaviour modifying moves, other control oriented strategies, like attentionals, rejections or failure to respond, can differentiate the two adults in their interactional intent, even if none of the features are remarkably high when measured in isolation.

For the purpose of studying the conversational strategies and the differences in these strategies of both of a child's parents in the bilingual family, conversational moves and/or subclasses of these moves were combined into clusters which indicate the parents' interactional intents.

All moves which continue a topic already introduced, were combined in the cluster *conversational drive*. This cluster consists of all topic re-initiations, all response-initiations and all follow-up-initiations. The number of parental moves in this cluster, expressed as a percentage of a parent's total moves to his/her child, indicates the parent's preoccupation with actively sustaining topics. This cluster reflects features of parents' verbal behaviour towards their young children as described in earlier investigations, such as extensions (Lieven 1978; Howe 1981; Barnes et al. 1983), semantically related utterances (Cross 1977, 1978) and incorporations of the child's topic (Brown et al. 1969; Hubbel 1977; Newport et al. 1977; Ellis and Wells 1980; among others). All of these studies suggested that children whose parents make use of topic continuing strategies frequently are likely to progress in their language development faster than children whose parents use them only infrequently.

Parents differ as to whether they take a more initiating or a more reacting part in conversations with their children and also as to how intense their reactions are, in terms of multiple follow-ups, for instance. The cluster *responsiveness* reflects this by combining all the responses, follow-ups, response-initiations and follow-up-initiations; it is expressed as a percentage of the total number of the parent's moves. This cluster reflects the extent of a parent's interactional effort at direct reactions to the child's conversational contributions. It includes measures like expansions, repetitions, positive reinforcements and verbal reflectives, which have been studied elsewhere and which have been associated with children's faster language development and sustenance of conversation (cf. Hubbel 1977; Cross 1977, 1978; Lieven 1978; Wells 1980; Wells et. al. 1981; McDonald and Pien 1982; Moerk 1983a; Stella-Prorok 1983).

The parents' intention to elicit continuing verbal participation from their children is accounted for in the cluster *conversation oriented initiations*. In this cluster, all questions, including re-initiating questions, all tag-questions and all topic re-initiating non-sequential moves, were totalled and percentaged against all the initiations, including re-initiations, of the speaker. This cluster pays tribute to initiating features in the parents' language which assist in sustaining conversations with young children, as have been studied by Hubbel (1977), Wells et al. (1981) and Stella-Prorok (1983). It is also closely related to McDonald and Pien's (1982) notion of parents' conversational intent. All of the interactional features of this cluster of moves have been associated with faster language development in other studies (cf. Cross 1977, 1978; Lieven 1978; Newport, Gleitman and Gleitman 1977; Gleitman, Newport and Gleitman

1984; and others). Also, successful sustenance of discourse is associated with the promotion of children's language development in general (Wells et al. 1979; Wells 1980; Wells and Montgomery 1981; Kielhöfer and Jonekeit 1983).

The parents' orientation towards controlling the children, rather than conversing with them, is reflected in the cluster *control oriented initiations*. This cluster combines all the behaviour modifying moves, attentionals, summonses and non-sequential moves which introduce new topics. The control oriented initiations were percentaged against all the initiations of the speaker, including re-initiations. In contrast to non-sequential moves which re-initiate an already established topic, non-sequential moves which initiate new topics are adult centred rather than child centred, and were therefore attributed to a parental orientation towards controlling the child. This group is closely related to McDonald and Pien's (1982) notion of parents' control orientation, which, in turn, comprises several of the features in parents' language to their young children connected with slower language development (cf. Newport et al. 1977; Cross 1978, 1981) and with low sustenance of discourse (Hubbel 1977; Stella-Prorok 1983).

The degree to which parents fail to respond to their children's communicative attempts is represented by the cluster *no-response*. A parent's failure to respond is calculated by percentaging all interruptions, overtalk and failures to respond to sequential initiations against all sequential initiations of the child. Re-initiations are to be disregarded here, since a failure to respond to a string of re-initiations is only counted once. The lack of response has only been studied marginally so far. But negative effects on the child's language development have been implied (cf. Lieven 1978). Quite obviously, the interactional features comprised in this cluster are contrary to all efforts regarding the sustenance of conversations.

Since to interrupt or not to respond to a conversational partner is a form of exerting control as well, a cluster *control orientation plus no-response* needed to be established. Similarly, negative reactions have strong controlling functions. Therefore, this cluster consists of all the control oriented initiations, no-response, corrections and rejections, and is percentaged against all moves of the parent and the child. In contrast to the cluster "control oriented initiations", *control orientation plus no-response* comprises initiative and reactive measures which constitute parents' control orientation. This cluster reflects reactive features in parents' verbal behaviour which have been associated with children's slower language development, such as corrections and rejections (Lieven 1978; McDonald and Pien 1982).

Summonses, attentionals, queries, inappropriate reactions, behaviour modifying openings and re-initiations, except for tag-questions, are all devices to make a speaker's conversational move more likely to succeed. An accumulation of them indicates communication problems between the interactants. Accordingly, these types of moves were combined into a cluster called *communication problems* and percentaged against all the moves of the speaker. Several of the features in this cluster have been associated with children's slower language development. They were studied in form of self-replies (Cross 1981), self-repetitions (Newport et al. 1977; Furrow et al. 1979; Cross 1981), attentionals (Cross 1981; McDonald and Pien 1982) and adult paraphrases (Cross 1978). Queries have been the focus of a number of studies with contradictory results (Garvey 1977; Langford 1981). Whereas some researchers claim them to be a feature of parents' verbal interaction with linguistically less advanced children (Lieven 1978) and group them with other high-constraint questions (Barnes et al. 1983), other scholars consider them to have rather positive effects on the children's linguistic progress (Käsermann 1980). For the present chapter, however, they will only be considered in their function as a means of repair for communication problems.

The seven interactionally relevant clusters of moves, thus formed, are concerned with the ways in which parents sustain conversations with their young children, as well as with the parents' needs and methods for exerting verbal control when interacting with their children. The following four measures will give an indication of how much parent-child dyads pursue topics, how intensive the verbal exchange is and how strongly the parent participates in conversation.

The measure *exchanges per topic* reflects the topic maintenance in number of exchanges. It is calculated by dividing all initiations (I) and all topic re-initiations (T/Ir) of two interactants by the total number of initiations (I) of both of them. This measure indicates the effort which is being put into pursuing a once established topic by the two interactants of a dyad. It corresponds to the measures *moves per topic* and *moves per exchange*, both of which reflect the intensity of verbal interaction in the dyads. *Moves per topic* are calculated by dividing all moves of a dyad by the total number of initiations (I) of the two interactants; the measure *moves per exchange* is established by calculating all moves of a dyad, except for opening markers, against the total number of initiations (I) and topic re-initiations (T/Ir) of both interactants. In the light of the studies on child language development and discourse sustenance, high rates of topic maintenance can be expected to be related to the parents' skills of engaging the child in conversations and to their sensitivity to the child's contributions to conversation. The three measures of *exchanges per topic, moves per topic* and *moves per exchange* are not identical, but shed light on the differences in strategies involved in maintaining a topic. The fourth measure *moves per topic: parent to child* differentiates the contribution to topic maintenance made by the parent from the contribution made by the child. For this measure, all moves of the parent, except for opening markers, are calculated against the total number of initiations (I) of both parent and child.

The interactionally relevant clusters of moves, formed in this section, are all constituted by moves which pursue the same interactional direction. However, many of the interactional moves are relevant constituting factors for more than one cluster. This is due to the multi-layered function of most moves. The formation of interactionally relevant clusters of moves will allow for the parents in the bilingual families of the present sample to be compared in terms of the communicative strategies they employ when interacting with their children.

In order to assess the conversational involvement of the children with each of their two parents, four of the seven interactionally relevant clusters of moves were calculated for the children as well. A fifth cluster, called *child-initiative in conversation*, was added. The cluster *child-initiative in conversation* consists of all questions, tag-questions, non-sequential new topic initiations and non-sequential topic re-initiations, all of which were percentaged against the total number of moves of the child. This cluster reflects the extent to which a child uses verbal strategies for conversational purposes. In contrast to the verbal behaviour of adults towards young children, the success of the children's communicative attempts towards the adults is not likely to be dependent on topic-incorporating and low-constraint strategies as expressed by the clusters *conversational drive* and *conversation oriented initiations*. Furthermore, a failure to respond cannot be considered as means of control which young children possess in interaction with their parents. The cluster *control orientation plus non-response* is, therefore, irrelevant as well. This leaves the clusters *responsiveness, no-response, communication problems, control-oriented initiations* and *child-initiative in conversation* to be calculated for the children.

4.3 Discourse structures in the families

The discourse model which was described in section 4.2.5 was used for analyzing the discourse structures in each of the six bilingual families. The analysis was done separately for each mother-child dyad and for each father-child
dyad. Subsequently, the interactionally relevant clusters of moves were calculated.

It was hypothesized that a child would be more likely to make active use
of the minority language, German, if the interaction between child and German-speaking parent was equally or more child centred than the interaction
between child and English-speaking parent. I consider a child centred mode
of interaction to be one which is responsive to the child's contributions to the
conversation, which works to maintain a topic once introduced, and which is
more oriented towards conversing with the child than controlling the child. The
number of communication problems are taken as an indication of how approachable the child is for the parent.

The children's involvement in conversational interaction with each of their
parents was defined in terms of high levels of *responsiveness* and *child-initiative in conversation*, and low levels of *no-response*, *communication problems* and *control oriented initiations*. Degree of involvement in conversational
interaction was expected to be directly related to the parents' interactional styles
as well as to the children's willingness and ability to use German actively.

4.3.1 Comparison across the sample

The comparison of the parents' verbal behaviour towards their children was
expected to display similarities between the parents of the two actively German-speaking children, Keith and Fiona, and to display differences between
Keith's and Fiona's parents, on the one hand, and the other children's parents
on the other hand. The results are summarized in Tables 4.2 to 4.5, separated
for German-speaking parent-child dyads and English-speaking parent-child
dyads, as well as recording time.

The cross-sample comparison showed only limited correlations between
the parents' scores in the interactionally relevant clusters of moves and the
children's willingness and ability to use German "originally and intentionally". Of the eleven measures (plus dominance) which were investigated, it was
only in the cluster *conversational drive* that a clear agreement was shown in

Table 4.2: Discourse behaviour of German-speaking parents – first recording

	Alice	Keith*	Jacob	Agnes	Fiona*	Trudy
conversational drive	26.1%	31.9%	26.6%	20.8%	28.5%	21.2%
responsiveness	31.3%	47.9%	35.8%	20.7%	27.9%	24.7%
no-response	24.3%	4.7%	13.0%	28.1%	16.2%	9.7%
communication probl.	12.4%	15.6%	21.4%	25.4%	22.7%	25.5%
conversation orien.init.	56.8%	57.9%	43.2%	23.0%	40.0%	43.3%
control orien.initiation	36.5%	27.7%	41.8%	59.4%	51.0%	45.6%
control orient.+no-resp.	20.9%	15.1%	20.5%	32.6%	25.0%	28.3%
exchanges per topic	1.70	2.26	2.16	1.35	1.98	1.63
moves per topic	3.84	5.93	5.38	3.31	4.63	4.01
moves per exchange	2.22	2.59	2.40	2.26	2.18	2.47
moves/topic: P to C	2.10	3.59	3.07	2.08	2.69	2.91
dominance	1.20	1.50	1.27	1.48	1.33	2.64

* actively German-speaking children

Table 4.3: Discourse behaviour of English-speaking parents – first recording

	Alice	Keith*	Jacob	Agnes	Fiona*	Trudy
conversational drive	42.3%	32.2%	33.0%	30.0%	22.0%	30.1%
responsiveness	48.3%	37.8%	38.9%	33.9%	41.5%	20.7%
no-response	23.7%	22.4%	13.1%	26.9%	3.6%	15.5%
communication probl.	6.3%	16.5%	19.8%	14.5%	22.3%	26.6%
conversation orien.init.	66.3%	43.7%	57.0%	49.7%	41.2%	49.1%
control orien.initiations	31.2%	33.0%	28.0%	32.0%	47.7%	41.9%
control orient.+no-resp.	17.5%	20.0%	14.0%	20.6%	17.0%	24.6%
exchanges per topic	2.83	1.69	2.44	1.69	1.95	2.02
moves per topic	7.03	3.49	6.85	4.29	5.15	4.52
moves per exchange	2.47	1.99	2.72	2.44	2.51	2.24
moves/topic: P to C	3.37	1.82	3.99	2.39	3.10	3.15
dominance	0.93	1.09	1.35	1.18	1.39	2.27

* actively German-speaking children

the discourse behaviour to which the two actively German-speaking children were exposed by their German-speaking parents during the first recording. During the second recording, the scores for the cluster *control orientation plus no-response* were different for Keith's and Fiona's German-speaking parents compared with the other children's German-speaking parents. However, when the children were divided into the two age groups of 2;8 and 2;4 (at the time of the first recording, Alice, Keith, Jacob and Agnes were aged 2;8, and Fiona and Trudy were aged 2;4), the scores for both Keith's and Fiona's German-speaking parents were similar and contrasted with those for the other German-speaking parents in the children's respective age groups in so far as they were higher in *responsiveness, exchanges per topic* and *moves per topic* and lower in *control orientation plus no-response* during the first recording. However, no such tendencies were observed during the second recording.

Table 4.4: Discourse behaviour of German-speaking parents – second recording

	Alice	Keith*	Jacob	Agnes	Fiona*	Trudy
conversational drive	24.2%	24.0%	26.2%	18.6%	24.1%	22.7%
responsiveness	24.0%	51.6%	29.0%	28.2%	27.6%	28.7%
no-response	17.1%	12.1%	16.0%	38.7%	14.7%	3.2%
communication probl.	27.6%	16.9%	17.5%	15.6%	16.2%	23.2%
conversation orien.init.	43.3%	57.6%	48.1%	42.6%	41.4%	45.7%
control orien.initiations	54.3%	31.8%	50.6%	49.0%	46.4%	44.0%
control orient.+no-resp.	28.9%	16.2%	26.6%	30.2%	23.0%	26.2%
exchanges per topic	1.44	1.71	1.67	1.30	1.52	1.84
moves per topic	2.98	4.08	3.28	2.63	3.43	4.45
moves per exchange	2.07	2.39	1.97	2.02	2.19	2.35
moves/topic: P to C	1.61	2.34	1.82	1.64	2.04	3.02
dominance	1.25	1.37	1.27	1.66	1.46	2.41

* actively German-speaking children

At both times of recording, the scores for the English-speaking parents of the children who did not use German actively were higher than were the scores for the English-speaking parents of Keith and Fiona in the cluster *conversation oriented initiations*, and lower in the cluster *control oriented initiations*. Their scores were also lower than were those of Keith's and Fiona's English-speaking parents in the cluster *control orientation plus no-response* during the second recording. When the children were divided into age groups, the scores

Table 4.5: Discourse behaviour of English-speaking parents – second recording

	Alice	Keith*	Jacob	Agnes	Fiona*	Trudy
conversational drive	31.9%	22.9%	38.6%	32.0%	25.1%	28.4%
responsiveness	27.1%	40.7%	28.1%	49.3%	30.1%	35.7%
no-response	13.5%	22.6%	19.2%	17.9%	7.5%	13.1%
communication probl.	12.9%	13.0%	17.1%	21.3%	16.3%	18.1%
conversation orien.init.	60.1%	39.7%	63.4%	46.7%	42.1%	54.4%
control orien.initiations	33.4%	56.0%	31.4%	31.1%	50.0%	34.4%
control orient.+no-resp.	18.3%	26.9%	18.1%	17.9%	21.7%	17.8%
exchanges per topic	2.09	1.50	2.09	1.61	1.61	1.83
moves per topic	4.41	2.88	4.72	3.42	3.68	3.93
moves per exchange	2.11	1.91	2.25	2.12	2.20	2.02
moves/topic: P to C	2.74	1.44	2.53	1.76	2.09	2.14
dominance	1.67	1.02	1.27	1.06	1.29	1.43

* actively German-speaking children

for the English-speaking parents of the children who did not use German "originally and intentionally" were also higher on the measure *moves per topic: parent to child*, and these parents were more dominant in the verbal interaction with their children than were the English-speaking parents of Keith and Fiona in the children's respective age groups, during the second recording.

The children's discourse behaviour is summarized in Tables 4.6 to 4.9.

Table 4.6: Child to German-speaking parent – first recording

	Alice	Keith*	Jacob	Agnes	Fiona*	Trudy
responsiveness	49.5%	50.2%	32.5%	44.4%	37.7%	63.6%
no-response	20.4%	18.3%	22.5%	29.4%	24.4%	30.3%
communication probl.	16.4%	12.1%	23.1%	23.8%	21.9%	6.8%
control orient.initiations	51.5%	43.1%	38.8%	48.8%	59.8%	51.7%
child-initiative in conv.	31.0%	35.4%	38.5%	19.1%	24.6%	22.9%

* actively German-speaking children

Table 4.7: Child to English-speaking parent – first recording

	Alice	Keith*	Jacob	Agnes	Fiona*	Trudy
responsiveness	49.0%	24.0%	36.5%	52.5%	46.0%	61.1%
no-response	10.5%	23.7%	21.7%	19.2%	20.0%	29.3%
communication prob.	13.4%	25.3%	24.3%	17.7%	10.2%	11.2%
control orien.initiations	35.0%	71.8%	38.4%	67.7%	27.5%	47.8%
child-initiative in conv.	40.3%	22.0%	31.9%	11.1%	43.3%	23.4%

* actively German-speaking children

Table 4.8: Child to German-speaking parents – second recording

	Alice	Keith*	Jacob	Agnes	Fiona*	Trudy
responsiveness	37.8%	33.0%	30.2%	44.6%	40.3%	41.5%
no-response	35.4%	15.1%	25.4%	51.0%	15.3%	30.9%
communication probl.	19.9%	15.2%	22.8%	16.3%	17.2%	11.2%
control orien.initiations	56.9%	35.0%	47.7%	80.4%	46.7%	52.7%
child-initiative in conv.	30.9%	54.0%	39.7%	13.9%	38.6%	29.8%

* actively German-speaking children

Table 4.9: Child to English-speaking parent – second recording

	Alice	Keith*	Jacob	Agnes	Fiona*	Trudy
responsiveness	64.0%	20.4%	39.8%	30.0%	48.2%	30.6%
no-response	15.6%	34.8%	19.8%	60.9%	20.2%	20.3%
communication probl.	5.5%	23.9%	25.9%	20.0%	13.5%	15.9%
control orien.initiations	35.6%	55.6%	33.9%	70.6%	49.0%	46.4%
child-initiative in conv.	25.3%	47.8%	45.8%	22.9%	34.3%	37.6%

* actively German-speaking children

The cross-sample comparison of the children's discourse behaviour towards their German- and English-speaking parents indicated that Keith and Fiona displayed less responsive behaviour towards their English-speaking parents than did the other children in their respective age groups during the first recording (cf. *responsiveness*). Likewise, Keith's and Fiona's scores were lower in the cluster *no-response* in interaction with their German-speaking parents than were the other children's scores in their respective age group during the first recording, and lower *per se* during the second recording. Also during the second recording, Keith and Fiona used strategies from the cluster *control oriented initiations* less with their German-speaking parents than did the other children. Lastly, Keith and Fiona showed more *child-initiative in conversation* with their German-speaking parents than did the other children in their respective age groups during the second recording.

As can be seen from Tables 4.2 to 4.9, the comparison across the sample did not yield the expected results in any straight forward way. Similarities in the discourse behaviour of Keith's and Fiona's parents and in Keith's and Fiona's own verbal strategies did not contrast with the discourse behaviour of the other children's parents or the other children's own verbal strategies consistently over both times of recording.

This failure of finding consistent results which differentiate the two actively bilingual children from the four passive bilinguals is an indication of the difficulties encountered in comparing the linguistic input which children receive in different families. Lieven (1984) argued convincingly that most children acquire language in spite of their parents providing very different linguistic input; she discussed examples from a variety of cultures as well as a variety of verbal behaviours displayed by American mothers and the children's strategies to make optimal use of that input in their attempts at learning to speak. The type of linguistic input which another child receives is of no consequence to the individual child. Instead, he/she has to make do with whatever linguistic input is available.

4.3.2 Discussion of each individual family

As shown in section 4.3.1, the comparison across the sample did not render the anticipated explanation as to why Keith and Fiona were willing and able to use German "originally and intentionally", but the other children were not. In addition to the short-comings of cross-sectional comparisons of parents' interactive styles already described, the insufficiency of the cross-sectional comparison of this very small sample of children is also due to the fact that, in spite of the major social variables being kept stable, the interactive and communicative situations within the families were hardly comparable. The families differed in terms of interactive situations taking place on the days of recording, such as work load, the presence of visitors, and emotional preoccupation with people and things other than the child. They differed in terms of the division of chores between the parents, and they differed in the demands being made on the parents by the children. All of these factors affected the parents' verbal behaviour towards their children. Although some of these differences might have been chosen by the parents and were, therefore, a relatively stable factor in the family life, such as the division of chores for instance, others were unique to a particular day. The children's mood and behaviour were also likely to be dependent on the circumstances of a particular day. The families will, therefore, be looked at individually.

Although the general family situation of a particular day is comparable for both parents in a family, the ways in which the parents cope with external influences and with the demands which are placed on them by the child will be different for each of the two parents. Therefore, children have different experiences when interacting with each of their parents. The situations in which the father interacts with the child are in most families different from the situations in which the mother interacts with the child (Döpke 1987). They might be chosen by the parents or by the child. Likewise, the type of language to which the child is exposed while interacting with each of his/her parents will be unique to the parent-child dyad in question, for the language used is often a result of the activity chosen. Children in bilingual families are, therefore, likely to be exposed to different interactive strategies in the two languages of their two parents. Provided that the sort of verbal interaction which children are involved in does in fact influence their pace of language acquisition, then the way in which the German-speaking parent's interactive strategies differ from the English-speaking parent's interactive strategies can result in the child acquiring one language rather than the other, due to the child's greater linguistic orientation towards one parent than the other. For this reason, the interactive strategies of each child's German-speaking parent was compared with that of his/her English-speaking spouse.

It was hypothesized that the interaction between the child and his/her German-speaking parent must be enjoyable and rewarding for the child in order to motivate the child to use the minority language actively. In order to achieve this goal for the individual child, the German speaking parent's interactive strategies must be compatible with the English-speaking parent's interactive strategies in terms of being oriented towards the child's momentary interest and communicative needs. It was expected to be favourable for the child's willingness to actively acquire German when the German-speaking parent used the clusters *conversational drive, responsiveness* and *conversation oriented initiations* more often or equally as often compared with the English-speaking parent. The scoring was defined as being equal when the parents' scores did not differ by more than three percent. For the clusters *no-response, control oriented initiations* and *control orientation plus no-response*, it was expected to be favourable when the German-speaking parent produced less moves or equally as many moves in these clusters than did the English-speaking parent. Again, equal scoring was defined as not differing by more than three percent. Likewise, the cluster *communication problems* ought to be less or equally represented in the discourse behaviour of the German-speaking parent compared with that of the English-speaking parent, and equal scoring was defined as not exceeding a difference of three percent. The remaining measures of *exchanges per topic, moves per topic, moves per exchange* and *moves per topic: parent to child* were all assumed to be favourably higher or equally represented in the discourse of the German-speaking parent and the child compared with the discourse of the English-speaking parent and the child. Equal scoring was defined as +0.1 exchanges in the measure *exchanges per topic* and as +0.6 moves in the other three measures. Cut-off points between equal and differential scoring were derived empirically: their purpose was to assist in distinguishing between the active bilinguals (Keith and Fiona) and the passive bilinguals (Alice, Jacob, Agnes and Trudy). Positive and negative signs indicate the way in which the German-speaking parents differ from the English-speaking parents with respect to their use of moves in a particular interactionally relevant cluster of verbal moves.

In order to compare the children's degree of involvement in conversations with each of their two parents, the children's verbal behaviour towards their German-speaking parents was contrasted with the verbal behaviour towards their English-speaking parents. The differences in scoring in each of the five clusters, *i.e., responsiveness, no-response, communication problems, control oriented initiations* and *child-initiative in conversations*, were expected to give an indication of the children's verbal involvement with each of their parents, and to be related to the parents' child centredness of behaviour as well as the children's willingness and ability to use German actively. The results will be discussed separately for each family.

4.3.2.1 Alice. A comparison of the discourse behaviour of Alice's German-speaking mother with that of her English-speaking father yielded some interesting points. The results from the first recording are shown in Tables 4.10 and 4.11.

The parents' scores on measures of *conversation oriented initiations* and *control oriented initiations* in Table 4.10 showed that they were both oriented more towards conversing with Alice than towards controlling her. The comparison of the parents in Table 4.11, however, revealed that Alice's German-speaking mother rated lower than did the English-speaking father on the measure of *conversation oriented initiations* and also lower on the measures of *conversational drive* and *responsiveness*. She rated higher than did the father on the measures of *control oriented initiations*, *control orientation plus no-response* and *communication problems*. The parents scored equally on the measure of *no-response*. The topic length in the father-child dyad exceeded that in the mother child dyad in "exchanges per topic" and "moves per topic". The

Table 4.10: Discourse behaviour of Alice's parents – first recording

	Mother	Father
conversational drive	26.1%	42.3%
responsiveness	31.3%	48.3%
no-response	24.3%	23.7%
communication problems	12.4%	6.3%
conversation oriented initiations	56.8%	66.3%
control oriented initiations	36.5%	31.2%
control orientation plus no-response	20.9%	17.5%
exchanges per topic	1.70	2.83
moves per topic	3.84	7.63
moves per topic	2.22	2.47
moves per topic: parent to child	2.10	3.37

Table 4.11: Comparison of Alice's parents regarding their discourse behaviour – first recording

conversational drive	-16.2%
responsiveness	-17.0%
no-response	0.6%
communication problems	6.1%
conversation oriented initiations	-9.5%
control oriented initiations	5.3%
control orientation plus no-response	3.4%
exchanges per topic	-1.13
moves per topic	3.19
moves per exchange	-0.25
moves per topic: parent to child	-1.27

length of exchanges can be considered equal, since the mother-child dyad generated exchanges which were, on the average, only 0.25 moves per exchange shorter than those which were generated by the father-child dyad.

The analysis of Alice's verbal behaviour (Tables 4.12 and 4.13) shows that her behaviour differed according to whether she was interacting with her mother or with her father.

Table 4.12: Alice's discourse behaviour towards her parents – first recording

	Mother	Father
responsiveness	49.5%	49.0%
no-response	20.4%	10.5%
communication problems	16.4%	13.4%
control oriented initiations	51.5%	35.0%
initiative in conversation	31.0%	40.3%
parent's dominance	1.20	0.93

Table 4.13: Differences in Alice's discourse behaviour between interaction with her mother and interaction with her father – first recording

responsiveness	0.5%
no-response	9.9%
communication problems	3.0%
control oriented initiations	16.5%
initiative in conversation	-9.3%

The major part of Alice's participation in the verbal interaction with her parents was responsive. Nearly fifty percent of all her moves were scored in the cluster *responsiveness*. Indeed, she exceeded her parents on this measure. The measure of *no-response*, however, showed her to be less responsive to her mother than to her father. The cluster *control oriented initiations* indicated that Alice was more likely to address requests to her mother than to her father. At the same time, she was more initiative on a conversational level in interaction with her father than in interaction with her mother. The cluster *communication problems* was represented equally in her verbal behaviour towards both parents. The mother was slightly more dominant than the child, and the father was slightly less dominant than Alice.

The analysis of the communicative situation in Alice's family appears to confirm the parents' opinion that the father's interaction with Alice was more intense than was the mother's. His high scores in *conversational drive, responsiveness* and topic length indicate a very child centred mode of interaction. This was possibly the basis for the close relationship between father and daughter which both parents pointed out in the initial interview. The father's child centred mode of interaction was rewarded by the child's intensive verbal participation. The mother's less child centred mode of interaction resulted in the child's higher proportion of failure to respond and her subdued *initiative in conversations*. On the other hand, Alice's high level of *responsiveness* towards her mother was remarkable. Nevertheless, Alice was less involved in conversations with her mother than she was with her father.

During the second recording (Tables 4.14 and 4.15) Alice's mother rated lower than Alice's father in the clusters *conversational drive, responsiveness* and *conversation oriented initiations*. She rated higher in the remaining clusters of *no-response, communication problems, control oriented initiations* and *control orientation plus no-response*. The measures regarding the topic length indicated that the mother-child dyad engaged in shorter topics than did the father-child dyad. There were fewer *exchanges per topic* and fewer *moves per topic* in the mother-child dyad than were in the father-child dyad. This was

Table 4.14: Discourse behaviour of Alice's parents – second recording

	Mother	Father
conversational drive	24.2%	31.9%
responsiveness	24.0%	27.1%
no-response	17.1%	13.5%
communication problems	27.6%	12.9%
conversation oriented initiations	43.3%	60.1%
control oriented initiations	54.3%	33.4%
control orientation plus no-response	28.9%	18.3%
exchanges per topic	1.44	2.09
moves per topic	2.98	4.41
moves per exchange	2.07	2.11
moves per topic: parent to child	1.61	2.74

Table 4.15: Comparison of Alice's parents regarding their discourse behaviour – second recording

conversational drive	-7.7%
responsiveness	-3.1%
no-response	3.6%
communication problems	14.7%
conversation oriented initiations	-16.8%
control oriented initiations	20.9%
control orientation plus no-response	10.6%
exchanges per topic	0.65
moves per topic	-1.43
moves per exchange	-0.04
moves per topic: parent to child	-1.13

due primarily to the mother contributing less to an ongoing topic than the father, as expressed by the measure *moves per topic: parent to child*. The only mea-sure in which mother and father scored equally during the second recording was *moves per exchange*.

Alice was less responsive towards her mother than towards her father during the second recording (Tables 4.16 and 4.17) and had more *communication problems* with her mother as well. If Alice wanted something done for herself, she was more likely to turn to her mother. This is indicated by Alice's rating in the cluster *control oriented initiations*. Nevertheless, on the measure *child-initiative in conversations*, Alice scored slightly higher in interaction with her mother than with her father. During the second recording, both parents were dominant in the verbal interaction with Alice. The mother's dominance had changed little since the first recording, but the father, who was less dominant than Alice during the first recording, was even more dominant than the mother during the second recording.

Table 4.16: Alice's discourse behaviour towards her parents – second recording

	Mother	Father
responsiveness	37.8%	64.0%
no-response	35.4%	15.6%
communication problems	19.9%	5.5%
control oriented initiations	56.9%	35.6%
initiative in conversation	30.9%	25.3%
parent's dominance	1.25	1.67

Table 4.17: Differences in Alice's discourse behaviour between interaction with her mother and interaction with her father – second recording

responsiveness	-26.2%
no-response	19.8%
communication problems	14.4%
control oriented initiations	21.3%
initiative in conversation	5.6%

The analysis of the discourse behaviour employed by parents and child during the second recording closely resembled the results of the first recording. Although the scoring in each of the groups differed greatly for the two recordings, the German-speaking mother scored towards the hypothesis, *i.e.* more than or as child centred as the father, in only two out of eleven interactionally relevant clusters of moves during the first recording and in only one out of eleven clusters during the second recording. On all other measures the father scored more child centred than did the mother. On the measure *moves per exchange*, the parents scored equally during both recordings, but the equal scoring for the cluster *no-response* during the first recording was not replicated during the second.

The discourse strategies which Alice used during the second recording were slightly different from those which she used during the first recording. Alice was less responsive to her mother than to her father and had slightly more *communication problems* with her mother during the second recording. In contrast to the first recording, she engaged in more conversations in interaction with her mother than in interaction with her father during the second recording. However, Alice was overall still more involved in conversational types of interaction with her father than with her mother during both recordings.

Since the results for both recordings are similar, Alice's unwillingness or inability to use German actively was likely to be related to the father's more child centred verbal behaviour and Alice's, consequently, higher involvement in verbal interactions with him.

4.3.2.2 Keith. The mother- and father-child dyads in Keith's family differed greatly in the amount of verbal interaction which took place during the first recording. In spite of this, Keith's mother and father scored equally on the measure of *conversational drive* (Tables 4.18 and 4.19). They also scored equally on *communication problems*. In all of the other clusters, the German-speaking father scored more favourably towards the hypothesis than did the English-speaking mother. The father's score exceeded the mother's score in *responsiveness* and in *conversation oriented initiations*. His score was lower than the mother's score on the measures of *control oriented initiations, no-*

Table 4.18: Discourse behaviour of Keith's parents – first recording

	Father	Mother
conversational drive	31.9%	32.3%
responsiveness	47.9%	37.8%
no-response	4.7%	22.4%
communication problems	15.6%	16.5%
conversation oriented initiations	57.9%	43.7%
control oriented initiations	27.7%	33.0%
control orientation plus no-response	15.1%	20.0%
exchanges per topic	2.26	1.69
moves per topic	5.93	3.49
moves per exchange	2.59	1.99
moves per topic: parent to child	3.59	1.82

Table 4.19: Comparison of Keith's parents regarding their discourse behaviour – first recording

conversational drive	-0.4%
responsiveness	10.1%
no-response	-17.7%
communication problems	-0.9%
conversation oriented initiations	14.2%
control oriented initiations	-5.3%
control orientation plus no-response	-4.9%
exchanges per topic	0.57
moves per topic	2.44
moves per exchange	0.60
moves per topic: parent to child	1.77

response and *control orientation plus no-response*. In length of topic, the father-child dyad exceeded the mother-child dyad in *exchanges per topic*, *moves per topic*, and *moves per exchange*. On average, the father addressed 1.77 times more moves to the child than did the mother in the course of a topic.

More than fifty percent of all the moves which Keith addressed to his father were responsive, but only a quarter of his moves to his mother were responsive (Tables 4.20 and 4.21). He also failed to respond to his mother more often than to his father. 25.3% of all his moves to his mother indicated *communication problems*, but only 12.1% of his moves to his father indicated the same. With requests for action, complaints and rejections, Keith was more likely to turn to his mother than to his father: this was shown in the different ways with which he made use of strategies in the cluster *control oriented initiations*. Keith also showed considerably more *initiative in conversations* with his father than with his mother. However, the father was more dominant in the parent-child dyad than was the mother. Overall, Keith seemed to be more involved in conversations when talking to his father than when talking to his mother.

Table 4.20: Keith's discourse behaviour towards his parents – first recording

	Father	Mother
responsiveness	50.2%	24.0%
no-response	19.3%	23.7%
communication problems	12.1%	25.3%
control oriented initiations	43.1%	71.8%
initiative in conversation	35.4%	22.0%
parent's dominance	1.50	1.09

Table 4.21: Differences in Keith's discourse behaviour between interaction with his father and interaction with his mother – first recording

responsiveness	26.2%
no-response	-5.4%
communication problems	-13.1%
control oriented initiations	-28.7%
initiative in conversation	13.4%

The analysis of the communicative situation in Keith's family showed that the father spent much time at home in verbal interaction with Keith. However, he not only talked more to his son than did the mother, but also more intensively, as can be shown by topic length in *exchanges per move* and *moves per topic*. His mode of interaction was more child centred than was hers, which is indicated by the measures of *conversation oriented initiations, responsiveness* and *no-response*. It is remarkable that the father's percentages in the clusters *control oriented initiations* and *control orientation plus no-response* were both below those of the mother, even though he performed most of the child-care procedures that day (*e.g.* bathing and dressing Keith). The percentage of *communication problems* is inflated because the father made many *queries* in order to prod Keith into speaking German to him instead of English.

This analysis confirms the mother's and maternal grandmother's opinions that Keith and his father had a very close relationship. It also contributes towards an explanation for Keith's willingness to make active use of the minority language to which he was exposed through his father.

During the second recording, Keith's father again scored towards the hypothesis in nearly all of the interactionally relevant clusters. The results are presented in Tables 4.22 and 4.23

Table 4.22: Discourse behaviour of Keith's parents – second recording

	Father	Mother
conversational drive	24.0%	22.9%
responsiveness	51.6%	40.7%
no-response	12.1%	22.6%
communication problems	16.9%	12.9%
conversation oriented initiations	57.6%	39.7%
control oriented initiations	31.8%	56.0%
control orientation plus no-response	16.2%	26.9%
exchanges per topic	1.71	1.50
moves per topic	4.08	2.88
moves per exchange	2.39	1.91
moves per topic: parent to child	2.34	1.44

The father scored similarly to the mother in the cluster *conversational drive*, but higher than the mother in *responsiveness* and *conversation oriented initiations*, and lower than the mother in the clusters *no-response, control oriented initiations* and *control orientation plus no-response*. Only on the measure *communication problems* did he score contrary to the hypothesis with a score of 4% higher than that for the mother. The father-child dyad engaged in longer topics on all four levels of measurement.

Table 4.23: Comparison of Keith's parents regarding their discourse behaviour – second recording

conversational drive	1.1%
responsiveness	10.9%
no-response	-10.5%
communication problems	4.0%
conversation oriented initiations	17.9%
control oriented initiations	-24.2%
control orientation plus no-response	-10.7%
exchanges per topic	0.21
moves per topic	1.20
moves per exchange	0.48
moves per topic: parent to child	0.90

Accordingly, Keith scored towards the hypothesis, and thus towards high involvement in conversational activities with his father, in all five of the calculated clusters of moves (Tables 4.24 and 4.25).

Table 4.24: Keith's discourse behaviour towards his parents – second recording

	Father	Mother
responsiveness	33.0%	20.4%
no-response	15.1%	34.8%
communication problems	15.2%	23.9%
control oriented initiations	35.0%	55.6%
initiative in conversation	54.0%	47.8%
parent's dominance	1.25	1.67

Table 4.25: Differences in Keith's discourse behaviour between interaction with his father and interaction with his mother – second recording

responsiveness	12.6%
no-response	-19.7%
communication problems	-8.7%
control oriented initiations	-20.6%
initiative in conversation	6.2%

Keith was more responsive to his father than to his mother as shown in the clusters *responsiveness* and *no-response*, and he contributed more initiating conversational moves to the verbal interaction with his father. For requests of all types, he was more likely to turn to his mother. He also had more *communication problems* with his mother than with his father. The degree of parental dominance remained fairly stable from the first to the second recording, with the father being more dominant than the mother.

The comparative results for the parental discourse behaviour showed that the father rated towards the hypothesis in the vast majority of all measures during both recordings. Consequently, Keith was more involved in conversational types of interaction with his father than with his mother. The differences in discourse behaviour of Keith's parents were not only substantial but also stable; therefore, Keith's success in acquiring the minority language, German, actively, was most probably strongly related to his father's more child centred style of interaction.

4.3.2.3 Jacob. The results from the analysis of the discourse behaviour as employed by Jacob's parents during the first recording are shown in Tables 4.26 and 4.27.

Although both parents scored higher on the measure of *conversation oriented initiations* than on the measure of *control oriented initiations*, the scores for the English-speaking father exceeded those for the German-speaking mother in all positive measures. The father rated higher on *conversational drive*, *responsiveness*, *conversation oriented initiations* and *topic length*, and there were more *exchanges per topic* and more *moves per topic* in the father-child dyad than in the mother-child dyad. The father contributed 0.92 *moves per topic* more

Table 4.26: Discourse behaviour of Jacob's parents – first recording

	Mother	Father
conversational drive	26.6%	33.4%
responsiveness	35.8%	38.9%
no-response	13.0%	13.1%
communication problems	21.4%	19.8%
conversation oriented initiations	43.2%	57.0%
control oriented initiations	41.8%	28.0%
control orientation plus no-response	20.5%	14.0%
exchanges per topic	2.16	2.44
moves per topic	5.38	6.85
moves per exchange	2.40	2.72
moves per topic: parent to child	3.07	3.99

Table 4.27: Comparison of Jacob's parents regarding their discourse behaviour – first recording

conversational drive	-6.4%
responsiveness	-3.1%
no-response	-0.1%
communication problems	1.6%
conversation oriented initiations	-13.8%
control oriented initiations	13.8%
control orientation plus no-response	6.5%
exchanges per topic	-0.28
moves per topic	-1.47
moves per exchange	-0.32
moves per topic: parent to child	-0.92

than did the mother. The scores for the mother exceeded those for the father in the clusters *control oriented initiations* and *control orientation plus no-response*. The parents scored equally in the clusters *no-response* and *communication problems*. Both dyads also generated exchanges which were similar in length.

About one third of Jacob's moves addressed to both of his parents were responsive, and another third of his moves were *initiatives in conversations* (Tables 4.28 and 4.29).

Table 4.28: Jacob's discourse behaviour towards his parents – first recording

	Mother	Father
responsiveness	32.5%	36.5%
no-response	22.5%	21.7%
communication problems	23.1%	24.3%
control oriented initiations	38.8%	38.4%
initiative in conversation	38.5%	31.9%
parent's dominance	1.27	1.35

Table 4.29: Differences in Jacob's discourse behaviour between interaction with his mother and interaction with his father – first recording

responsiveness	-4.0%
no-response	0.8%
communication problems	1.2%
control oriented initiations	0.4%
initiative in conversation	6.6%

Whereas Jacob was slightly more responsive in interaction with his father, he was more initiating while having conversations with his mother. Nearly a quarter of his verbal participation was scored in the cluster *communication problems*, and scoring was equal for both parents. His scoring on the measure *no-response* was also the same for both parents. Jacob turned with requests of all sorts to both parents equally. The father was slightly more dominant in the verbal interaction than was the mother.

Thus the analysis of the communicative situation in Jacob's family showed the following: whereas Jacob was equally involved when conversing with each of his parents, the father's interaction with the child was more child centred than the mother's (*conversational drive, responsiveness, control* versus *conversational orientation*). This might have been due partly to the distribution of activities. The interaction was also more intense in the father-child dyad (*length of topic*). The scores for both parents appeared to be more or less equal on the measures of *communication problems* and *no-response*, and Jacob behaved similarly on these measures towards both of them. The fact that both these scores were fairly high, especially his *no-response* measure, which was quite a bit higher than those of his parents, as well as the measure of *responsiveness* being the lowest of all the children's in the German-speaking dyads and second lowest in the English-speaking dyads, could possibly be attributed to his "difficult" temperament as indicated by the Toddler Temperamental Scale (cf. 2.2).

During the second recording (Tables 4.30 and 4.31), the scores for the mother were lower than those for the father in the clusters *conversational drive* and *conversation oriented initiations*, and higher than those for the father in the clusters *control oriented initiations* and *control orientation plus no-res-*

Table 4.30: Discourse behaviour of Jacob's parents – second recording

	Mother	Father
conversational drive	26.2%	38.6%
responsiveness	29.0%	28.1%
no-response	16.0%	19.2%
communication problems	17.5%	17.1%
conversation oriented initiations	48.1%	63.4%
control oriented initiations	50.6%	31.4%
control orientation plus no-response	26.6%	18.1%
exchanges per topic	1.67	2.09
moves per topic	3.28	4.72
moves per exchange	1.97	2.25
moves per topic: parent to child	1.82	2.53

Table 4.31: Comparison of Jacob's parents regarding their discourse behaviour – second recording

conversational drive	-12.4%
responsiveness	0.9%
no-response	-3.2%
communication problems	0.4%
conversation oriented initiations	-15.3%
control oriented initiations	19.2%
control orientation plus no-response	8.5%
exchanges per topic	-0.42
moves per topic	-1.44
moves per exchange	-0.28
moves per topic: parent to child	-0.71

ponse. In the remaining three interactionally relevant clusters of moves, the mother's scores tended towards the hypothesis, *i.e.* the parents had comparable scores in the clusters *responsiveness* and *communication problems* and in the cluster *no-response* the mother's rating was slightly more favourable than was the father's. In the four measures which establish the topic length in the dyads, the parents rated equally only on *moves per exchange*. On *exchanges per topic*, *moves per topic* and *moves per topic: parent to child*, the scores for the German-speaking dyad lagged behind those for the English-speaking dyad.

Jacob's ratings in the interactionally relevant clusters of moves resembled the results of his parents (Tables 4.32 and 4.33). The only cluster which implied somewhat more satisfying interaction between mother and son than between father and son was the cluster *communication problems*. In all of the other clusters, Jacob rated more favourably in interaction with his father. He scored lower in *responsiveness* and *child-initiative in conversations* in interaction with his mother, and higher in *no-response* and *control oriented initiations*. Both parents were equally dominant over Jacob in their verbal contributions.

Table 4.32: Jacob's discourse behaviour towards his parents – second recording

	Mother	Father
responsiveness	30.2%	39.8%
no-response	25.4%	19.8%
communication problems	22.8%	25.9%
control oriented initiations	47.7%	33.9%
initiative in conversation	39.7%	45.8%
parent's dominance	1.27	1.27

Table 4.33: Differences in Jacob's discourse behaviour between interaction with his mother and interaction with his father – second recording

responsiveness	-9.6%
no-response	5.6%
communication problems	-3.1%
control oriented initiations	13.8%
initiative in conversation	-6.1%

Out of eleven calculated measures, the scores for Jacob's mother tended towards the hypothesis three times during the first recording and four times during the second recording. Three of these measures were the same for both recordings, namely *no-response, communication problems* and *moves per exchange*. The scores for the parents were equal in the cluster *responsiveness* during the second recording and only slightly outside the range of equal scoring during the first recording.

The scores for Jacob himself were equal in interaction with both his parents in three out of five clusters during the first recording, *i.e.* in *no-response*, communication problems and control oriented initiations. However, he was more initiating with his mother and more responsive to his father. He seemed, therefore, equally involved in conversational types of interaction with his father and with his mother. During the second recording, only the cluster communication problems indicated a slightly more successful verbal relationship between mother and son. According to the other four clusters, Jacob appeared to be more involved in conversations with his father than with his mother during the second recording.

Although the scoring in the various interactionally relevant clusters of moves were not as clear-cut in Jacob's family as they were in Keith's family, Jacob's lack of readiness to speak German was nevertheless likely to be, amongst other factors, related to the difference in interactional experience which Jacob had when interacting with his mother rather than with his father.

4.3.2.4 *Agnes*. In Agnes's family, the English-speaking father rated considerably higher than did the German-speaking mother in *conversational drive*, responsiveness, *conversation oriented initiations* and length of topic during the first recording, with more *exchanges per topic* and more *moves per topic* than the mother (Tables 4.34 and 4.35). The mother exceeded the father in the clusters *control oriented initiations, control orientation plus no-response* and *communication problems*. The parents scored equally on the measures of *no-response, moves per exchange* and *moves per topic: parent to child*.

Table 4.34: Discourse behaviour of Agnes's parents – first recording

	Mother	Father
conversational drive	20.8%	30.0%
responsiveness	20.7%	33.9%
no-response	28.1%	26.9%
communication problems	25.4%	14.5%
conversation oriented initiations	23.0%	49.7%
control oriented initiations	59.4%	32.0%
control orientation plus no-response	32.6%	20.6%
exchanges per topic	1.35	1.69
moves per topic	3.31	4.29
moves per exchange	2.26	2.44
moves per topic: parent to child	2.08	2.39

Table 4.35: Comparison of Agnes's parents regarding their discourse behaviour – first recording

conversational drive	-9.2%
responsiveness	-13.2%
no-response	1.2%
communication problems	10.9%
conversation oriented initiations	-26.7%
control oriented initiations	27.4%
control orientation plus no-response	12.0%
exchanges per topic	-0.34
moves per topic	-0.98
moves per exchange	-0.18
moves per topic: parent to child	-0.31

Nearly half of Agnes's participation in the verbal interaction with her parents was responsive (Tables 4.36 and 4.37), but she scored higher on this measure in interaction with her father than with her mother. Instead, she contributed more initiating moves to the conversations with her mother. She chose more often not to respond to her mother's verbal approaches towards her than to her father's, and had more difficulties approaching her mother as indicated by the score for the cluster *communication problems*. Agnes was more likely to turn to her father than to her mother with requests. In spite of the limited interaction which took place between mother and daughter, the mother was slightly more dominant in the interaction with Agnes than was the father.

Table 4.36: Agnes's discourse behaviour towards her parents – first recording

	Mother	Father
responsiveness	44.4%	52.5%
no-response	29.4%	19.2%
communication problems	23.8%	17.7%
control oriented initiations	48.8%	67.7%
initiative in conversation	19.1%	11.1%
parent's dominance	1.48	1.18

Table 4.37: Differences in Agnes's discourse behaviour between interaction with her mother and interaction with her father – first recording

responsiveness	-8.1%
no-response	10.2%
communication problems	6.1%
control oriented initiations	-18.9%
initiative in conversation	8.0%

The time spent with everyday tasks was relatively short in Agnes's family, and the amount of speech exchanged between parents and child fairly low in comparison with the other families in the sample (cf. 2.4). However, the analysis of the discourse structures showed that the interaction between father and child was more child centred than was the interaction between mother and child. This supported the parents' feeling that Agnes talked more to her father than she did to her mother, and it indicated why he understood her better than she did. The analysis of the discourse structures between Agnes and her parents suggests the basis for her closer relationship with her father.

The scores for both parents were lower in topic length, *i.e. moves per topic*, than were the scores for any other of the parents in the sample, and the mother rated lowest on *conversational drive, responsiveness, conversation oriented initiations* and highest on *control oriented initiations* and *control orientation plus no- response* of all parents in the sample. Not only did Agnes not speak German, but she was also the least linguistically developed of the children aged 2;8 when the first recording took place.

Similarly with the first recording, the mother scored lower than the father during the second recording in the clusters conversational drive, responsiveness and conversation oriented initiations, and higher than the father in the clusters control oriented initiations and control orientation plus no-response (Tables 4.38 and 4.39).

The mother's score in the cluster communication problems was lower than that of the father during the second recording, and thus different from the first recording, and her score was higher in the cluster no- response, which previously was equal to the father's score. The father-child dyad generated longer topics than did the mother-child dyad as measured in exchanges per topic and moves per topic, but exchanges which were again similar in length with those of the mother-child dyad. The parents' involvement in topic development was also similar again, suggesting it was Agnes's differential participation which caused the father-child topics to be longer than the mother-child topics.

Table 4.38: Discourse behaviour of Agnes's parents – second recording

	Mother	Father
conversational drive	18.6%	32.0%
responsiveness	28.2%	49.3%
no-response	38.7%	17.9%
communication problems	15.6%	21.3%
conversation oriented initiations	42.6%	46.7%
control oriented initiations	49.0%	31.1%
control orientation plus no-response	30.2%	17.9%
exchanges per topic	1.30	1.61
moves per topic	2.63	3.42
moves per exchange	2.02	2.12
moves per topic: parent to child	1.64	1.76

Table 4.39: Comparison of Agnes's parents regarding their discourse behaviour – second recording

conversational drive	-13.4%
responsiveness	-12.1%
no-response	20.8%
communication problems	-5.7%
conversation oriented initiations	-4.1%
control oriented initiations	17.9%
control orientation plus no-response	12.3%
exchanges per topic	-0.31
moves per topic	-0.79
moves per exchange	-0.10
moves per topic: parent to child	-0.12

Agnes's discourse behaviour was reversed during the second recording. Instead of being non-responsive towards her mother and control-oriented towards her father, she was more responsive (cf. *responsiveness* and *no-response*) and also more control-oriented (cf. *control oriented initiations*) towards her mother than towards her father (Tables 4.40 and 4.41). The scores for the cluster *communication problems* indicated that it was easier for Agnes to get through to her mother than to her father this time. The scores for the cluster *child-initiative in conversations* were reversed as well. Since the father was less involved than the mother in child-care tasks during the second recording, a relatively higher proportion of conversational initiations were directed towards him. The mother was again dominant over Agnes in her verbal contributions to the interaction than was the father.

Table 4.40: Agnes's discourse behaviour towards her parents – second recording

	Mother	Father
responsiveness	44.6%	30.0%
no-response	51.0%	60.9%
communication problems	16.3%	20.0%
control oriented initiations	80.4%	70.6%
initiative in conversation	13.9%	22.9%
parent's dominance	1.66	1.06

Table 4.41: Differences in Agnes's discourse behaviour between interaction with her mother and interaction with her father – second recording

responsiveness	14.6%
no-response	-9.9%
communication problems	-3.7%
control oriented initiations	9.8%
initiative in conversation	-9.0%

Since Agnes had reversed her strategies in so far as she was more initiating and less responsive towards her mother during the first recording, but more responsive and less initiating during the second recording, none of the tendencies of Agnes's scores were repeated from the first to the second recording. Agnes's verbal participation appeared to be dependent on the type of activity her parents engaged in when interacting with her. Agnes tended to be more responsive and more control-oriented towards the parent who performed child-care tasks and who was therefore responsible for fulfilling her needs. Most of those child-care tasks, like feeding, bathing and putting to bed, were left to the mother during the second recording, but were performed by the father during the first recording.

The analysis of the discourse strategies in Agnes's family suggests a correlation between Agnes's unwillingness and/or inability to use German actively and the mother's less child centred mode of interaction in comparison with the father's mode of interaction with the child. Although the scores for the parents in each of the clusters were more similar to those of the other parents' scores in the sample during the second recording, Agnes's linguistic skills still lagged noticeably behind those of the other children in her age group. The relative brevity of evening activities in Agnes's family, compared with the other families in the sample, was a result of Agnes's parents not being in the habit of spending time at play with Agnes or involving her in their own activities.

4.3.2.5 *Fiona*. The results obtained from the analysis of the discourse structures in Fiona's family are shown in Tables 4.42 and 4.43.

Fiona's German-speaking mother rated higher than did her English-speaking father in the cluster *conversational drive* and equal to him in the measure of *conversation oriented initiations, communication problems, exchanges per topic, moves per topic, moves per exchange* and *moves per topic: parent to child*. These seven measures point towards the child's successful acquisition of an active command of the minority language. In the remaining four clusters, the father's scores indicated more child centredness than did the mother's. The mother was less responsive than was the father, she rated high-

Table 4.42: Discourse behaviour of Fiona's parents – first recording

	Mother	Father
conversational drive	28.5%	22.0%
responsiveness	27.9%	41.5%
no-response	16.2%	3.6%
communication problems	22.7%	22.3%
conversation oriented initiations	40.0%	41.2%
control oriented initiations	51.0%	47.7%
control orientation plus no-response	25.0%	17.0%
exchanges per topic	1.98	1.95
moves per topic	4.63	5.15
moves per exchange	2.18	2.51
moves per topic: parent to child	2.69	3.10

Table 4.43: Comparison of Fiona's parents regarding their discourse behaviour – first recording

conversational drive	6.5%
responsiveness	-13.6%
no-response	12.6%
communication problems	0.4%
conversation oriented initiations	-1.2%
control oriented initiations	3.3%
control orientation plus no-response	8.0%
exchanges per topic	0.03
moves per topic	-0.52
moves per exchange	-0.33
moves per topic: parent to child	-0.41

er on the measures of *no-response*, issued more *control oriented initiations* and scored higher in the cluster *control orientation plus no-response*. Whereas the mother's scores in *conversational drive* and *responsiveness* were similar, the father produced nearly twice as many moves in the cluster *responsiveness* than in the cluster *conversational drive*. Nearly a quarter of both parents' moves fell into the cluster *communication problems*.

Fiona was more responsive than initiating in interaction with both her parents. However, complementary to her father's high *responsiveness*, Fiona's *initiative in conversations* was proportionally higher in interaction with her father than in interaction with her mother (Tables 4.44 and 4.45).

Fiona took a more responding role in interaction with her father than with her mother, and she failed to respond more often in interaction with her mother than with her father. Moreover, she had more *communication problems* with her mother than with her father. Fiona was also more likely to turn to her mother with requests. Both parents were dominant in their interaction with Fiona.

Table 4.44: Fiona's discourse behaviour towards her parents – first recording

	Mother	Father
responsiveness	37.7%	46.0%
no-response	24.4%	20.0%
communication problems	21.9%	10.2%
control oriented initiations	59.8%	27.5%
initiative in conversation	24.6%	43.4%
parent's dominance	1.33	1.39

Table 4.45: Differences in Fiona's discourse behaviour between interaction with her mother and interaction with her father – first recording

responsiveness	-8.3%
no-response	4.4%
communication problems	11.7%
control oriented initiations	32.3%
initiative in conversation	-18.7%

The analysis of the communicative situation in Fiona's family rendered problems: the scores for the mother indicated a more child centred type of verbal interaction in only the cluster *conversational drive* compared with the verbal interaction of the father. This cluster was inflated by a high number of topic re-initiating behaviour modifying moves (T/Ir-bm). In addition, the scores for the mother were equal to those for the father in six more clusters, including *conversation oriented initiations* and *communication problems*. The child, on the other hand, appeared to be more involved in conversations with her father. With regard to child centredness and also in comparison with Keith's family, the parents' interactive styles were only barely balanced in Fiona's family. However, Fiona acquired German equally as well as she did English. It is, therefore, necessary to point out that the day on which taping took place was a rather difficult one for the mother. Fiona's maternal grandparents were staying with the family on their holidays, the newly born baby sister needed much of the mother's attention, and Fiona was in a very bad mood because her father had forbidden her to suck her thumb earlier that afternoon. Part of the mother's high rating on *no-response* and the child's high rating on *communication problems* were caused by all this. The father, on the other hand, had come home early from work because he did not feel well, and spent the afternoon lying in bed and talking to Fiona in leisure. He also performed very few of the child-care tasks. The mother's scores in the discourse functions must be considered in the light of all this. In spite of her demanding role in the family, for that afternoon at least, her scores were equal to or more child centred than those of the father in seven out of eleven measures. Although Fiona's stronger involvement in conversations with her father that afternoon suggested a closer relationship with her father than with her mother, which would be contrary to the parents' and my own intuition, the parents' very similar discourse behaviour did not support this suggestion.

During the second recording (Tables 4.46 and 4.47), the scores for the mother and for the father were equal in the clusters *conversational drive*, responsiveness, conversation oriented initiations and control orientation plus no-response. The scores for the mother were slightly lower than those for the father in the cluster control oriented initiations, but higher than those for the fa-

Table 4.46: Discourse behaviour of Fiona's parents – second recording

	Mother	Father
conversational drive	24.1%	25.1%
responsiveness	27.6%	30.1%
no-response	14.7%	7.5%
communication problems	16.2%	16.3%
conversation oriented initiations	41.4%	42.1%
control oriented initiations	46.4%	50.0%
control orientation plus no-response	23.0%	21.7%
exchanges per topic	1.52	1.61
moves per topic	3.43	3.68
moves per exchange	2.19	2.20
moves per topic: parent to child	2.04	2.09

Table 4.47: Comparison of Fiona's parents regarding their discourse behaviour – second recording

conversational drive	-1.0%
responsiveness	-2.5%
no-response	7.2%
communication problems	-0.1%
conversation oriented initiations	-0.7%
control oriented initiations	-3.6%
control orientation plus no-response	1.3%
exchanges per topic	-0.09
moves per topic	-0.25
moves per exchange	-0.01
moves per topic: parent to child	-0.05

ther in the cluster no-response. The scores for the parents were equal for all four measures of topic maintenance, i.e. exchanges per topic, moves per topic, moves per exchange and moves per topic: parent to child.

Fiona was less responsive and more initiating with her mother than with her father during the second recording (Tables 4.48 and 4.49). With *control oriented initiations* she was equally likely to turn to her father or to her mother. Although Fiona failed less often to respond to her mother, she caused her mother slightly more *communication problems* than she did her father. Both parents were again dominant in their verbal interaction with Fiona.

Table 4.48: Fiona's discourse behaviour towards her parents – second recording

	Mother	Father
responsiveness	40.3%	48.2%
no-response	15.3%	20.2%
communication problems	17.2%	13.5%
control oriented initiations	46.7%	49.0%
initiative in conversation	38.6%	34.3%
parent's dominance	1.46	1.29

Table 4.49: Differences in Fiona's discourse behaviour between interaction with her mother and interaction with her father – second recording

responsiveness	-7.9%
no-response	-4.9%
communication problems	3.7%
control oriented initiations	-2.3%
initiative in conversation	4.3%

Fiona's mother scored towards the hypothesis in seven out of eleven measures during the first recording, and in ten out of eleven measures during the second recording. All of the seven measures from the first recording were also scored towards the hypothesis during the second recording. However, the scores for all measures but one were due to the parents' equal use of the inter-actional strategies comprised in the clusters at both times of recording.

Whereas Fiona appeared to be far more involved in conversations with her father than with her mother during the first recording, she showed equal in-volvement in conversational types of interaction with both her parents during the second recording. As discussed above, the results of the first recording were likely to be distorted by the difficult situation in which the mother and the child were on that particular day. Fiona's equal involvement in conversations with both parents during the second recording, however, paralleled the parents' similar interactional strategies towards her.

In contrast with Keith's father, Fiona's German-speaking parent, her mother, did not employ a mode of interaction which would be more likely to foster Fiona's language development than would her father's mode of inter-action. However, in contrast with the other parents in the sample, Fiona's mother and father interacted with their daughter in much the same way, thereby providing her with equally satisfying experiences with German and English. The ease with which Fiona acquired both languages simultaneously is likely to be, at least partially, related to the emotional compatibility of the two lan-guages.

4.3.2.6 Trudy. The results obtained from the analysis of Trudy's parents' dis-course behaviour during the first recording are presented in Tables 4.50 and 4.51. Whereas the scores for the German-speaking mother were lower than those for the English-speaking father in the cluster *conversational drive*, the mother scored higher than did the father in the cluster *responsiveness*. In the cluster *conversation oriented initiations* her scores were lower than those for the father, and higher in the clusters *control oriented initiations* and *control orientation plus no-response*. The parents rated equally on the measure of *communication problems*. The mother-child dyad produced slightly shorter topics, with fewer *exchanges per topic* and fewer *moves per topic* than did the father-child dyad. Except for *exchanges per topic*, however, the measures re-lated to topic maintenance can be considered to be equal.

Table 4.50: Discourse behaviour of Trudy's parents – first recording

	Mother	Father
conversational drive	21.2%	30.1%
responsiveness	24.7%	20.7%
no-response	9.7%	15.5%
communication problems	25.5%	26.6%
conversation oriented initiations	43.3%	49.1%
control oriented initiations	45.6%	41.9%
control orientation plus no-response	28.3%	24.6%
exchanges per topic	1.63	2.02
moves per topic	4.01	4.52
moves per exchange	2.47	2.24
moves per topic: parent to child	2.91	3.15

Table 4.51: Comparison of Trudy's parents regarding their discourse behaviour – first recording

conversational drive	-8.9%
responsiveness	4.0%
no-response	-5.8%
communication problems	-1.1%
conversation oriented initiations	-5.8%
control oriented initiations	3.7%
control orientation plus no-response	3.7%
exchanges per topic	-0.39
moves per topic	-0.53
moves per exchange	0.23
moves per topic: parent to child	-0.24

The scores for Trudy were similar in interaction with both her parents in the clusters *initiative in conversations, responsiveness* and *no-response* (Tables 4.52 and 4.53). However, she had less *communication problems* with her mother than she did with her father. Trudy was slightly more likely to address *control oriented initiations* to her mother than to her father. Both parents were fairly dominant in the verbal interaction.

Table 4.52: Trudy's discourse behaviour towards her parents – first recording

	Mother	Father
responsiveness	63.6%	61.1%
no-response	30.3%	29.3%
communication problems	6.8%	11.2%
control oriented initiations	51.7%	47.8%
initiative in conversation	22.9%	23.4%
parent's dominance	2.64	2.27

Table 4.53: Differences in Trudy's discourse behaviour between interaction with her mother and interaction with her father – first recording

responsiveness	2.5%
no-response	1.0%
communication problems	-4.4%
control oriented initiations	3.9%
initiative in conversation	-0.5%

The analysis of the communicative situation in Trudy's family showed that the parents were rather similar in their discourse behaviour towards Trudy, with the father being slightly more child centred than the mother (cf. *conversational drive, conversation oriented initiations, control oriented initiations, control orientation plus no-response*). Accordingly, Trudy was equally involved in conversations with both her parents. At the time of the first recording, Trudy still used German to both her parents in about fifty percent of her utterances.

During the second recording (Tables 4.54 and 4.55), the scores for the mother tended towards the hypothesis in only one of the interactionally relevant clusters, *i.e.* in the cluster no-response. They were lower than those for the father in the clusters *conversational drive, responsiveness* and *conversation oriented initiations*, and higher than those for the father in the clusters *communication problems, control oriented initiations* and *control orientation plus no-response*. The parents rated equally on three of the four measures of topic length, namely *exchanges per topic, moves per topic* and *moves per exchange*. However, the mother addressed more moves per topic to the child than did the father.

Table 4.54: Discourse behaviour of Trudy's parents – second recording

	Mother	Father
conversational drive	22.7%	28.3%
responsiveness	28.7%	35.7%
no-response	3.2%	13.1%
communication problems	23.2%	18.1%
conversation oriented initiations	45.7%	54.4%
control oriented initiations	44.0%	34.4%
control orientation plus no-response	26.2%	17.8%
exchanges per topic	1.84	1.83
moves per topic	4.45	3.93
moves per exchange	2.35	2.02
moves per topic: parent to child	3.02	2.14

Table 4.55: Comparison of Trudy's parents regarding their discourse behaviour – second recording

conversational drive	-5.6%
responsiveness	-7.0%
no-response	-9.9%
communication problems	5.1%
conversation oriented initiations	-8.7%
control oriented initiations	9.6%
control orientation plus no-response	8.4%
exchanges per topic	0.01
moves per topic	0.52
moves per exchange	0.33
moves per topic: parent to child	0.88

Trudy behaved differently towards each of her parents (Tables 4.56 and 4.57). She was mainly responsive in interaction with her mother, and far less initiative with her than she was with her father. However, she failed to respond to her mother more often than she did to her father. Trudy was more success-ful in approaching her mother than she was in approaching her father as is shown by the difference in the scores for *communication problems*. With re-quests of all sorts, Trudy turned more often to her mother than to her father. Both parents were dominant in their interaction with Trudy.

Trudy's mother scored towards the hypothesis in six out of eleven meas-ures during the first recording and in five out of eleven measures during the second recording. The results for the measures of *no-response, moves per topic, moves per exchange* and *moves per topic: parent to child* were repeated from one recording to the next. The results for the other two interactionally relevant clusters in which the mother scored towards the hypothesis during the first recording, i.e. *responsiveness* and *communication problems*, did not show favourable results for the acquisition of German during the second recording. Instead, *exchanges per topic* were scored towards the hypothesis.

Table 4.56: Trudy's discourse behaviour towards her parents – second recording

	Mother	Father
responsiveness	41.5%	30.6%
no-response	30.9%	20.3%
communication problems	11.2%	15.9%
control oriented initiations	52.7%	46.4%
initiative in conversation	29.8%	37.6%
parent's dominance	2.41	1.43

Table 4.57: Differences in Trudy's discourse behaviour between interaction with her mother and interaction with her father – second recording

responsiveness	10.9%
no-response	10.6%
communication problems	-4.7%
control oriented initiations	6.3%
initiative in conversation	-7.8%

Accordingly, Trudy showed equal involvement in conversational types of interaction with both parents during the first recording: for three clusters her scores were equal in interaction with both her parents, and, for the remaining two clusters, one of her scores favoured interaction with her mother and the other favoured interaction with her father. At the time of the second recording, however, she seemed more involved in conversations with her father. This is indicated by the fact that the scores for only two clusters suggested more successful and more conversation oriented interaction with the mother than with the father, whereas her scores for the other three clusters indicated more conversational types of interaction with the father.

Whereas Trudy spoke both German and English to both her parents during the first recording, she had started to openly refuse to speak German or to sing German songs by the time of the second recording. Interestingly, the father had more or less stopped speaking German to Trudy some time between the first and the second recording, because Trudy had outgrown his mastery of the language. It might, therefore, be argued that Trudy's willingness to speak German until she was two and a half years of age stemmed more from her father's speaking German to her than from her mother's efforts.

4.3.3 Cross-sectional results

The percentages by which each German-speaking parent scored differently from his/her English-speaking spouse were compared and listed for the purpose of comparison across the sample in Tables 4.58 and 4.59. The number of items which scored towards the hypothesis were totalled for each German-speaking parent.

Alice's, Jacob's and Agnes's German-speaking parents all scored only between one and four out of eleven items at each recording in the way which was predicted to be supportive for the child's willingness to acquire German

Table 4.58: *Comparison of German- and English-speaking parents with regard to their discourse behaviour – first recording*

	hypoth.	"="	Alice	Keith**	Jacob	Agnes	Fiona**	Trudy
conversational drive	=/+	±3%	-16.2%	-0.4%*	-6.4%	-9.2%	6.5%*	-8.9%
responsiveness	=/+	±3%	-17.0%	10.1%*	-3.1%	-13.2%	-13.6%	4.0%*
no-response	=/-	±3%	0.6%*	-17.7%*	-0.1%*	1.2%*	12.6%	-5.8*
communication problems	=/-	±3%	6.1%	-0.9%*	1.6%*	10.9%	0.4%*	-1.1%*
conversation oriented initiations	=/+	±3%	-9.5%	14.2%*	-13.8%	-26.7%	-1.2%*	-5.8
control oriented initiations	=/-	±3%	5.3%	-5.3%*	13.8%	27.4%	3.3%	3.7%
control orientation + no-response	=/-	±3%	3.4%	-4.9%*	6.5%	12.0%	8.0%	3.7%
exchanges per topic	=/+	±0.1	-1.13	0.57*	-0.28	-0.34	-0.03*	0.39
moves per topic	=/+	±0.6	-3.19	2.44*	-1.47	-0.98	-0.52*	0.53*
moves per exchange	=/+	±0.6	-0.25*	0.60*	-0.32*	-0.18*	-0.33*	0.23*
move per topic: parent to child	=/+	±0.6	-1.27	1.77*	-0.92	-0.31*	-0.41*	0.24*
items scored by German-speaking parent:			2	11	3	3	7	6

* items scored towards the hypothesis   ** actively German-speaking children

Table 4.59: *Comparison of German- and English-speaking parents with regard to their discourse behaviour – second recording*

	hypoth.	"="	Alice	Keith**	Jacob	Agnes	Fiona**	Trudy
conversational drive	=/+	±3%	-7.7%	1.1%*	-12.4%	-13.4%	-1.0%*	-5.6%
responsiveness	=/+	±3%	-3.1%	10.9%*	0.9%*	-12.1%	-2.5%*	-7.0%
no-response	=/-	±3%	3.6%	-10.5%*	-3.2%*	20.8	7.2%	-9.9%*
communication problems	=/-	±3%	14.7%	4.0%	0.4%*	-5.7%*	-0.1%*	5.1%
conversation oriented initiations	=/+	±3%	-16.8%	17.9%*	-15.3%	-4.1%	-0.7%*	-8.7%
control oriented initiations	=/-	±3%	20.9%	-24.2%*	19.2%	17.9%	-3.6%*	9.6%
control orientation plus no-response	=/-	±3%	10.6%	-10.7%*	8.5%	12.3%	1.3%*	8.4%
exchanges per topic	=/+	±0.1	-0.65	-0.21*	-0.42	-0.31	-0.09*	0.01*
moves per topic	=/+	±0.6	-1.43	1.20*	-1.44	-0.79	-0.25*	0.52*
moves per exchange	=/+	±0.6	-0.04*	0.48*	-0.28*	-0.10*	-0.01*	0.33*
move per topic: parent to child	=/+	±0.6	-1.13	0.90*	-0.71	-0.12*	-0.05*	0.88*
items scored by German-speaking parent:			1	10	4	3	10	5

* items scored towards the hypothesis   ** actively German-speaking children

actively. None of the three children used German "originally and intentional-ly" at either time of recording. In contrast to this, Keith's father scored ten out of eleven items in the direction of the hypothesis, and Keith used German to his father as often as he was able to. The scores for the parents of the two younger children, Fiona and Trudy, showed less clear results. During the first recording, the scores for Fiona's and Trudy's mothers tended towards the hypothesis for seven and six of the eleven items, respectively. However, by the time of the second recording, the differences between the scores for the two mothers had widened: the scores for Fiona's mother tended towards the hypothesis for ten items, and thus they became comparable with those for Keith's father. On the other hand, the scores for Trudy's mother tended towards the hypothesis for only five items which made her verbal behaviour resemble more that of Alice's, Jacob's and Agnes's mothers. It can be assumed that the diffi-cult home situation in Fiona's case during the first recording influenced the verbal strategies of her mother on that particular day resulting in less conver-sational orientation.

The children's involvement in conversational types of interaction resem-bled their parents' more or less child centred mode of interaction (cf. Tables 4.60 and 4.61).

At both times of recording, Keith scored all of the five items in favour of more extensive conversational involvement with his German-speaking father than with his English-speaking mother. This paralleled the greater child cen-tredness of his father's language at both times of recording. Moreover, Alice, who did not use German "originally and intentionally" and whose German-speaking mother employed a less child centred mode of interaction than did her English-speaking father during the first and second time of recording, proved to be more involved in conversational types of interaction with her English-speaking father than with their German-speaking mother at both times of recording. Jacob, who also did not speak German and whose English-speaking father interacted in a somewhat more child centred way with him than did his German-speaking mother, appeared to be equally involved in conver-sational types of interaction with both parents during the first recording, but was more conversation oriented in interaction with his father during the second recording. Agnes's verbal participation appeared to depend on the division of responsibilities among her parents: she was more responsive towards the parent who was feeding and bathing her and also directed her requesting behaviour predominantly towards that parent, but she initiated conversational types of interaction more often with the parent who was less involved in caring for her

Table 4.60: Differences of child's discourse behaviour from interaction with German-speaking parent to interaction with English speaking parent – first recording

	hypoth.	"="	Alice	Keith	Jacob	Agnes	Fiona	Trudy
responsiveness	=/+	±3%	0.5%*	26.2%*	-4.0%	-8.1%	-8.3%	2.5%*
no-response	=/-	±3%	9.9%	-5.4%*	0.8%*	10.2%	4.4%	1.0%*
communication problems	=/-	±3%	3.0%*	-13.1%*	-1.2%*	6.1%	11.7%	-4.4%*
control oriented initiations	=/-	±3%	16.5%	-28.7%*	0.4%*	-18.9%*	32.3%	3.9%
initiative in conversation	=/+	±3%	-9.3%	13.4%*	6.6%*	8.0% *	18.7%	-0.5%*
items scored in favour of interaction with the German-speaking parent:			2	5	4	2	0	4
parent with whom the child is more involved in conversations:			English speaking parent	German speaking parent	equally involved	English speaking parent	English speaking parent	equally involved
child speaks German			no	yes	no	no	yes	yes

* items scored towards the hypothesis

Table 4.61: Differences of child's discourse behaviour between interaction with German-speaking parent and interaction with English speaking parent – second recording

	hypoth.	"="	Alice	Keith	Jacob	Agnes	Fiona	Trudy
responsiveness	=/+	±3%	-26.2%	12.6%*	-9.6%	14.6%*	-7.9%	10.9%*
no-response	=/-	±3%	19.8%	-19.7%*	5.6%	-9.9%*	-4.9%*	10.6%
communication problems	=/-	±3%	14.4%	-8.7%*	-3.1%*	-3.7%*	3.7%	-4.7%*
control oriented initiations	=/-	±3%	21.3%	-20.6%*	13.8%	9.8%	-2.3%*	6.3%
initiative in conversation	=/+	±3%	5.6%*	6.2%*	-6.1%	-9.0%	4.3%*	-7.8%
Items scored in favour of interaction with the German speaking parent:			1	5	1	3	3	2
parent with whom the child is more involved in conversation:			English speaking parent	German speaking parent	English speaking parent	German speaking parent	equally involved	English speaking parent
child speaks German			no	yes	no	no	yes	no

* items scored towards the hypothesis

needs and who therefore talked less to her. The father was more involved in child-care activities than was the mother during the first recording, but the mother looked after Agnes nearly exclusively by herself during the second recording. Hence Agnes reoriented her verbal behaviour from the first to the second recording from being more involved with her English-speaking father to being more involved with her German-speaking mother. This happened in spite of the father's language being more child centred than the mother's at both times of recording. Like Jacob and Alice, Agnes did not use German actively. The verbal strategies of Trudy's parents were more comparable than were those of Alice's, Jacob's and Agnes's parents, but Trudy spoke German "originally and intentionally" during the first recording only. This was paralleled by the mother's language being slightly less child centred during the second recording, and also, and probably more importantly so, by the fact that the father had discontinued speaking German to Trudy some time between the first and the second recording. Trudy appeared to be equally involved in conversations with both her parents during the first recording, but was more involved in conversational types of interaction with her father than with her mother during the second recording. Fiona's discourse behaviour reflected her parents' verbal behaviour at the two times of recording as well. During the difficult first time of recording, Fiona was clearly more involved in conversational types of interaction with her father than she was with her mother. During the second time of recording, however, when both parents interacted with her in very similar ways, Fiona appeared to be equally involved in conversational types of interaction with both of them.

4.4 Conclusions

The analysis of the discourse structures in the six bilingual families showed that parents as well as children differed from one family to the next in their scoring in the interactionally relevant clusters. These differences were in part due to the character and temperament of each individual parent and child. Other contributing factors were the situational features in the families on the particular days during which recordings were made, and the demands put on the parents by the children. As a result of these differences, each family was discussed separately, and the German-speaking parent and English-speaking parent of each family were compared with each other in terms of the verbal strategies employed when they were interacting with the child. This enabled the most

drastic discrepancies in the uncontrollable independent variables to be elimi-
nated. Remaining differences in the activities and chores of each of the parents
must be considered elective and part of the reality of life in the family.

It was predicted that the child's success in acquiring German in addition
to English would be positively related to the child centredness of his/her German-speaking parent's verbal strategies in comparison with the interactional
strategies employed by the English-speaking parent. As with those monolingual
children who tend to learn to speak faster, or who are more motivated to
continue their participation in a conversation because the parent or the adult
interlocutor is more responsive to the child, addresses more topic incorporating utterances to the child, and is generally more oriented towards conversing
with the child than controlling the child, so children with parents from different
language backgrounds have good reasons for preferring to model their language
production on the parent who is more skilful in incorporating the child's perspective and needs into the verbal interaction.

It was possible to demonstrate that the children studied here tended to
converse more with the parent who displayed a more child centred type of
verbal interaction. In the cases of Alice, Jacob and Agnes, it was the English-
speaking parents who displayed more child centred types of verbal behaviour,
and so the children did not speak German "originally and intentionally". In the
case of Keith, the German-speaking father related more intensively to the
child's intentional and attentional needs than did the English-speaking mother, and the child was more involved in conversational types of interaction with
his father than with his mother. Consequently, he spoke German with his father most of the time. In the case of Fiona, who was the only other child who
spoke German actively, the child was more involved in conversational types
of interaction with her English-speaking father during the first recording when
the father displayed a slightly more child centred type of verbal behaviour than
did the mother. During the second recording when the parents' behaviour was
very similar, she was equally involved in conversations with both her parents.
However, her willingness and ability to speak German was probably due not
only to the parents' similar interactional strategies towards her, but also to other
factors in the family situation. These have already been discussed in Chapter
3. The same is true for Trudy: the language of the German-speaking mother was
the slightly more child centred one during the first recording, and that of the
English-speaking father was the slightly more child centred one during the
second recording. Although Trudy spoke both German and English during the
first recording, she did not want to speak German any more during the second

recording. Factors discussed in Chapter 3 are likely to have been important in influencing this development.

The strategies employed by the parents in verbal interaction with their young children appear to influence the children's language development not only in a monolingual environment, as has been studied many times before, but also in a bilingual environment. Rather than resulting in a faster or slower rate of language acquisition, the parents' verbal strategies may determine that a child acquires only one of the languages instead of both of them. However, verbal strategies are only one of many influencing aspects in the success of active child bilingualism. Factors like those discussed in the previous chapter, and those which will be discussed in the following chapter, also have to be taken into consideration when evaluating the extent of the parents' contribution to their children's bilingual development.

5. Teaching Techniques

5.1 Introduction

The examination of the teaching techniques which the parents employed during the recorded and transcribed interaction with their children, is the next step in the analysis of the quality of input in each of the two languages to which the children were exposed in their homes. This chapter differs from the preceding one in that it is not so much concerned with interactional categories, but with more formal linguistic categories. I will first present some of the evidence which has been accumulated to prove that parents do in fact have a teaching function in their children's language development, and then outline the concept of teaching technique as it has been used for this analysis. The theoretical introduction will be finished off with the stating of the particular hypothesis for this chapter. In the empirical part of this chapter, I will first describe the method employed in establishing, assigning and evaluating the parental teaching techniques. Then the results will be discussed in terms of which parental teaching behaviour differentiates Keith's and Fiona's parents from the other children's parents. Finally, each family will be considered separately.

5.2 Parents as teachers

5.2.1 Theoretical discussion

It has been well established by now that the speech which adults address to young children differs considerably from the speech they address to other adults. The extent to which these modifications are related to the children's language acquisition, however, has not yet been fully determined.

Ever since Chomsky's (1959, 1964, 1965) strong and convincing reactions to the approach to language acquisition held by the American behaviouristic school, researchers in the field of first language acquisition have become very insecure about the possible parental effects on children's language development, at times even denying or not further pursuing evidence to that respect (cf. Brown, Cazden and Bellugi 1969; Brown 1973). It has also been argued that children's imitations of adult models would not foster language development (Ervin 1964), and that, in fact, children hardly ever imitate verbal models (Brown and Bellugi 1964; Brown 1968; Slobin 1968; Rodd and Braine 1970; Slobin and Welsh 1971), or that obvious grammatical progression from spontaneous to imitated utterances is due to lighter performance constraints, but not to the learning functions which the imitation of adult models might have for young children (Menyuk 1963; Slobin 1968; Smith 1970).

It has taken the field more than a decade to turn around and come back to the starting point of believing, or at least considering, that children learn language from their parents, and that parents are aware of their teaching function, albeit to varying degrees of explicitness. The value and function of imitations in children's speech has been re-evaluated (Bloom, Hood and Lightbown 1974; Clark 1977; Moerk and Moerk 1979; among others). By re-defining imitations in a less restrictive way, that is, by not limiting imitations to child utterances which immediately follow the adult model and by not excluding partial imitations (Clark 1977; Moerk and Moerk 1979), it was not only possible to show that children imitate much more than was formerly believed, but also that their imitations are grammatically more complex and richer in vocabulary than their spontaneous utterances. Clark (1977) pointed out that many ill-formed utterances from children are likely to be unanalysed imitations of parents' subordinate clauses, rather than spontaneous constructions due to a grammatical system originated by the children themselves (cf. example in 1.2.5). As far as adult input is concerned, Moerk convincingly argued against many of the positions held by Brown and associates. Moerk's re-analysis of the material collected from Eve, Adam and Sarah showed that input frequencies did in fact play a significant role in the acquisition of certain morphemes and syntactic structures for these three children (Moerk 1980), and that they could also account, to a certain degree, for the children's unequal language growth rate. Moreover, Moerk (1985a) presented evidence that both Adam's and Eve's mothers employed verbal teaching techniques, but Eve's mother did so more consistently, with the effect that Eve learned to talk faster than did Adam. Moerk (1985a:138) argued that "the major cognitive burden for analyzing and abstracting language structure does not fall upon the child, but (...) the mother does it for the child in her teaching techniques". Moerk (1983a) presented evidence that many of the learning-theoretical phenomena like conditioned positive reinforcements, linguistic corrections, linguistic modelling and three-term contingency patterns of stimulus-response-reinforcement existed in the speech of Adam's and Eve's mothers and occurred with higher than chance frequencies. Contrary to Brown (1973), Moerk (1983a,b, 1985a) found numerous corrections in the speech of Eve's mother. He attributed this discrepancy to different definitions of correction in Brown's and his own work. Whereas Moerk included positive and constructive corrections like expansions, substitutions, specification requests and contrasting corrections (cf. Moerk 1985a:131) in the class of corrections, Brown seemed to have only counted negative corrections as such (Moerk 1983b:104).

Studies on the routines of picture-book reading with young children showed that these routines provided a well-suited format for the teaching and learning of labels (Ninio and Bruner 1978; Ninio 1980a,b; Moerk 1985b). Within the frame of adult presentation, adult requests for pointing and adult elicitation of labels from the child, the child learns to decode and encode meaning in unambiguous and stable situations (Ervin-Tripp and Miller, 1977; Ninio and Bruner 1978; Snow and Goldfield 1983). Similar teaching frames take place in other interactive situations as well, like free-play or feeding (Moerk 1974). Snow (1983) demonstrated the use of deferred imitations in the picture-book reading context by her son. These much delayed imitations were more complex than his own spontaneous speech at the time. The higher verbal complexity was only integrated into his spontaneous speech after it had been used in imitated utterances.

The originally disappointing results of intervention studies (Cazden, 1965) were later re-evaluated and constructively criticized (Brown, Cazden and Bellugi 1969; Moerk 1972; Wells 1980). K.E. Nelson (1977) conducted a laboratory study by means of which he was able to relate an increase in verb and question complexity in the children's speech to higher frequencies of complex verbs and questions in the adults' speech. He pointed out that the evaluation of the Cazden-study was probably correct. Children learn best from the provision of new verbal material which is closely related to their momentary focus of attention. A number of the studies centred around this assumption have been presented in the preceding chapter.

In his search for stronger evidence that parents do in fact see themselves as mediators of language and are conscious of their function as language teachers, Moerk (1983b) reanalysed the speech of Eve's mother with great precision. He found that Eve's mother used an abundance of techniques aimed at modelling language for her daughter and breaking down linguistic structures for her. He also found an average of about one testing question per every two minutes of interaction wherein the mother checked whether the child had mastered a specific item of linguistic knowledge. He pointed out that these findings "belie the assertion of many authors that mothers are generally unaware that they teach language" (Moerk 1983b:32).

The concept of teaching technique as it has been derived from this theoretical discussion will be presented in the next section.

5.2.2 The concept of "teaching technique"

Any feature which differentiates speech to young children from speech to adults or older children can be considered a potential teaching technique. However, only a limited number of linguistic features have so far been shown to make any difference to the rate of children's language acquisition or have been related conceptually to children's linguistic progress. Moerk (1976b:1065) summarized the scope of conceivable teaching techniques as

> corrective feedback provided by the mother; an utterance of the mother
> that supplied linguistic information and to which the child responded by
> incorporating or acknowledging the input; questions asked by the mother to test the linguistic skills of the child; and the mother's modelling of
> the translation of environmental and behavioural structures, including
> pictures, into the linguistic medium on occasions when the child attended
> to both aspects of the interaction and responded to the mother's tutorial
> activity.

Similarly for the present analysis, parental utterances were considered teaching techniques when they presented the child with verbal models, rehearsed language information for the child, made pattern structures transparent, or elicited verbalizations from the child. Due to the often delayed or deferred learning effect of adult models on children's linguistic performance (Moerk and Moerk 1979; Snow 1983), and the limited data collection and familiarity between researcher and subjects, the presence of a learning strategy on the child's part was not made the defining feature of an adult teaching technique.

In the framework of the present study, parental teaching techniques are considered an aspect of the quality of input which children receive from their parents. Their expected effect on the children's active acquisition of both the majority language, English, and the minority language, German, will now be discussed.

5.2.3 The relevance of teaching techniques for bilingual families

The purpose of this study was to find correlations between the extent of the parents' instructional speech and the children's active acquisition of the minority language. As in the case of interactive styles (cf. Chapter 4), the teaching techniques used by the parents were expected to differ greatly from family to family and even from father to mother within the same family. The extent to which parents employ teaching techniques is likely to be due to their personality as well as to the choice of activity in which they get involved with the child. The results were expected to complement the results from the preceding chapter: a relatively high overall level of teaching techniques in the German-speaking parents' speech and a relatively higher level of teaching techniques in the speech of the German-speaking parent than in the speech of the English-speaking parent were both expected to be of assistance in the children's active acquisition of German. Child centredness in the parents' interactive style and awareness of their function as a language teacher were assumed to be related.

5.3 Method

In contrast to the analysis reported in the last chapter, which was concerned with the interactive direction of the parents' speech to their children, the analysis presented in this chapter was based on formal linguistic properties of the parents' speech. The basic unit of analysis was, therefore, the utterance. The beginning and end of an utterance was defined for sentences by their linguistic completeness, and for elliptical utterances by their semantic completeness. Thus, expressions like "yes, that is a car" or "Johnnie give me the spoon" were coded as one unit each. Linguistic complexes consisting of one main clause and one or more subordinate clauses were also coded as one unit. However, in the case where two or more main clauses were joined by conjunctions, each main clause was coded as one individual unit.

The analytical categories were closely modelled on the teaching techniques established by Moerk (1983b), but they were somewhat reduced and simplified on the one hand, and adapted to the bilingual situation of the subjects in the present study on the other hand. Moerk's categories were employed if their original definition matched their appearance in the present data. They were changed or collapsed into one if the original definition was too specialized; this avoided the case where a category would contain only a few isolated examples. A new category was established if several occurrences of nearly identical form, meaning or function were encountered in any one family (cf. Moerk, 1976b:1066). Again following Moerk (1983b), utterances were multiply coded whenever necessary, with three codings being the maximum for any one utterance. Teaching techniques which were intrinsically part of another teaching technique were not double coded; instead, the more encompassing of the two techniques was chosen.

Each parental utterance was examined for its teaching properties. They were identified as either vocabulary teaching techniques, grammar teaching techniques, techniques with unspecified goals, or no teaching oriented utterances. Vocabulary and grammar teaching techniques were subdivided into modelling techniques, patterning techniques, rehearsing techniques and eliciting techniques (cf. Döpke 1988).

The *vocabulary teaching techniques* consisted of eight *modelling techniques*, two *rehearsing techniques*, one *patterning technique* and seven *eliciting techniques*.

a. Modelling techniques:

provision of label: Utterances which consisted of one single content element only, as in "This is ..." or "There are ...", were coded in this category. Utterances with more than one content element were coded as *mapping*.

mapping: Utterances which consisted of two or more content elements and which mapped observable reality with syntactic structures were coded in this category.

semantic correction: This category was assigned to contrastive corrections, as in:

C: *this is a mouse.*
P: *this is a cat.*

Semantic corrections were often combined with negative feedback.

chaining: If parents combined new content elements with elements which had already been introduced by either themselves or the child, this category was assigned to the utterance.

translation: For this category to be assigned, the parent had to translate all or part of the child's utterance. In some cases, parents translated their own or another adult's utterance. The extent to which a parent made use of this technique was not only related to the child's use of the inappropriate language, but also to parents' consciousness of their role as the teacher of the language. The difficulties encountered in using this category will be discussed in more detail at a later point.

feature elaboration: A parent who used this category commented upon already introduced content elements in terms of their qualities, i.e., mainly abstractly as in "The beans taste nice". Utterances like "This is red" were coded as *provision of label.*

functional elaboration: Utterances coded as *functional elaboration* explained the function of an object, as in "The car is to ride in".

general paraphrase: A general paraphrase conveyed the same meaning with different words. Utterances were only coded in this category if there was no structural relationship between the original and the rephrased utteranceses.

b. Rehearsing techniques:

vocabulary perseveration: In contrast to Moerk's (1983b) definition, the coding of utterances in this category was not limited to new or rare vocabulary items, both of which would have needed more extensive data and more intensive familiarity between researcher and subjects. Instead, it was assigned whenever parents repeated their own or the child's utterance fully or in part for no other apparent reason but to repeat vocabulary. Pronunciation corrections were included in this category, but self-repetitions due to the child's failure to respond were coded elsewhere.

incorporation: At times, parents incorporated all or part of a child's utterance into their own speech. This technique was often coded together with translation or vocabulary perseveration.

c. Patterning techniques:

contrasting provision of label: For this technique, the parent provided both labels of a contrast pair, as in:

> P: *your hands are all dirty. -*
>   *now they are clean.*

The contrasting labels did not have to be adjoining, but they had to be interactionally related. This technique was also coded when the parent provided a contrasting label in a child-initiated sequence.

d. Eliciting techniques:

request for label: This category comprised test questions and real questions which required a single content element for an answer, as in "What is this?" or "What are you having for lunch?"

choice question: Occasionally, parents asked a "or"-type question, and, thereby, provided two labels from which the child was supposed to choose one. This type of question can be used for testing, but was more often used for real questions.

request for insertion: Some parents elicited verbal responses from their children by providing slots for the child to fill in, as in:

> P: *that is the -*
> C: *wolf.*

These sequences tended to be the more successful the more they were part of a routine.

contrasting polar questions: Utterances coded in this category were testing questions which provided the child with labels for opposites and other contrastive items. This technique was not used in all dyads, but for those parents who did use it, it was another strong routine verbal game, which secured the child's close attention because of the challenge involved.

where-is questions: Only questions which allowed pointing or deixis for an answer were coded in this category. If the answer had to, or did, consist of a full prepositional phrase, the question was coded as a *request for PP extension.*

what-doing question: This technique was coded for questions which could be answered just with a verb. If the answer had to contain a verb plus one or more complements, the question was assigned to the category *request for VP extension.*

request for translation: The parent who used this elicitation technique asked the child to translate a specific item or a whole utterance. As with *trans-*

lation, the use of the technique *request for translation* was not only related to the child's inappropriate language choice, but also to parents' personality and their estimation of the parent-child relationship (cf. 3.4.2.2 and 5.4.1.4).

The *grammar teaching techniques* consisted of seven *modelling techniques*, three *rehearsing techniques*, three *patterning techniques* and four *eliciting techniques*:

a. Modelling techniques:

expansion: In agreement with numerous other studies, this category was coded for parental utterances which structurally expanded a child's one- or multi-word utterance. On some rare occasions, it was coded in combination with *adult self-repetition*, which effectively made it an *adult self-expansion*. It could also be combined with the *translation* of the child's utterance.

optional transformation: Changes in sentence type from, for example, declarative to question or imperative, were coded in this category. This technique was usually combined with *self-repetition*.

morpheme correction: For this technique, the parent corrected a morpheme by providing the correct morpheme in a contrasting manner, as in:

> C: *I goed shopping*
> P: *oh you went shopping.*

This technique was usually used in combination with *minor substitution*, as in the above example, but not necessarily so. Like *semantic correction*, it could also be combined with negative feedback.

complex extension: If parents extended their own utterance or the child's utterance by more than one syntactic element or by a subordinate clause, the utterance was put into this category.

NP extension: For an utterance to be assigned to this category, parents had to extend their own or the child's utterance by a subject or object noun phrase. In German, in particular, this involves the modelling of specific grammatical forms.

PP extension: For this category to be coded, parents had to extend their own or the child's utterance by a full prepositional phrase, which again calls for specific grammatical forms in German.

VP extension: This category was coded when the parent extended a one or two word utterance of the child by a verb or a verb phrase.

b. Rehearsing techniques:

morpheme perseveration: This technique was coded when parents repeated a morpheme for no other apparent reason than to rehearse it. They could do this with the same or a new vocabulary item. A cluster of, for example, present perfect forms in German were consequently assigned to this category, even if the forms were not identical. For example:

> P: *du hast dich verSTECKT.*
> 'you are HIDing'.
> *jetzt hab ich dich geFUNDen.*
> 'now I have FOUND you'.

The first participle is derived from a regular verb, the second participle from an irregular verb.

self-reduction: If parents reduced their own utterance by one or more syntactic elements or subordinate clauses, this category was coded.

minor substitution: For this technique to be assigned, parents had to substitute grammatical elements in their own or the child's utterance without changing the content, for example, pronouns for nouns, second person for first person, determiners, prepositions or prefixes of separable verbs.

c. Patterning techniques:

major substitution: The parent substituted content elements or auxiliary verbs for others. This could take place in the same-speaker sequence or in a two-speaker sequence.

frame variation: This technique was coded when the parent repeated the content of an utterance, but changed the syntactic frame, as in:

> P: *bring me the ball -*
> *bring it to me.*

morpheme substitution: This category was assigned when parents substituted a morpheme in their own or the child's speech for another, for example, plural for singular, past tense for present tense, or the like.

d. Eliciting techniques

request for NP extension: In this category, parents asked the children a question, the answer to which required them to extend their own or the parent's utterance by a subject or object noun phrase. This technique was different from the *request for label* technique insofar as the response to a *request for NP extension* had to form part of a sentence and comply with particular grammatical constraints in German.

request for PP extension: The parent asked for an adverbial response which could not be given through pointing or deixis, but only by means of a prepositional phrase.

request for VP extension: The parent asked a what-doing type of question which could only be answered sufficiently with a full verb phrase.

request for complex extension: The parent asked a why-question.

Six further techniques, which could not be placed into either the set of vocabulary teaching techniques or the set of grammar teaching techniques, were coded. These techniques were modifications of speech which are characteristic of adult speech to young children, but which occurred with varying direction of educational intent. Hence they were termed *techniques with unspecified goals.*

self-repetition: This category was coded when parents repeated themselves as a result of the child's failure to respond. Self-repetitions without such motivation were coded as *vocabulary perseveration* or *morpheme perseveration.*

provision of answer: At times, parents provided the answers to their own questions because the child either failed to respond or the parent anticipated that the child would not be able to do so. This technique might provide the child with unknown vocabulary and syntactic information.

query: A query was made in cases of misunderstanding or not understanding. Queries have been found to motivate the child to modify the original utterance on the syntactic, phonetic or vocabulary level (cf. Käsermann 1980; Langford 1981). In the bilingual families of the present study, a *translation* was often accompanied with a query, as in:

> C: *I want an apple*
> P: *möchtest du einen Apfel?*

This technique differed from a straight forward translation in that it required a verification from the child. Similar monolingual sequences were coded as *vocabulary perseveration plus query*:

> C: *I want an apple*
> P: *do you want an apple?*

request for repetition: The parent asked the child to repeat an utterance in full or part, as in:

> P: *say I want an apple.*

positive feedback: This category was coded when a parent signalled to the child that the child's last utterance was linguistically good, correct or acceptable.

negative feedback: For this category to be assigned a parent signalled to the child that the child's last utterance was not acceptable. This technique was usually combined with one of the correction techniques.

All utterances which could not be identified as any of these techniques were coded as *no teaching oriented utterance*. This included utterances which were not related to the "here and now" and were, therefore, not decodable by means of the properties of the current situation.

In order to allow the twelve parents to be compared, the data had to be adjusted for its unequal length. This was done by calculating percent frequencies for each parent, with the total number of utterances coded for each parent as 100%. The children's German- and English-speaking parents were compared across the sample as well as within each family.

Since Keith and Fiona were the only two of the six children who used German "originally and intentionally", the most prevailing question was: to what extent did Keith and Fiona receive a similar linguistic input from their parents, and to what extent did this input differ from the input the other four children received. The results were, therefore, examined for similarities between Fiona's and Keith's German- and English-speaking parents on the one hand, and differences between Fiona's and Keith's German- and English-speaking parents and the other children's parents on the other hand.

5.4 Parental teaching behaviour

5.4.1 Comparison across the sample

The parents are first compared at the levels of *vocabulary teaching techniques*, *grammar teaching techniques*, *techniques with unspecified goals* and *no teaching oriented utterances*. The special nature of the technique *translation* will lead to a recalculation of the *specified teaching techniques*. Following this, the results from several individual techniques and sub-groupings will be presented.

5.4.1.1 No teaching oriented utterances. Scores in the set *no teaching orient-ed utterances* ranged from 16% to 63%, with most of the scores being between 40% and 50%. This contrasts with the results of Moerk (1976b, 1983a) who reported much higher frequencies of teaching techniques in the speech of the mothers whom he investigated. This discrepancy may be due to the shorter re-cording sessions in Moerk's studies, during which the mothers were better able to monitor their speech than were the mothers and fathers during the lengthy recording sessions of the present investigation. Although Moerk (1972:230) doubted the mother's ability to suddenly change familiar interaction patterns, an increase in routinized teaching sequences is likely to have occurred (Clark 1977; Graves and Glick, 1978). This, of course, only stresses Moerk's argu-ment that mothers are aware of their teaching role.

As can be seen from Table 5.1, the cross-sectional comparison of the par-ents' lack of teaching orientation yielded little in terms of differences between Keith and Fiona on the one hand, and the other children in the sample on the other hand.

Table 5.1: Parents' use of "no teaching oriented utterances"

language	rec.	Keith	Fiona	Alice	Jacob	Agnes	Trudy
German	1st	18.7%	47.3%	52.6%	44.1%	63.4%	42.4%
	2nd	16.3%	47.0%	57.1%	50.0%	51.9%	53.8%
English	1st	55.1%	54.6%	52.5%	39.7%	58.2%	36.3%
	2nd	53.3%	56.5%	45.1%	55.7%	53.9%	44.7%

Table 5.2: Comparison of German- and English-speaking parents with regard to their use of "no teaching oriented utterances"

recording	Keith	Fiona	Alice	Jacob	Agnes	Trudy
1st	-36.4%	-7.3%	0.1%	4.4%	5.2%	6.1%
2nd	-37.0%	-9.5%	12.0%	-5.7%	-2.0%	9.1%

The comparison on the intrafamilial level in Table 5.2, however, showed that only Fiona's and Keith's German-speaking parents used teaching tech-niques more often than did their English-speaking parents at both times of re-cording. In the remaining four families, the German-speaking parents used either lower or in Alice's case, equal proportions of teaching techniques com-pared with the English-speaking parents during the first recording. For the second recording, only the results for Trudy's parents remained similar to those for the first recording. The results for Jacob's and Agnes's parents were both reversed, and the results for Alice's parents indicate that they changed in fa-vour of the English language environment.

5.4.1.2 Teaching techniques with unspecified goals. The scores for the *techniques with unspecified goals* ranged from 7% to 26%. Tables 5.3 and 5.4 show that the presence of *teaching techniques with unspecified goals* in the parents' speech did not indicate any correlation with the children's use or non-use of German.

Table 5.3: Teaching techniques with unspecified goals

language	rec.	Keith	Fiona	Alice	Jacob	Agnes	Trudy
German	1st	22.6%	10.4%	12.3%	12.5%	17.8%	16.7%
	2nd	25.9%	9.9%	17.5%	10.2%	15.6%	10.7%
English	1st	14.3%	13.0%	3.6%	7.0%	13.9%	13.4%
	2nd	12.8%	10.7%	6.8%	9.1%	16.7%	12.2%

Table 5.4: Comparison of German- and English-speaking parents with regard to their use of "teaching techniques with unspecified goals"

recording	Keith	Fiona	Alice	Jacob	Agnes	Trudy
1st	8.3%	-2.6%	8.7%	5.5%	3.9%	3.3%
2nd	13.1%	-0.8%	10.7%	1.1%	-1.1%	-1.5%

5.4.1.3 Specified teaching techniques. The scores for *vocabulary teaching techniques* and *grammar teaching techniques* ranged from 12.9% to 44.3% and from 5.8% to 17.2%, respectively. The predominance of *vocabulary teaching techniques* over *grammar teaching techniques* might indicate that the parents were more conscious of their role as vocabulary teachers. The extent to which parents made use of techniques in either of these two sets showed some similarity between Keith's and Fiona's parents as opposed to the other children's parents. However, the combination of the two sets gave an even clearer picture. The results are illustrated in Figure 5.1 and 5.2 and Table 5.5. They have to be looked at on two levels: cross-sectional and intrafamilial.

Table 5.5: Specified teaching techniques

language	rec.	Keith	Fiona	Alice	Jacob	Agnes	Trudy
German	1st	58.7%	42.3%	35.1%	43.4%	15.8%	40.7%
	2nd	57.8%	43.1%	24.7%	39.8%	32.6%	35.5%
English	1st	30.6%	32.4%	45.2%	53.4%	27.9%	50.3%
	2nd	33.9%	32.6%	48.1%	35.2%	30.0%	43.2%

Keith's and Fiona's German-speaking parents were using more *specified teaching techniques* than were the other German-speaking parents during the second recording, and more than the other German-speaking parents except for

a) German-speaking parents

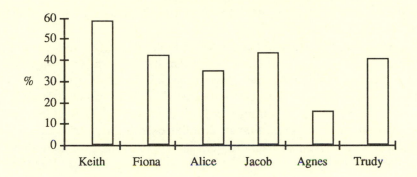

b) English-speaking parents

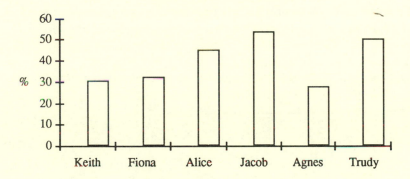

Figure 5.1: Specified teaching techniques - first recording

Jacob's mother during the first recording. This was complemented by Keith's and Fiona's English-speaking parents using less *specified teaching techniques* than did the other English-speaking parents during the first recording, with the exception of Agnes, whose parents used the least proportion of *specified teaching techniques* of all parents in the sample. During the second recording, only Alice's and Trudy's English-speaking parents used more *specified teaching techniques* than did Keith's and Fiona's English-speaking parents. Agnes's and Jacob's English-speaking father used *specified teaching techniques* to much the same extent as did Keith's and Fiona's English-speaking parents.

It is, therefore, necessary to have a closer look at the intrafamilial comparison in order to resolve the question of whether the linguistic environments in Jacob's and Agnes's families were favouring German or English.

The calculation of the differences between the German- and English-speaking parents in each of the families in Table 5.6 revealed that the German-speaking parents in Keith's and Fiona's families used higher percentages of *specified teaching techniques* than did the English-speaking parents in these two families during the first recording. In the remaining four families, the English-speaking parents used proportionally more *specified teaching techniques* than did the German-speaking parents. Although Jacob's mother seemed to use more *specified teaching techniques* than did Fiona's mother in the cross-sectional comparison, the comparison on the intrafamilial level showed that Fiona's mother used about 10% more *specified teaching techniques* than did Fiona's father, whereas Jacob's mother used about 10% less *specified teaching techniques* than did Jacob's father. The linguistic balance was, therefore, more tipped towards German in Fiona's family, but more tipped towards English in Jacob's family.

Table 5.6: Comparison of German- and English-speaking parents with regard to their use of "specified teaching techniques"

recording	Keith	Fiona	Alice	Jacob	Agnes	Trudy
1st	28.1%	9.9%	-10.1%	-10.0%	-12.5%	-9.6%
2nd	24.0%	10.5%	-23.4%	4.5%	2.6%	-7.7%

During the second recording, both Keith's and Fiona's German-speaking parents used proportionally more *specified teaching techniques* than did their English-speaking parents. However, only Alice's and Trudy's German-speaking mothers used lower proportions of *specified teaching techniques* than did their English-speaking fathers. Agnes's and Jacob's German-speaking mothers used higher percentages of *specified teaching techniques* than did their husbands. For an assessment of whether the linguistic environments were as favourable for the acquisition of German in the last two families, as they were

a) German-speaking parents

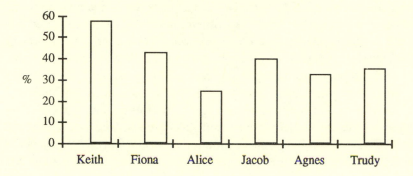

b) English-speaking parents

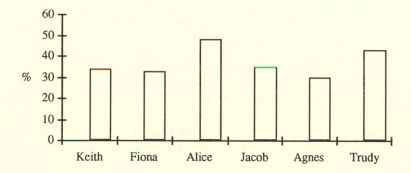

Figure 5.2: Specified teaching techniques - second recording

in Keith's and Fiona's families during this recording, it is necessary to compare Agnes's and Jacob's parents with Keith's and Fiona's parents on both levels simultaneously, i.e., on the cross-sectional as well as on the intrafamilial level. Agnes's family shall be examined first.

Agnes's English-speaking father used less *specified teaching techniques* than did any of the other English-speaking parents at both times of recording, and Agnes's German-speaking mother used the lowest proportion of *specified teaching techniques* of all parents during the first recording, and as little during the second recording as the German-speaking parents of the other children who did not use German "originally and intentionally". It can be assumed that the general level of *specified teaching techniques* in German was too low in Agnes's family for Agnes to profit from them enough to acquire German actively, and the greater usage of *specified teaching techniques* by the mother rather than by the father during the second recording was not significant.

During the second recording, like Agnes's mother, Jacob's German-speaking mother used a higher proportion of *specified teaching techniques* than did Jacob's English-speaking father, but a lower proportion of them than did Fiona's mother. Moreover, the score for Jacob's mother was only about 5% more than that for Jacob's father, the difference being half as much as the difference between the scores for Fiona's parents. This combination of factors allows us to argue that the linguistic environment in Fiona's family was more favourable for the acquisition of German than it was in Jacob's family. However, the differences were slim, and other factors, such as have been discussed in the preceding chapters, were necessary for these parents' attempts to result in Fiona's successful, but Jacob's unsuccessful active acquisition of German.

5.4.1.4 The special role of the technique of translation. At this point, the nature of the technique of *translation* needs to be discussed. In the six bilingual families of the present sample, parental *translations* were most definitely a form of *vocabulary teaching technique* and not a form of *grammar teaching technique*. None of the children ever made an incorrect or inappropriate language choice by supplying German lexical items with English grammatical markers in the German-speaking environment, or English lexical items with German grammatical markers in the English-speaking environment. However, there was no direct relationship between the relative frequency with which parents used this technique and the children's active acquisition of German. On the contrary, it should, ideally, be the nature of this technique that it be used less the more appropriate the children's language choice was. In this way, the significance of *translations* is very different from that of the other *vocabulary teaching techniques*. In practice, parents' awareness of children's language choice, and their determination to teach the child, also influenced the frequency with which this technique was employed. Furthermore, some of the English-speaking parents used this technique, not in order to provide the child with correct English words where the child seemed to only know the German equivalent, but they translated from English into German. Such translations do not belong to *teaching techniques* in an environment of 'one parent-one language'. The corresponding elicitation technique *request for translation* was used or misused in much the same way.

5.4.1.5 *Specified teaching techniques minus translation and request for translation.* Since the teaching value of translations was of an ambiguous nature, the *specified teaching techniques* were re-calculated excluding of *translations* and *requests for translation*. Figures 5.3 and 5.4 and Table 5.7 show the results obtained this way.

Table 5.7: Specified teaching techniques minus translation and request for translation

language	rec.	Keith	Fiona	Alice	Jacob	Agnes	Trudy
German	1st	50.5%	40.0%	29.1%	31.6%	13.8%	38.4%
	2nd	56.8%	41.6%	19.5%	30.3%	25.9%	31.3%
English	1st	30.6%	29.9%	43.1%	52.6%	27.4%	47.6%
	2nd	33.1%	31.3%	46.7%	32.4%	30.0%	40.6%

During both times of recording, Keith's and Fiona's German-speaking parents used more *specified teaching techniques minus translation and request for translation* than did the other German-speaking parents, although the difference between the scores for Fiona's and Trudy's mothers was very slim during the first recording. Correspondingly, the English-speaking parents of the children who did not speak German actively used more *specified teaching techniques minus translation and request for translation* than did Keith's and Fiona's English-speaking parents during the first recording. The only exception was Agnes's father. However, he used an extremely low level of teaching techniques, to the point that Agnes's preference for English over German could not possibly be credited to the father. The result from the first recording was not repeated during the second recording: Jacob's father did not use relatively more *specified teaching techniques minus translation and request for translation* than did Keith's and Fiona's English-speaking parents. Therefore, the German- and English-speaking parents of each family had to be compared again.

The comparison of the *specified teaching techniques minus translation and request for translation* on the intrafamilial level supported the argument that the linguistic environments favoured German more in Keith's and Fiona's

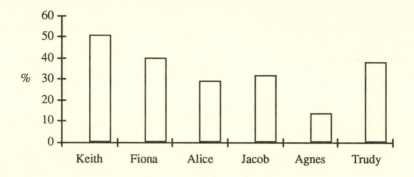

a) German-speaking parents

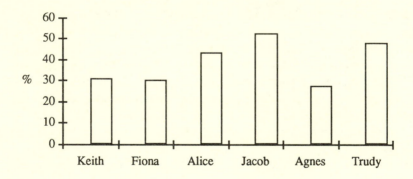

b) English-speaking parents

*Figure 5.3: Specified teaching techniques minus translation and request for translation –
first recording*

families than in the other children's families (Table 5.8). Both Keith's and
Fiona's German-speaking parents used more *specified teaching techniques
minus translation and request for translation* than did Keith's and Fiona's

a) German-speaking parents

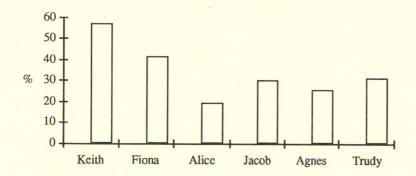

b) English-speaking parents

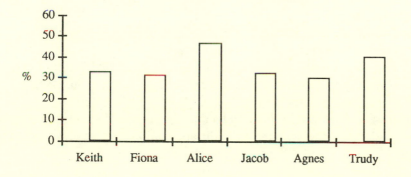

Figure 5.4: Specified teaching techniques minus translation and request for translation –
second recording

English-speaking parents during both times of recording. The other children's
German-speaking parents used less of them than did their English-speaking
spouses.

Table 5.8: Comparison of German- and English-speaking parents with regard to their use of "specified teaching techniques minus translation and request for translation"

recording	Keith	Fiona	Alice	Jacob	Agnes	Trudy
1st	19.9%	10.1%	-14.0%	-21.0%	-13.6%	-9.2%
2nd	25.8%	10.3%	-27.2%	-2.1%	-4.1%	-9.3%

A closer look was taken at individual techniques as well as some more specific groupings of techniques. More detailed results were expected with regard to which teaching techniques, or which types of teaching techniques would be most beneficial for the active acquisition of German. However, not much of that sort could be found. Those individual techniques and sets of techniques which differentiated Keith's and Fiona's German- or English-speaking parents from the other children's parents consistently, at both times of recording, will be presented in the remaining part of this section. The first four sets of techniques and individual techniques will demonstrate similarities and differences between the German-speaking parents. This will be followed by one set for which similarities and differences between the English-speaking parents were found. Finally, four further sets of techniques and individual techniques showed consistent intrafamilial differences between the German- and English-speaking parents at both times of recording.

5.4.1.6 Vocabulary perseveration. As demonstrated in Table 5.9, Keith's and Fiona's German-speaking parents applied the technique *vocabulary perseveration* relatively more often than did the other four German-speaking parents. This tendency was consistent for both times of recording. The significance of this tendency was further supported by the comparison of the German- and English-speaking parents with regard to the application of this technique (Table 5.10).

Table 5.9: Vocabulary perseveration – German-speaking parents

recording	Keith	Fiona	Alice	Jacob	Agnes	Trudy
1st	13.1%	12.3%	8.5%	6.9%	4.0%	9.1%
2nd	19.4%	10.5%	4.7%	6.4%	3.7%	7.4%

Table 5.10: Comparison of German-and English-speaking parents with regard to the relative use of the technique "vocabulary perseveration"

recording	Keith	Fiona	Alice	Jacob	Agnes	Trudy
1st	9.0%	4.1%	-2.9%	-9.2%	-1.3%	-3.6%
2nd	8.2%	4.0%	-7.7%	-1.5%	-3.0%	-2.4%

Table 5.10 shows that the German-speaking parents in the two families where the children were willing and able to use German "originally and intentionally" devoted higher proportions of their speech to vocabulary rehearsing routines than did their English-speaking spouses. Correspondingly, the four German-speaking parents of the children who did not use German actively used this technique to a lower extent than did the English-speaking parents.

5.4.1.7 Rehearsing. A further result could be obtained by grouping all vocabulary and grammar rehearsing techniques together.

Table 5.11: Rehearsing techniques – German-speaking parents

recording	Keith	Fiona	Alice	Jacob	Agnes	Trudy
1st	16.1%	18.4%	12.8%	11.9%	7.0%	11.6%
2nd	23.1%	15.3%	9.1%	14.0%	9.1%	12.7%

We can see from Table 5.11 that the German-speaking parents of Keith and Fiona engaged in relatively more rehearsing routines than did the other children's German-speaking parents at both times of recording. Moreover, the comparison of the scores for German- and English-speaking parents in each family (Table 5.12) shows the balance between parental rehearsing techniques in German and English to be leaning more towards German in Keith's and Fiona's families, but either more towards English or being balanced in the other children's families.

Table 5.12: Comparison of German- and English speaking parents with regard to the use of "rehearsing techniques"

recording	Keith	Fiona	Alice	Jacob	Agnes	Trudy
1st	11.3%	8.0%	-2.2%	-8.0%	2.8%	-4.8%
2nd	9.5%	3.6%	-8.1%	-0.1%	-1.0%	0.0%

A slight exception to this rule was found in Agnes's family during the first recording. Her mother used somewhat more rehearsing techniques than did her father, but the difference between their scores was considerably lower than was the difference between the scores for Keith's and Fiona's mothers and fathers. In combination with the general low level of linguistic input in Agnes's family, this result does not present any challenge to the hypothesis.

5.4.1.8 Self-repetition. The technique *self-repetition* has been found to differentiate the linguistic environment of slow language learners from that of normal or advanced language learners (Cross 1981). Its significance for the smooth conversational flow has been discussed in the preceding chapter. The technique was included in the analysis of the parents' teaching techniques following Moerk's (1983b) example. Only the results for the German-speaking parents showed any relation between the parents' usage of this technique and the children's success or failure to acquire an active command of German (Table 5.13).

Table 5.13: Self-repetition – German- speaking parents

recording	Keith	Fiona	Alice	Jacob	Agnes	Trudy
1st	2.0%	4.0%	5.3%	4.9%	8.9%	5.6%
2nd	0.9%	0.9%	7.6%	3.3%	5.4%	1.9%

According to Table 5.13, Keith's and Fiona's German-speaking parents had to repeat themselves less frequently than did the other children's German-speaking parents at both times of recording. Hence, this technique is unlikely to have furthered the process of acquiring active language skills in German. The comparison of the scores for the German- and English-speaking parents cast further doubt on the notion of *self-repetition* as a teaching technique (Table 5.14).

Table 5.14: Comparison of German- and English-speaking parents with regard to their use of the technique "self-repetition"

recording	Keith	Fiona	Alice	Jacob	Agnes	Trudy
1st	0.6%	-0.8%	4.5%	3.3%	6.5%	0.7%
2nd	-1.2%	-2.0%	6.4%	0.9%	0.4%	0.3%

During the first recording, the scores for Keith's and Fiona's parents indicated that neither their German- nor their English-speaking parents used the technique of *self-repetition* more frequently than did their respective spouses. Alice's, Jacob's and Agnes's German-speaking parents had higher proportions of *self-repetitions* in their speech than did their English-speaking parents. The scores for Trudy's parents were similar again. During the second recording, Keith's and Fiona's German-speaking parents used this technique less than did their English-speaking parents, whereas the other children's German-speaking parents used *self-repetitions* either more or to the same extent as did their English-speaking parents. The general trend of these results seems to favour the argument that *self-repetition* is in fact not a teaching technique. The inclusion of *self-repetitions* into the bulk of *no teaching oriented utterances* replicated the original results for the set *no teaching oriented utterances* in every respect.

5.4.1.9 Patterning. The scores for the combination of all the vocabulary and grammar patterning techniques yielded another result. However, it only applied to the German-speaking parents. Table 5.15 shows the result.

Table 5.15: Patterning – German-speaking parents

recording	Keith	Fiona	Alice	Jacob	Agnes	Trudy
1st	6.0%	5.3%	2.1%	4.0%	2.0%	3.2%
2nd	4.1%	3.6%	1.3%	2.0%	1.3%	2.8%

At both times of recording, Keith's and Fiona's German-speaking parents provided more vocabulary and grammar patterning techniques than did the other German-speaking parents.

5.4.1.10 Modelling. Modelling, and especially vocabulary modelling, which would have been expected to play a major role in distinguishing the German-speaking parents of the children who used German actively from those who did not, failed to yield results to that effect. It did, however, separate Keith's and Fiona's English-speaking parents from the English-speaking parents of the other children. Table 5.16 presents the results for the combined set of all modelling techniques.

Table 5.16: Modelling – English-speaking parents

recording	Keith	Fiona	Alice	Jacob	Agnes	Trudy
1st	12.3%	10.8%	22.0%	22.0%	11.6%	20.5%
2nd	14.0%	12.7%	17.3%	15.8%	11.7%	23.1%

With the exception of Agnes's father, the English-speaking parents of the children who did not use German actively modelled more linguistic data for their children than did Keith's and Fiona's English-speaking parents. A closer look at the modelling techniques revealed that it was the *vocabulary modelling techniques* which differentiated the English-speaking parents in that way: the *grammar modelling techniques* alone did not produce the same differences. Table 5.17 presents the results concerning all the *vocabulary modelling techniques*, and Table 5.18 presents the results concerning all the *vocabulary modelling minus translation* techniques.

Table 5.17: Vocabulary modelling – English-speaking parents

recording	Keith	Fiona	Alice	Jacob	Agnes	Trudy
1st	10.2%	6.9%	14.7%	15.0%	5.7%	14.3%
2nd	11.1%	6.9%	12.7%	12.4%	6.7%	16.3%

Table 5.18: Vocabulary modelling minus translation – English-speaking parents

recording	Keith	Fiona	Alice	Jacob	Agnes	Trudy
1st	10.2%	5.4%	12.6%	14.2%	5.2%	11.6%
2nd	10.3%	5.9%	11.3%	11.0%	6.7%	13.7%

Again, Agnes's father's speech did not show the same properties as did the speech of Alice's, Jacob's and Trudy's fathers.

5.4.2 Discussion of each individual family

The language of the parents within each family was compared in order to ascertain those teaching behaviours which distinguished most strongly the language of one parent from that of the other. Only techniques or sets of techniques will be reported which distinguished between the language of the parents consistently over both recordings, with a score of at least one percent.

5.4.2.1 Alice. Alice's English-speaking father differed from Alice's German-speaking mother most of all in his general *modelling* and *rehearsing* behaviour. With *modelling*, he displayed a more teaching oriented behaviour in both vocabulary and grammar modelling. The only individual modelling technique in which the father's score surpassed the mother's was *feature elaboration.* With regard to *rehearsing, vocabulary rehearsing techniques*, especially *vocabulary perseveration*, were most characteristic of the father's teaching behaviour. He also employed a generally wider range of techniques than did the mother.

Alice's mother used more *translations* and *where-is questions* than did the father. Other than that, her score exceeded his only in the use of *unspecified techniques*, especially *self-repetitions* and *queries*.

This comparison of Alice's parents suggests a clear difference in their awareness of their functions as language teachers, which was probably instrumental in Alice's preference for English over German.

5.4.2.2 Keith. The teaching behaviour scores for Keith's German-speaking father exceeded those for his English-speaking mother in three of the four areas of *specified teaching techniques*, namely *modelling, eliciting* and *rehearsing*. His scores indicated higher frequencies of modelling techniques in both vocabulary and grammar modelling. However, no one individual technique stood forth. The rehearsing techniques were more prominent in the father's speech than in the mother's speech in both areas as well. Among the vocabulary rehearsing techniques, the technique *vocabulary perseveration* was the distinguishing factor, and among the grammar rehearsing techniques it was the technique *expansion*. With the eliciting techniques, only vocabulary eliciting techniques differentiated the parents; in particular, *requests for label, where-is questions* and *what-doing questions*. Moreover, the father employed relatively more feedback techniques, especially positive feedback, than did the mother. Generally, his range of techniques was wider than was the mother's.

The mother's score did not exceed the father's in any of the sets. Instead, she displayed higher proportions of no teaching oriented behaviour at both times of recording.

The differences between Keith's German- and English-speaking parents were substantial. The father provided Keith with a much richer linguistic input than did the mother. Consequently, Keith was able to acquire a good command of German from his father.

5.4.2.3 Jacob. The scores for Jacob's German-speaking mother surpassed those for Jacob's English-speaking father in modelling techniques, especially *vocabulary modelling*. The only individual techniques which were consistently higher over both recordings were *mapping* and *translation*. The mother also provided more feedback and employed a generally wider range of techniques than did the father. Jacob's father made consistently more use of the techniques *feature elaboration* and *vocabulary perseveration*.

With the other areas of analysis, the difference between the scores for Jacob's parents was slim. The discussion in 5.3.1.3, however, showed that in comparison with the other children, in particular Fiona, the degree of teaching oriented input which Jacob received was somewhat more favourable for English. I doubt, though, that this difference was great enough to be a major contributing factor in Jacob's reluctance to speak German.

5.4.2.4 Agnes. Agnes's German-speaking mother differed from Agnes's English-speaking father in *vocabulary modelling*, due to the mother's more frequent use of *translations*. She also used more *self-repetitions* and *queries* than he did. Agnes's father's scores did not consistently exceed the mother's in any of the teaching techniques.

Agnes's parents' scores were very similar with regard to their low levels of teaching techniques. As argued before, it seemed to be both parents' generally low level of linguistic input, as well as their low level of input tailored to needs of the language learning child, to which Agnes's inability or unwillingness to speak German must be attributed.

5.4.2.5 Fiona. The scores for Fiona's German-speaking mother surpassed those for Fiona's English-speaking father in general modelling behaviour, and especially in *vocabulary modelling*. She also rehearsed the linguistic information more than did the father, particularly the vocabulary. As discussed earlier, *vocabulary perseveration* was the most distinguishing single technique. Among the *grammar teaching techniques*, *grammar eliciting techniques* and *major substitution* differentiated the mother consistently from the father.

Although scores indicate that the mother used more *grammar eliciting techniques* than did the father, the father used a higher overall frequency of eliciting techniques, and predominantly *vocabulary eliciting techniques*. Among the *vocabulary eliciting techniques*, *contrasting polar questions* were the only single differentiating technique. The father also provided higher frequencies of the only *vocabulary patterning technique*, i.e. *contrasting provision of label*. However, he consistently employed higher proportions of *no teaching oriented utterances* than did the mother.

As also indicated on the other levels of analysis, Fiona's parents were more linguistically similar than were most of the other children's parents. In addition, the German-speaking mother tended to provide somewhat more teaching oriented linguistic input than did the English-speaking father. Her teaching behaviour, therefore, added to the generally favourable language environment for German (cf. Chapters 3 and 4). Accordingly, Fiona acquired a very good command of German.

5.4.2.6 Trudy. The scores for Trudy's English-speaking father exceeded those for Trudy's German-speaking mother in *modelling techniques*, especially *vocabulary modelling*, *vocabulary rehearsing techniques*, especially *vocabulary perseveration*, and *grammar eliciting techniques*. The scores for Trudy's mother did not exceed those for Trudy's father in any of the teaching techniques or sets of teaching techniques. In contrast, she used higher proportions of *no teaching oriented utterances* at both times of recording.

In the area of teaching techniques, the father clearly tailored his input more to the learning needs of the child than did the mother. He thereby contributed to a linguistic environment which made Trudy acquire more language from him than from the mother.

5.5 Conclusions

The analysis of the teaching techniques showed that the parents differed in the extent to which they employed teaching techniques in verbal interaction with their children. The German-speaking children in the sample received a linguistic input from their German-speaking parents which was richer in teaching techniques than was the linguistic input that the other four children received from their German-speaking parents. It was also more consistently applied. On the other hand, the children who did not use German actively, received a more consistently teaching oriented input from their English-speaking parents than did Keith and Fiona. At the same time, Keith's and Fiona's German-speaking parents engaged in more teaching oriented behaviour than did their English-speaking parents, whereas the other children's English-speaking parents tended to surpass their German-speaking spouses in that respect.

However, these differences were not as striking in some families as they were in others. Although one can suspect that parental application of teaching techniques plays a major role in the children's willingness or ability to use German actively in Keith's, Alice's and Trudy's families, further explanations are necessary to account for the course which Fiona's, Jacob's and Agnes's bilingual development has taken. This has been attempted in the other analytical chapters of this investigation.

6. Summary and Conclusions

6.1 Introduction

In the foregoing study, I have compared the macro- and micro-linguistic environments of six young Australian children, who were exposed to German and English through the 'one parent-one language' principle. It is a reality in Australia, as well as in other predominantly monolingual Western societies, that children from bilingual families often do not even start to develop an active command of the minority language in spite of their parents' intentions to raise them bilingually. The aim of this study was to find features in the verbal environments of the subjects which differentiated between those who acquired an active command of German and those who learned to understand it only. In order to do some justice to the complexity of the matter, I opted for an indepth analysis of a small number of families. Consequently, this is a collection of case studies, and no statistical validity was to be expected.

In this final chapter, the results will be summarized and the factors which determined each child's degree of bilingualism will be described separately. Next, the relationship of the results to the hypotheses will be considered. This will be followed by an outline of the children's further bilingual development. Finally, a number of general issues which arose from the study will be discussed.

6.2 Summary of results

6.2.1 Children's linguistic proficiency

All six children had age-appropriate receptive knowledge of German at both times of recording. This was measured by means of a translated version of the Zimmermann et al. (1979) "auditory comprehension test". For all children, English was the dominant language. Dominance was indicated through language choice and linguistic complexity. Language choice was measured in percentage of moves in the appropriate and non-appropriate language to each parent; linguistic complexity was measured in words per utterance. The analysis of the children's language choice further revealed that Keith and Fiona used German in interaction with their German-speaking parents more consistently than did Alice, Jacob and Agnes in all types of investigated moves, namely polar responses, reiterations, imitations, translations and, most importantly, original utterances.

The children's use of original German utterances was most indicative of the children's intentional language use. The notion of "original and intentional" use of German divided the sample most sharply: whereas Keith and Fiona spoke more German during the second recording than they had done during the first recording, Alice's, Jacob's and Agnes's "original and intentional" use of German had decreased to isolated tokens. Parallel to the increase in the amount of German spoken, Keith's and Fiona's German grew in complexity from the first to the second recording; the complexity of Alice's, Jacob's and Agnes's German decreased.

Trudy's language choice resembled that of Keith and Fiona during the first recording, but was more like that of Alice, Jacob and Agnes during the second recording, especially with regard to her "original and intentional" use of German. The complexity of Trudy's German utterances did, however, increase from the first to the second recording, indicating that her change towards English was a case of conscious rejection of German and that it was more recent than that of Jacob, whose behaviour indicated conscious rejection as well. Whether Alice and Agnes were not willing or were not able to speak more German than they did cannot be decided, and neither can it be decided whether or not Jacob could have spoken more German.

Within Taeschner's (1983) frame of bilingual development, all children were at the second stage during the first recording, but only Keith and Fiona had progressed into the third stage by the time of the second recording.

6.2.2 The macro-linguistic environment

The language environment was principally similar for all children: they grew up as first-born children in linguistically mixed German-English middle class families in Australia, where German is only marginally maintained in such situations.

The children's contact with German varied: Fiona's and Jacob's mothers were native speakers of German, and their families had relatively more contact with German-speaking people than did the other families in the sample. Both children were read to extensively, they sang songs with their parents and, generally, spent considerable time playing with their German-speaking mothers as well as with their English-speaking fathers. The parents estimated that the children heard more German than English in the course of a day.

Trudy's mother was born in Australia and had grown up bilingually herself. Trudy saw her maternal grandparents regularly and heard German from them as well as from her mother. Her, for all practical purposes, monolingual English-speaking father also tried to speak as much German to Trudy as he could. Both parents read, sang and played with Trudy extensively. In the course of a day, she heard more German than English.

Keith, Alice and Agnes were all reported to hear less German than English. Alice's mother was a second-generation German-Australian like Trudy's mother, but Alice's maternal grandparents did not speak German to Alice because Alice always spoke English to them. Moreover, the family had hardly any German-speaking friends or acquaintances. The father played relatively more with Alice than did the mother, and both parents read books to her in English. German books were not as readily available for her.

Agnes's mother was a native speaker of German, but the family had only very little contact with other German-speaking people in Australia. Instead, the mother had extensive contact with English-speaking neighbours and friends. Neither of Agnes's parents played or read much with her.

Keith was the only child in the sample whose German-speaking parent was the father rather than the mother. Moreover, the father was a native speaker of English, but whose love for German motivated him to raise his son bilingually. Consequently, the family did not have any German-speaking relatives and only very few German-speaking friends, most of whom were second-language speakers as well. As with the other families, the child was cared for at home by the mother and the father pursued outside work. When at home, the father played with Keith intensively, and consciously tried to compensate for the lack of exposure to German by providing Keith with books, songs and films in German.

All German-speaking parents were very consistent in their language choice when addressing their children. The greatest variation in consistency was caused through English-speaking fathers being less consistent or the parents alternating between German and English when addressing each other. In Keith's and Fiona's families the German- and English-speaking parents were equally consistent in their language choice towards the child (>99% consistency) and always spoke English to each other. This correlated with the children's willingness and ability to use German actively. Agnes's and Alice's parents were only slightly less consistent (>95% consistency) in their language choice towards their children and also spoke English to each other all the time. Alice and Agnes hardly ever used German "originally and intentionally" but readily imitated German or produced German words when prodded to do so. Jacob's and Trudy's parents displayed the least overall consistency. In Jacob's case the parents nearly always addressed Jacob in their respective languages (>98% consistency), but they alternated between English and German when talking to each other. Trudy's parents were the least consistent in the sample (M>95%; F>73%/1st. rec. and >79%/2nd rec.). Both Jacob and Trudy openly rejected the use of German.

There was little insistence on German in any of the families when the children used English in interaction with their German-speaking parents. However, Keith's and Fiona's German-speaking parents did use insisting strategies more regularly than did the other children's German-speaking parents. Moreover, they tended to choose strategies which put higher constraints on the ongoing interaction, like for example, content questions and requests for translation, than did the other children's parents. The other children's parents never, or only in isolated cases, used high-constraint strategies, but instead just continued in German themselves or, at the most, translated the child's English utterances before they continued. This difference increased from the first to the second recording, with Keith's and Fiona's German-speaking parents using greater proportions of high-constraint strategies and the other children's German-speaking parents using as few or fewer as they did during the first recording.

The attitudes towards bilingualism were generally positive and optimistic. Only Agnes's parents were wondering whether the exposure to two languages was causing Agnes's slow language development, and Trudy's mother was very conscious of being different from others in, for example, the playgroup setting.

6.2.3 The micro-linguistic environment (1): discourse structures

The analysis of the discourse structure was the first step in analyzing the children's micro-linguistic environments. Each interactional move between parents and children was coded for its interactive relevance. Subsequently, the moves were grouped into seven interactionally relevant clusters of moves: *conversational drive*, *responsiveness*, *no-response*, *communication problems*, *conversation oriented initiations*, *control oriented initiations* and *control orientation plus no-response*. The extent to which the parents made use of interactive moves in any of the interactionally relevant clusters was calculated in percentages. Additionally, four measures of topic maintenance were computed: *exchanges per topic*, *moves per topic*, *moves per exchange*, and *moves per topic: parent to child*. These eleven measures were taken as indications of the parents' relative child centredness. A child centred mode of interaction was described as one which is responsive to the child's contributions to the conversation, which works to maintain a once introduced topic, and which is more oriented towards conversing with the child than controlling the child. Communication problems were taken as an indication of how approachable the child was for the parent.

The German- and English-speaking parents in each family were compared with each other. The results lend support to the view that parental child centredness and children's degree of bilingualism are related. Alice, Jacob and Agnes, who did not acquire an active command of German, had English-speaking fathers who interacted with them in more child centred ways than did their German-speaking mothers. Keith learned to understand and speak German from his German-speaking father, who was much more child centred in his verbal interaction with Keith than was his English-speaking mother. Fiona's and Trudy's German-speaking mothers and English-speaking fathers differed much less from each other than did the other children's mothers and fathers. The mothers were equally as child centred or slightly more child centred than were the fathers during the first recording. However, during the second recording, Trudy's English-speaking father behaved in a more child centred manner than did Trudy's German-speaking mother, whereas Fiona's parents' verbal behaviour was very similar again. This was paralleled by both children's "original and intentional" use of German during the first recording. The argument that parental child centredness and the children's active acquisition of the minority language are related derives strong support from Alice's, Jacob's, Agnes's and Keith's cases and somewhat weaker support from Fiona's and Trudy's cases.

The children's involvement in conversational types of interaction with each of their parents was investigated as well. The interactionally relevant clusters *responsiveness, no-response, communication problems, control oriented initiations* plus the children-specific cluster *child-initiative in conversations* were calculated separately for each child's interaction with his/her father and his/her mother and then compared.

In most cases, the children's involvement in conversational types of interaction paralleled the parents' relative child centredness: Keith was more involved in conversational types of interaction with his German-speaking father than he was with his English-speaking mother at both times of recording; Alice was less involved in conversational types of interaction with her German-speaking mother than she was with her English-speaking father; Trudy was equally involved in conversational types of interaction with both her parents during the first recording, but more so with her English-speaking father than with her German-speaking mother during the second recording. However, Jacob was equally involved in conversational types of interaction with both his parents during the first recording in spite of his English-speaking father's more child centred behaviour, but conversed relatively more with him than with his German-speaking mother during the second recording. Agnes's case is difficult to interpret: she appeared to be most responsive but also most control oriented towards the parent who was more involved in child-care activities, and irresponsive but initiating towards the parent who initiated less interaction him/herself. During the first recording, it was the father who looked after her more than did the mother, and during the second recording, the mother attended to her physical needs; hence Agnes's reorientation from more intense, albeit not conversation oriented, interaction with her father during the first recording to more intense, but again not conversation oriented, interaction with her mother during the second recording. Fiona was more involved in conversational types of interaction with her father during the first recording, but equally involved in such verbal activities with both her parents during the second recording; this was paralleled by the father's slightly more child centred behaviour during the first recording as well as the parents' similar behaviour during the second recording.

These results are in agreement with insights gained from studies of verbal interaction between monolingual mothers and their children, who have been shown to acquire language at a faster or slower rate depending on the mothers' child centredness in interaction, and their skilfulness in sustaining conversations with their young children. In the bilingual environment created by the 'one parent-one language' approach, the relative child centredness of the minority language-speaking parent and his/her skilfulness in actively involving the children in conversational exchanges is related to the degree of bilingualism achieved by this approach.

6.2.4 The micro-linguistic environment (2): teaching techniques

The analysis of the teaching techniques employed by the parents was the second step in analyzing the children's micro-linguistic environments. Teaching techniques were described as linguistic features which differentiate adults' language to young children from adults' language to other adults. The coding of teaching techniques followed in part Moerk (1983b). Additional teaching techniques were defined, congruent with the special situation of the bilingual families. Four major sets of techniques evolved: *vocabulary teaching techniques*, *grammar teaching techniques*, *techniques with unspecified goals* and *no teaching oriented utterances*. Each parental utterance was coded, and a parent's relative use of each technique was expressed as a percentage of this parent's total utterances to the child. Comparisons were made on the inter- and intrafamilial level.

The linguistic environments of the two actively German-speaking children, Keith and Fiona, could not be distinguished from the other children's linguistic environments with respect to their parents' use of *teaching techniques with unspecified goals*. The comparison of the parents' use of utterances belonging to the set "no teaching oriented utterances", however, showed that only Keith's and Fiona's German-speaking parents used utterances which were not teaching oriented less than did their English-speaking parents at both times of recording.

With regard to *vocabulary teaching techniques* and *grammar teaching techniques* the only individual techniques which stood out as distinguishing between the verbal input Keith and Fiona received and the verbal input the other children received, was the technique *vocabulary perseveration*. Keith's and Fiona's German-speaking parents used this technique more often than did the other German-speaking parents at both times of recording. Moreover, the comparison of the German- and English-speaking parents on this measure revealed that only Keith's and Fiona's German-speaking parents used this technique more often than did their English-speaking parents. Such was the case at both times of recording.

Patterning, which was a subcategory of *vocabulary teaching techniques* and which consisted of a number of individual techniques itself, was used more by Keith's and Fiona's German-speaking parents than it was used by the other German-speaking parents at both times of recording.

Keith's and Fiona's English speaking-parents could be distinguished from the other children's English-speaking parents with respect to their use of *vocabulary modelling techniques*: both of them used *vocabulary modelling techniques* less frequently than did Alice's, Jacob's and Trudy's English-speaking parents at both times of recording. Agnes's father, however, used these types of teaching techniques least frequently of all the English-speaking parents in the sample.

The limited results achieved by comparing the parents on their use of individual teaching techniques were attributed to parents' preferences for certain types of teaching techniques. Consequently, *vocabulary teaching techniques* and *grammar teaching techniques* were combined into *specified teaching techniques*. After the exclusion of *translations* and *requests for translation*, which are primarily dependent on the child's language choice and only secondarily on parents awareness of their function as a teachers, the scores for *specified teaching techniques* clearly differentiated Keith's and Fiona's linguistic environments from those of the other children: firstly, Keith's and Fiona's German-speaking parents used *specified teaching techniques* relatively more often than did the German-speaking mothers of Alice, Jacob, Agnes and Trudy at both times of recording; secondly, Keith's and Fiona's English-speaking parents used *specified teaching techniques* relatively less often than did Alice's, Jacob's and Trudy's English-speaking fathers at both times of recording. As with *modelling techniques* alone, Agnes's father used *specified teaching techniques* less than did any of the other English-speaking parents, including Keith's and Fiona's; finally, Keith's and Fiona's German-speaking parents used *specified teaching techniques* relatively more often than did their English-speaking parents at both times of recording, while the other children's German-speaking mothers used them relatively less often than did their English-speaking fathers at both times of recording.

The results gained from the analysis of the parents' orientation towards language teaching resembled those of the analysis of the discourse structures in the families: those parents who were more child centred in their verbal behaviour towards their children were also more aware of what type of linguistic input enables children to learn to decode and encode successfully.

6.2.5 Lack of threshold levels

One of the most striking results of this investigation was the lack of threshold levels, *i.e.* the lack of clear-cut levels which would need to be reached by the German-speaking parents in any of the interactionally relevant clusters, or in any of the individual teaching techniques or sets of teaching techniques, in order to ensure that the children acquire an active command of German. Studies which investigated the relationship between parental input and child's rate of language acquisition usually assumed that mothers should differ significantly on one or more measures of adult modification towards young children. The limited amount of statistically valid results and the failure to replicate results were generally disappointing.

The results from the present investigation suggest a number of possible reasons for the lack of success in determining exactly the factors which promote or inhibit language development. Firstly, the matter is far too complex for it to be reduced to a few features in the mothers' language towards their children. Secondly, parents take different paths when interacting with their children: some display a great deal of initiative, others prefer to be responsive, or they balance their initiating and responding behaviour. Thirdly, the type of activity in which parents and children engage influences the parents' verbal strategies (Golinkoff and Ames 1979; Rondal 1980), and parents differ with regard to how often they choose to play with their children. Such differences must be accounted for in the research. A prescription of activities produces similarities in parents' interactive styles which cannot be found in unobserved day-to-day interaction. Fourthly, parents adjust their verbal behaviour to the age of the children as well as to the children's preferences for initiating verbal interaction or responding to verbal advances. Differences in the children's verbal participation may indicate types of verbal input which are most beneficial for the language acquisition by particular children.

In the context of bilingual families who follow the 'one parent-one language' principle, this means that even if the German-speaking parent of child A is as child centred in his/her verbal interaction with the child as is the German-speaking parent of child B, children A and B are not automatically similarly likely to acquire an active command of the minority language. Child A can only compare the German-speaking parent A with the English-speaking parent A, while child B can only compare the German-speaking parent B with the English-speaking parent B. Both children are likely to orient their language learning towards the parent who provides the most conducive input, which might not be the German-speaking parent in both cases. (Döpke 1990)

6.3 Determining factors for the individual children's degree of bilingualism

6.3.1 Alice

Alice's contact with German was restricted to the input she received from her mother. Although cared for by her mother at home, Alice played, read and sang more regularly with her English-speaking father than she did with her German-speaking mother. The mother was more consistent in her language choice than was the father, who liked to try out his minimal German on Alice. However, the mother did not insist that Alice addressed her in German; she simply continued in German herself or, at the most, translated Alice's English utterance into German before she went on.

The analysis of the micro-linguistic environment revealed that the English-speaking father was much more child centred than was the German-speaking mother. He was also more aware of his role as a language teacher.

Alice learned to understand German, but did not use German "originally and intentionally" at either time of recording. She did, however, imitate the mother's German at times or repeated a German word when asked to do so. She also knew a few fixed German utterances, which she at times called on to gain her mother's attention or to achieve some more material effect. Her general verbal participation indicated that she was more involved in conversational types of interaction with her father than she was with her mother. The interaction with her mother was characterized by demands and rejections.

6.3.2 Keith

Keith was the only child in the sample whose father was the transmitter of the minority language. Since the father had learned German as a second language, the family's contact with German-speakers was very limited. Keith heard German nearly exclusively from his father. Like Alice, he was cared for by his mother at home, but much of the father's time at home was spent playing, reading and singing with him. He also watched German films made for children or for foreign language learners on video.

Both parents were very consistent in their language choice. Keith's father insisted on Keith speaking German more than did any of the other German-speaking parents during the first recording, when Keith's language choice was still relatively inconsistent. There was less need for constant insistence on German during the second recording, because Keith appeared to have accepted the 'one parent-one language' principle. However, the types of insisting strategies employed by the father caused higher constraints for the ongoing interaction during the second recording than they did during the first recording. A feature which could not be captured by the audio-recordings in any systematic way was the father's tendency not to react at all when Keith spoke English. All this must have given Keith the impression that it was easier to speak German to his father than it was to speak English to him.

The analysis of the micro-linguistic environment showed that the German-speaking father was far more child centred when interacting verbally with Keith than was the English-speaking mother. He was also more aware of his role as a language teacher than she was.

The differences between the parents were substantial, and so were the differences between Keith's father and the other German-speaking parents. The input which Keith received from his German-speaking father was generally very rich, and richer than that which he received from his English-speaking mother. Consequently, Keith learned to use German actively and did so with much pleasure and pride. He was also more involved in conversational types of interaction with his father than he was with his mother, to whom he preferred to turn to in order to have his physical needs met.

6.3.3 Jacob

Jacob had more contact with German than did Alice and Keith. His mother was a native speaker of German who had a number of German-speaking friends. He also observed her speaking German to other children, although he did not interact with those children himself. Moreover, Jacob was looked after by a German-speaking baby-sitter for a couple of hours each week. Jacob played, read and sang extensively with both his parents.

The language choice of his parents followed the principle of 'one parent-one language' very consistently when addressing Jacob, but they alternated between German and English when talking to each other. The German-speaking mother used strategies, the function of which was to insist that Jacob spoke German to her, more often than did most of the parents, but still only in response to around 20% of Jacob's English utterances addressed to her. Most of these insisting strategies were non-sequential, and, therefore, put very little constraint on the ongoing interaction. Nearly all of her sequential insisting strategies required polar responses only.

The micro-linguistic analysis indicated that Jacob's English-speaking father was more child centred in his verbal approaches towards Jacob than was his German-speaking mother. The difference in the parents' awareness of their roles as language teachers was slight, but the mother employed a generally wider range of teaching techniques than did the father, and exceeded the father in the relative use of *specified teaching techniques* during the second recording.

Jacob's comprehension of German was very good, but he did not use German actively. In fact, he avoided imitating German and openly refused to repeat German words or utterances and to translate from English to German. The mother's lack of insistence on Jacob speaking German to her can probably be attributed to Jacob's overt rejection of German. Interestingly, he was the only child who scored "difficult" on the Toddler Temperamental Scale. Jacob was equally involved in conversational types of interaction with both his parents during the first recording, but more so with his English-speaking father than with his German-speaking mother during the second recording.

6.3.4 Agnes

Although Agnes spent most of her day at home with her native German-speaking mother, the parents felt that she heard more English than German in the course of a day. The mother had very little contact with other speakers of German, and spent much of her time in the company of English-speaking neighbours and friends. Agnes's mother did not usually play or sing with Agnes, and the reading of books was kept brief. German books were not readily available, but English books were translated into German. Agnes's mother felt that Agnes talked more to her father, and that he could understand Agnes better than she could.

Both Agnes's German-speaking mother and her English-speaking father were consistent in their language choice. However, they generally interacted very little with Agnes. Agnes's preference for English was met with low-constraint insisting strategies during the first recording; during the second recording, the mother did used a number of clarification requests, but most of them were genuine and hence not a strategy to insist on German.

Both parents appeared to be least child centred of all the parents in the sample on several measures during the first recording, but behaved more like the other parents did during the second recording. The English-speaking father was more child centred than was the German-speaking mother at both times of recording. The father's use of *specified teaching techniques* was lowest of all the English-speaking parents at both times of recording, and the mother's use of *specified teaching techniques* was the lowest of the German-speaking parents during the first recording and among the lowest during the second recording. Nevertheless, the father used *specified teaching techniques* more frequently than did the mother at both times of recording.

Agnes did not acquire an active command of German during the time of the investigation. Moreover, her knowledge of English seemed to be least developed of the children in her age group (*i.e.* Alice, Keith and Jacob), which was cause for some concern to the parents. Agnes did not get involved in conversational types of interaction with either of her parents very much, but was most responsive towards the parent who looked after her physical needs. Therefore, she interacted more with her father than with her mother during the first recording, and more with her mother than with her father during the second recording. Both Agnes's failure to acquire an active command of German and her slow development in English are most likely related to the fact that the parents did not talk to her very much, and much of the verbal input which Agnes did receive from them was not tailored to her linguistic and interactional needs. Hence, the difference between the mother's and the father's verbal behaviour towards her was probably of secondary importance.

6.3.5 Fiona

Fiona had the most contact with German-speaking people of all the children in the sample. Her mother was a native speaker of German, and the family received frequent long-term visits from the mothers' relatives in Austria. Moreover, the family had many German-speaking friends in Melbourne, and the paternal grandparents, who were Hungarian-Australians, spoke German to Fiona's mother as well. To Fiona they spoke either German or Hungarian. Mother and father regularly played, read and sang with Fiona.

Fiona's parents were very consistent in their language choice. The mother did not make use of strategies which insisted on Fiona speaking German very much, but when she did, she used greater proportions of high-constraint insisting strategies than did Alice's, Jacob's, Agnes's and Trudy's German-speaking mothers. Moreover, she changed the relative proportions of high- to low-constraint insisting strategies in favour of high-constraint insisting strategies from the first to the second recording.

Mother and father were similarly child centred in this family, and similarly aware of their functions as language teachers for their young daughter. The German-speaking mother, however, provided slightly more teaching oriented linguistic input than did the English-speaking father.

Due to a couple of complicating factors during the first recording (cf. 4.3.2.5), Fiona was more involved in conversational types of interaction with her father than with her mother at that time, but interacted in similar ways with both her parents during the second recording. The extensive contact with German as well as the parents' consistent adherence to the 'one parent-one language' principle was highly influential in Fiona's active acquisition of German. Both parents' similar ways of interacting with Fiona and their similarly teaching oriented linguistic input must, however, be considered important factors in Fiona's acceptance that both languages are useful communication tools.

6.3.6 Trudy

Trudy heard German from her second-generation German-Australian mother as well as during visits to her grandparents' home. Other than that, she did not have any contact with German-speaking people. However, the father had started to learn some German from his wife once Trudy was born, and always spoke German to Trudy until she was about two years old. From then on, he could not keep pace with Trudy's language acquisition, and he increasingly resorted to English. At some time between the first and the second recording, the grandparents went overseas, and on their return the grandfather became very ill. Thus, her contact with the grandparents became minimal. But since Trudy spent most of her days in the care of her mother, the parents felt that Trudy heard more German than she heard English in the course of a day anyway. Both parents regularly played, read and sang with Trudy.

Due to the father's use of German, the parents did not follow the 'one parent-one language' principle consistently. Moreover, Trudy's use of English was not met with much insistence by her German-speaking mother: she used only low-constraint insisting strategies for fear of upsetting her relationship with

Trudy. She was also anxious not to make Trudy feel awkward among her monolingual peers and only spoke very quietly to Trudy when monolingual children were around, so that they would not hear her speak German.

The parents were similarly child centred in interaction with Trudy during the first recording, but the English-speaking father proved to be slightly more child centred than did the German-speaking mother during the second recording. With regard to teaching techniques, the father appeared to be more aware of his function as a language teacher than did the mother at both times of recording.

Trudy spoke German and English in interaction with both her parents during the first recording. During the second recording, she spoke nearly only English to her father, and had also considerably reduced the amount of German she spoke to her mother. Most of the German she still used in interaction with her mother were imitations of her mother's preceding utterances and incorporations of just heard lexical items into her otherwise English sentences. Statements against German and self-corrections towards English when talking to her mother indicated that she was consciously refusing to speak German. The collaborated evidence points towards the assumption that Trudy wished to follow her father's linguistic model more than her mother's.

6.4 Relationship between results and hypotheses

6.4.1 Differences between fathers and mothers

A number of studies have shown that mothers and fathers do not differ linguistically when interacting with their young children. Such studies concentrated on MLU and pre-verb complexity (Gleason 1975; Golinkoff and Ames 1979; Masur and Gleason 1980; Kavanaugh and Jen 1981), usage of declaratives, interrogatives, repetitions and expansions (Giattino and Hogan 1975; Gleason 1975; Kavanaugh and Jen 1981; Masur 1982), types of semantic reference (Kavanaugh and Jen 1981; Masur 1982) and adjustment to the developing linguistic and cognitive abilities of the child (Rondal 1980; Masur 1982). The studies of Golinkoff and Ames (1979) and Rondal (1980) have also shown that the situation had corresponding effects on mothers' and fathers' speech: both mothers and fathers talked more in structured play situations and during story telling than during free play, and more during free play than during meal times. They also adjusted the type of talk to the situation: free play and

story telling elicited more words, lower utterance complexity, fewer declaratives, more questions, fewer joint and indirect requests for action, more verbal approvals and more expansions of child utterances from both parents than
did the meal situation (Rondal 1980).

Parents were found to differ with respect to talkativeness, degree of linguistic adjustment and general interactive style: mothers tended to talk more
than did fathers (Rebelsky and Hank 1971; Friedlander, Davis and Wetstone
1972; Gleason 1975; Rondal 1980) and adjusted their speech more to the
children's growing linguistic development than did fathers (Gleason 1975;
Gleason and Weintraub 1978; Rondal 1980; Kavanaugh and Jen 1981; Masur
1982; McLaughlin, White, McDevitt and Raskin 1983). Mothers also tended
to focus more on their relationship to the child, whereas the fathers concentrated
more on the activity itself and therefore involved the children less than did
mothers (Gleason 1975; Masur 1982; Pieper 1984).

In the present study, mothers and fathers were found to differ, with respect
to child centredness and the employment of teaching techniques, considerably
in some families and less so in others. In none of the families, however, was it
the mother who was the more child centred and the more didactic parent. At
the most, mothers and fathers were similar in those respects. This contradiction
to former studies must be attributed to the way in which the data were collected:
all the earlier studies investigated mothers' and fathers' verbal behaviour in
identical situations; for the present study, however, data were collected in the
children's homes, and the parents were advised to pursue their interactional
routines as usual. Hence mother-child dyads and father-child dyads engaged
in different activities and these activities had a bearing on the verbal behaviour
of the parents.

I would like to conclude that, even though mothers and fathers have been
shown to be similar in their verbal behaviour towards young children, or
mothers have been shown to be more linguistically accommodating than were
fathers while the situation was kept constant, an uneven distribution of activities
in a family can result in fathers and mothers behaving differently as well as
fathers' verbal input being more in tune with the children's development than
mothers' verbal input.

6.4.2 Children's orientation on the interactionally more child centred parent

Studies of parent-child interaction have striven to gain insight into aspects of parental speech likely to foster young children's language acquisition. It was possible to relate those features in parents' speech which display sensitivity to the child's focus of attention, structurally as well as with respect to content, to rapid language development in a variety of studies. Among the features studied were positive reinforcement (Cross 1978; Lieven 1978; Moerk 1983a; Nelson et al. 1983), questions (Cross 1978; Lieven 1978; Furrow et al. 1979; Howe 1981; Barnes et al. 1983) and semantic relatedness (Cross 1978; Lieven 1978; Howe 1981; Barnes et al. 1983; Nelson et al. 1983), all of which have also been shown to be instrumental in sustaining conversations with young children (Hubbel 1977; Wells, MacLure and Montgomery, 1981; McDonald and Pien 1982; Stella-Prorok 1983).

At the same time, mothers of children who developed language more slowly would characteristically use high proportions of directives (Newport et al. 1977; Cross 1978, 1981), attentionals (Cross 1981), rejections (Lieven 1978) and semantically unrelated utterances (Cross 1978); they would also ignore their children's communication attempts more often than mothers of children who were developing their language skills more rapidly (Lieven 1978). These ways of interacting with young children have been associated with mothers' orientation towards controlling the child (McDonald and Pien 1982) and are believed to counteract the child's active participation in conversations (Hubbel 1977; Wells, 1980; Wells, MacLure and Montgomery 1981).

The present study described features which were formerly associated with children's rapid language development as aspects of parental child centredness. It was found that the children tended to interact more intensively with the parent who displayed the more child centred behaviour. Moreover, those children whose English-speaking parents were more child centred in their verbal interaction with them than were the German-speaking parents did not acquire an active command of German, but those children who did acquire an active command of German had German-speaking parents who were more child centred than, or as child centred as, their English-speaking parents.

The lack of a threshold level of child centredness for the active acquisition of German supports the view that children acquire language from whatever input is available to them. Moreover, the data indicate that the children preferred to follow the linguistic model which attended to their interactive needs best. In the context of families who followed the 'one parent-one language' principle, that meant that the children acquired the minority language in those families where the interaction with the minority language-speaking parent was a generally rewarding experience for them. Where, however, the interaction with the majority language-speaking parent proved to be more enjoyable for them than that with the minority language-speaking parent, the children were not interested in using the minority language actively. Such unbalanced orientation towards one of the parent's verbal models is most likely to happen in monolingual families as well, but apart from snippets usually commented upon by surrounding adults with utterances like "she sounds just like her father", it is not easily traceable.

The reverse will of course not happen, that is, the majority language will always be acquired due to the accumulating effect of input from various sources and the communicative demands created by monolingual speakers in the society. Hence, the opposition is not between children's orientation on the parent who speaks the minority language and who therefore acquire the minority language and children's orientation on the parent who speaks the majority language and who therefore acquire the majority language. Instead, the opposition is between children who orient themselves on the minority language-speaking parent and who will learn both languages and become productive bilinguals on the one hand, and children who orient themselves on the majority language-speaking parent and who will acquire the majority language as expected but who will not develop an active command of the minority language, on the other hand.

6.4.3 Children's orientation on the more didactic parent

Mothers' awareness of their roles as language teachers has recently been re-evaluated and the importance of the linguistic input being tailored to the needs of the language learning child has been revisited (Clark 1977; Ninio and Bruner 1978; Moerk and Moerk 1979; Moerk 1980, 1983a,b, 1985b; Ninio 1980a,b; Snow 1983). It was found that mothers make use of teaching techniques much more than was formerly believed, as well as that mothers differ with regard to the extent with which they use teaching techniques (Moerk 1980, 1983a,b, 1985a,b): mothers of rapid language learners tended to provide input which was designed to teach formal aspects of the language more than did mothers of normally developing children.

The results of the present study indicate that there was a relationship between the parents' awareness of their roles as language teachers and the children's active acquisition of the minority language, in that those children whose minority language parent provided more structurally tailored input than did their majority language parent acquired an active command of the minority language. In the reverse case, *i.e.* where the majority language parent provided the more teaching oriented input, the children became receptive bilinguals only.

The results from the analysis of the parents' teaching orientation and those from the analysis of the parents' interactive child centredness complemented each other, due to the fact that both child centred interaction and teaching oriented linguistic input are more easily applied in playful activities than they are in more difficult-to-manage child caring activities. Moreover, they are both features of a parental personality which is conscious of the child's intellectual abilities and developmental needs. Therefore, the parents' personalities as well as the distribution of activities in the families appeared to be major factors contributing to the micro-linguistic environments of the children in the sample.

6.4.4 Relation between parents' insistence on the minority language and its active acquisition by the children

Saunders (1982b) and Taeschner (1983) both suggested that the use of insisting strategies of the "what? I don't understand"-type was instrumental in their children's active acquisition of the minority language. Studies of the effect of clarification requests on monolingual children's linguistic performance suggested that children re-evaluated, varied and often improved their original utterances. In the monolingual as well as the bilingual environment, clarification requests urge the child to greater approximation of the adult model. For the bilingual children, they additionally suggest a re-evaluation of their language choice. With respect to the organization of discourse, clarification requests produce side sequences which have priority over the main topic of the conversation (Jefferson 1972).

The results from the present study showed that the parents differed in their use of insisting strategies and that only those children who acquired an active command of German were met with high-constraint insisting strategies like unspecified clarification requests and requests for translation.

The importance of high-constraint insisting strategies for the child's active acquisition of the minority language lies in their ability to create a need to speak the minority language which does not automatically exist. Most of the majority language-speakers who children meet do not understand them when they speak the minority language; often that even includes their own parents. However, most or all of the minority language-speaking people the child meets are bilingual; and most importantly, their own minority language parent is bilingual. The relative artificiality of this method is of secondary importance. Primarily, the high-constraint insisting techniques interrupt the current interaction for as long as is necessary to conclude the associated repair sequence. Children will soon find out that passing through these side-sequences is in their interest and will eventually avoid these unwelcome diversions altogether.

6.4.5 Fathers' tendency to provide higher quality of interaction than mothers

Popular opinion suggests that children would learn a minority language from their mothers as a matter of course, but that a father would have little chance of transmitting a minority language in a situation where he is the main or only interlocutor of that language for the child. The underlying assumption is that mothers stay at home, spend a lot of time with the children and are consequently more important for their emotional and verbal development than are fathers, whose outside work only permits limited father-child contact. Döpke (1990) reported research into type and quality of interaction between mothers and their young children as well as between fathers and their young children. It was found that mothers spend surprisingly little time actively playing, cuddling and exploring stimulating objects with their children (Clarke-Stewart 1972) and that children responded more positively to play as well as physical contact with their fathers than with their mothers (Lamb 1975a,b); this was related to the fact that the fathers' play was more physical and their physical contact more play-related than was that of mothers, who spent much higher proportions of the time they had with their children in caretaking activities.

The results of the present study indicate that most fathers interacted with their children in a more child centred way and provided linguistic input which was more conducive to language acquisition than did mothers. This correlated with four of the six children not learning German from their mothers and one child learning German from his father.

The present study supports earlier findings concerning the relative quality of interaction in mother-child dyads and father-child dyads by means of linguistic analyses, showing that the quality of the verbal interaction can often be better in father-child dyads than in mother-child dyads. Thus, the more extensive exposure to language through the mother during the day is off-set by the more intensive exposure to language through the father during the evening.

The reasons for such differences in the quality of interaction are to be found in the unequal distribution of activities. Mothers at home are commonly responsible for housekeeping and child rearing. This means that they do not often engage in play exclusively, but tend to combine housework with play. Moreover, child-care activities, like bathing, dressing, disciplining etc., elicit high proportions of speech which does not motivate verbal interaction very much and which is not linguistically tailored to the needs of the language learning child. Fathers, on the other hand, engage less in housekeeping and child-care and do not feel responsible for house chores being done. Therefore, they are more likely to concentrate on playing exclusively or to extend child-care activities into playful activities. Consequently, father-child interaction can be more child centred and more tailored to the linguistic needs of the language learning child than can mother-child interaction.

The results from the present study give reason to believe that the quality of input is more important in the acquisition of a minority language than is the quantity of input when children are raised according to the principle of 'one parent-one language'.

6.5 Four years later

In the light of the foregoing discussion, it is interesting to see how the children's bilingualism developed further.

Trudy's and Alice's mothers eventually stopped speaking German to their children. By the time they entered school, the children had lost their passive knowledge of German except for some rudimentary vocabulary.

Jacob's and Agnes's families went to Germany for extensive stays of around six months when the children were three and a half to four years of age. On their return, both children were active bilinguals. During the following years, their German gradually faded, until the beginning of school finally set them back to their former stage of answering their German-speaking mothers only in English. When faced with an apparently monolingual German speaker, Jacob was still able to speak German, but kept the interaction to a minimum; Agnes mixed some German into her English. Jacob's mother reported that it was just too difficult for Jacob to talk about his school experiences in German and that it would require much more of her time than she was able to give to compensate for the English language experience in school with German language experience at home.

Keith never went to Germany, but he continued to speak German to his father until he entered school. During his pre-school years, he attended Jacob's mother's kindergarten once a week and was spoken to in German by her. He also participated in a one-hour-a-week German program for children run by the German Department of a local university. Once he had entered school, however, he did not participate in the program any more, nor did he any longer meet Jacob's mother. His father reported that Keith refused to speak German since the start of school and only did so accidentally at times. His father, however, had not yet stopped speaking German to Keith, but was uncertain of how long he would continue with it.

Fiona continued to receive a rich and varied input in German. Immediately after the second recording, she went to Austria for the first time, and again a second time twelve months later. Her maternal grandfather visited the family every year for a couple of months. The family also had two au-pair girls, one from Austria, the other one from Germany, each for half a year. Fiona never stopped speaking German. However, the beginning of school had its negative effects on the minority language even in this family: Fiona increasingly tried to speak English to her mother.

All of the six children eventually had younger siblings, and in all families the children spoke English to each other. Trudy's and Alice's younger siblings did not acquire any German, not even any receptive skills. Agnes's and Keith's younger brothers learned to understand German, but did not speak it. Jacob's younger sister did not mind speaking German at the age of four, but mixed German and English freely. Her mother thought that she "just [did] not care" about the differentiation between the two languages and at times even spoke some German to her monolingual English friends. Fiona had two younger siblings, both of whom became active bilinguals.

6.6 General issues

6.6.1 Direction of influence

One of the most controversial issues among researchers interested in children's language development and its relation to parental input is the question of whether the parents are masters of their language modifications in interaction with their young children or whether they simply respond to the particular child's interactional demands: in other words, are differences between parents (*i.e.* mostly mothers were investigated) in the way they make use of aspects of the linguistic system due to the parents' personalities or are they due to the children's personalities? Referring back to data collected in the seventies, Gleitman et al. (1984) and Furrow et al. (1986) debated this issue heatedly. Lieven (1978) reported that the researcher adjusted her speech styles along the lines of the respective mothers and suggested that this might be an indication that children elicit certain types of adult verbal behaviour. Wells et al. (1979:369) argued for the direction of influence going from the parent to the child (cited in 4.2.1). Smolak (1987) presented evidence of a complex interaction between maternal speech style and children's behaviour, with the mother probably setting a pattern which fosters certain behavioural traits in the child, but subsequently reacting to the child's behaviour.

The research on this issue has not yet progressed out of its initial stage of speculations and pilot studies. The difficulties are due to the complexity of the phenomenon and to problems arising from the attempt to find answers by looking at dyads of mothers and children rather than looking at groups of adults in relation to one child.

The present study compared mothers and fathers in interaction with their children. Thus, each child interacted with two adults. The results indicated that parents differed in type of verbal behaviour and linguistic modification towards the same child, some to a greater, some to a lesser extent.

Although the child's influences on the parent cannot be excluded (and by no means would I wish to do so), the fact that the adults differed in the ways they interacted with the same child and that these differences correlated with the children's degree of bilingualism across the sample, indicates that some force other than the child's temperament or the specific child's interactive demands must have been responsible for the behavioural differences of the adults. The situation as a factor which determines parents' relative child centredness and teaching oriented linguistic modifications has already been discussed. Personality factors, as proposed by Wells et al. (1979), are also likely to influence the degree to which adults adjust themselves to the interactional and linguistic needs of the child. Moreover, the extent to which adults choose to engage in playful and conversation oriented interaction is most probably not only a result of their traditional roles in the family, but is also related to characteristics of their personality. Further research into this question is called for.

6.6.2 Value of becoming a passive bilingual

Children's failure to acquire an active command of the minority language is usually disappointing to parents. However, several authors have pointed out the advantages of achieving passive or receptive bilingualism over becoming totally monolingual (Saunders 1982b; Porsché 1983; Harding and Riley 1986; Arnberg 1987). In the majority of reported cases, children with receptive knowledge of a second language converted this knowledge into the ability to speak in a surprisingly short time once they went to a country where the minority language was the only medium of communication (Leopold, 1957-8; Arnberg 1981b; Porsché 1983; Harding and Riley 1986). Visits from relatives who are monolingual in the child's passive language had a similar activating effect on some children (Arnberg 1987). In contrast to that, parents of monolingual children usually report that the child was just about ready to start speaking the second language when the visit was over (Arnberg 1987). The ability to at least understand the minority language of one's parent keeps options open: communicatively when meeting monolingual speakers of that language, emotionally when meeting one's own relatives and, of course, educationally when the child is to study that language formally in school.

For two of the children studied here, this was the case. They left for Germany as passive bilinguals and returned with active language skills in German.

6.6.3 Differences between first- and later-born children

Differences between first- and later-born children have not been studied very much. Wherever authors did refer to later-born children as distinct from first-born children, it has usually been ascertained that their language development took different paths to those of their older siblings. Nelson (1981) differentiated between children who were *expressive* and children who were *referential*, and found that later-born children tended to be *expressive* more often than were first-born children. Oldenburg (1986) employed a functional systemic framework when comparing her second-born daughter with Halliday's (1975) and Painter's (1984) first-born sons. She found that the second-born child developed the interpersonal mode faster than she did the experiential mode, and that she differed from the two first-born children in that respect. Oldenburg put that difference down to the younger child using the older child as a model, as well as the younger one having to compete with the older child for possessions, territory and parental attention.

Much of the research into monolingual parent-child interaction and children's linguistic growth rate only studied first-born children or did not discriminate on the basis of birth order. One study which did look at siblings' effects on the rate of language acquisition was done by Nelson et al. (1978). They found that short-lag later-borns, that is, children with a gap to the next older child of less than twenty four months, were superior to first-born and long-lag later-born children on measures of syntax and concept development. The authors attributed this difference to the younger children's profiting most from interactions between parents and short-lag older siblings as well as from directly interacting with and imitating their short-lag older siblings.

Later-born bilingual children were often reported to have become receptive bilinguals, even when their older siblings used the minority language actively (Leopold 1957-8; de Jong 1986; Arnberg 1987). The reasons for that are to be found in the input of the minority language being considerably reduced for the second child, due to the parent having more than one child to attend to as well as because children usually adopt the majority language as a means of communication among themselves (Clyne 1970; Arnberg 1987) The latter aspect results in peer group pressure being exerted onto the younger child at a much earlier age than it was experienced by the older child Moreover, younger children are often talked for by their older siblings and have less need to develop active language facilities in interaction with their parents than in interaction with their older brothers and sisters (de Jong 1986). I have never heard or read of a case where a child has become actively bilingual in spite of the first child exclusively using the majority language.

Of the few reports on second-born children who were exposed to the 'one parent-one language' principle, all but one involved second-born children who did become active bilinguals. Leopold's daughter Karla (Leopold 1949) only developed receptive knowledge of German in spite of her older sister talking German to their father. The age-gap between the two girls was six years, and Karla must, therefore, be considered a long-lag later-born. Saunders's (1982b), Kielhöfer and Jonekeit's (1983) and Taeschner's (1983) subjects, as well as the children of the non-linguist Finnish-Kurdish-Swedish family reported by Arnberg (1987), were all born in between thirteen and twenty three months of the older child and were, therefore, short-lag later-borns. One long-lag later-born active bilingual was reported by Hoffmann (1985), the age-gap between his sister and him being three years. Saunders's third child (1988) was born five years and four months after the second one and she, too, became actively bilingual. By then, however, there were already three people in the family who spoke German.

The children of the present study were purposely sampled as first-born children. Their younger siblings were all long-lag later-borns. The closest gaps were between Keith and his brother, who was twenty eight months his junior, and Fiona and her sister, who was born when Fiona was twenty seven months old. In spite of the fact that four of the younger siblings heard their older brothers and sisters speak German to one of their parents for at least a couple of years, only one child became actively bilingual.

Research into the different dynamics of language acquisition for later-born children is much called for; and especially the language environment of later-born bilingual children needs to be explored.

6.6.4 Parental effort in raising children bilingually

The final word will be devoted to the amount of parental effort which is necessary when parents who follow the 'one parent-one language' principle want their children to become productive bilinguals. Saunders (1982b), Harding and Riley (1986) and Arnberg (1987) as well as many of the parents Harding and Riley (1986), de Jong (1986) and Arnberg (1987) interviewed have all pointed out that great parental effort is involved in raising children to become productive bilinguals.

The present study additionally explored features of the interaction between parents and their young children which appeared to be influential in monolingual children's rate of language development and which were shown to also be influential in bilingual children's active acquisition of the minority language. Parents needed to create the necessity to talk the minority language by insisting that the children spoke it in interaction with them. Moreover, they had to create a micro-linguistic environment which was conducive to language acquisition in general, and which in these cases fostered the active acquisition of the minority language. The relationship between type of activity and parental input which is tailored to the needs of the language learning child suggests that parents who speak a minority language to their children should try and engage in playful activities with their children as much as possible and, if possible, more than does the parent who speaks the majority language.

Incidentally, parent intervention programs have shown that parents are able to alter their style of interaction when made aware of alternatives by professionals (cf. Hubbel 1977). Counselling or training should, therefore, be able to encourage parents to raise their level of child centredness as well as their level of teaching oriented behaviour by incorporating more play into activities which are not primarily designed for play.

For parents who follow the 'one parent-one language' principle or who intend to do so, this study suggests that there are criteria over which the parent can have influence to a certain degree, and that one's children's active acquisition of a minority language is not solely left to uncontrollable factors such as the child's temperament or being blessed with ethnic grandparents resident nearby.

Notes

1. For a more complete overview of the issues discussed in this section I would like to direct the interested reader to Döpke, McNamara and Quinn (1991)

2. 1;5 conventionally reads: one year and five months.

3. In spite of my doubts concerning the ultimate validity of the initial one-system hypothesis promoted by this model, its usefulness for the discussion of my data later on warrants its description at this point.

4. This turn of events is by no means restricted to families who pursue the 'one parent-one language' principle, but just as common in families where both parents speak the same minority language to the children, only that the reluctance to speak the minority language and the eventual refusal happens later and for different reasons.

5. Interactively coherent translation, although not literal.

References

Arnberg, L. 1979. "Language strategies in mixed nationality families". *Scandinavian Journal of Psychology* 20. 105-112.

Arnberg, L. 1981a. *The Effects of Bilingualism on Development During Early Childhood: A Survey on Literature.* Linköping: Linköping University, Department of Education.

Arnberg, L. 1981b. *Early Childhood Bilingualism in the Mixed-Lingual Family.* Linköping: Linköping University, Department of Education.

Arnberg, L. 1981c. *A Longitudinal Study of Language Development in Four Young Children Exposed to English and Swedish in the Home.* Linköping: Linköping University, Department of Education.

Arnberg, L. 1984. "Mother tongue playgroups for preschool bilingual children". *Journal of Multilingual and Multicultural Development* 5. 65-84.

Arnberg, L. 1987. *Raising Children Bilingually. The Preschool Years.* Clevedon: Multilingual Matters.

Arnberg, L. and P.W. Arnberg. 1985. "The relation between code differentiation and language mixing in bilingual three- to four-year-old children". *Bilingual Review* 12 (1-2): 20-32.

Bain, B. and A. Yu. 1980. "Cognitive consequences of raising children bilingually: one parent-one language". *Canadian Journal of Psychology* 34. 304-313.

Barnes, S., M. Gutfreund, D. Satterly and G. Wells. 1983. "Characteristics of adult speech which predict children's language development". *Journal of Child Language* 10. 65-84.

Beck, J. 1985. *How to Raise a Brighter Child. The Case of Early Learning.* Glasgow: Fontana/Collins.

Ben-Zeev, S. 1977a. "The influence of bilingualism on cognitive strategy and cognitive development". *Child Development* 48. 1009-1018

Ben-Zeev, S. 1977b. "Mechanism by which childhood bilingualism effects understanding of language and cognitive structures". *Bilingualism. Psychological, Social and Educational Implications,* ed. by P. Hornby. New York: Academic Press.

Bloom, L., L. Hood and L. Lightbown. 1974. "Imitation in language development: if, when and why". *Cognitive Psychology* 6: 380-420.

Brown, R. 1968. " The development of wh-questions in child speech." *Journal of Verbal Learning and Verbal Behaviour* 7. 279-290.

Brown, R. 1973. *A First Language. The Early Stages.* Cambridge, MA: M.I.T. Press.

Brown, R., C.B. Cazden and U. Bellugi. 1969. "The child's grammar from I to III". *Minnesota Symposium on Child Development. Vol.2.,* ed. by J.P. Hill. Minneapolis: University of Minnesota Press.

Brown, R. and U. Bellugi. 1964. "Three processes in the child's acquisition of syntax." In *New Direction in the Study of Language,* ed. by E.H. Lenneberg. Cambridge, MA: M.I.T. Press

Burling, R. 1959. "Language development of a Garo and English speaking child". Word 15. 45-68.

Cazden, C.B. 1965. "Environmental assistance to the child's acquisition of grammar". Ph.D. dissertation, Harvard University Press.

Chomsky, N. 1959. "Skinner: Verbal Behaviour". Language 35. 26-57.

Chomsky, N. 1964. "Formal discussion of W. Miller and S. Ervin 'The development of grammar in child language.'" In *The Acquisition of Language,* ed. by U. Bellugi and R. Brown. Monographs of the Society for Research in Child Development . 29 (Serial No. 92).

Chomsky, N. 1965. *Aspects of the Theory of Syntax.* Cambridge, MA: M.I.T. Press.

Clark, E.V. 1979. The *Ontogenesis of Meaning.* Wiesbaden: Akademische Verlagsgesellschaft.

Clark, R. 1974. "Performing without competence". *Journal of Child Language* 1. 1-10.

Clark, R. 1977. "What is the use of imitation?" *Journal of Child Language* 4. 241-358.

Clarke-Stewart, K.A. 1972. "Interactions between mothers and their young children: characteristics and consequences" Unpublished Ph.D. Thesis, Yale University.

Clyne, M. 1970. "Some aspects of the bilingualism and language maintenance of Australian-born children of German-speaking parents". *ITL Review of Applied Linguistics* 9. 35-47.

Clyne, M. 1982. *Multilingual Australia*. Melbourne: River Seine.

Clyne, M. 1985. "Bilingual language acquisition and language separation". *Journal of Intercultural Studies* 6 (1). 41-48.

Corsaro, W. 1977. "The clarification request as a feature of adult interactive style with young children". *Language in Society* 6 (2). 183-207.

Cross, T.G. 1977. "Mothers' speech adjustments: the contribution of selected child listener variables". IN *Talking to Children: Language Input and Acquisition.*, ed. by C.E. Snow and C.A. Ferguson. Cambridge: Cambridge University Press.

Cross, T.G. 1978. "Mothers' speech and its association with rate of linguistic development in young children". In *The Development of Communication*, ed. by N. Waterson and C. Snow. Chichester: Wiley.

Cross, T.G. 1981. "The linguistic experience of slow language learners". In *Advances in Child Development*, ed. by A.R. Nesdale, C. Pratt, R. Grieve, J. Field, D. Illingworth and J. Hogben. Nedlands, W.A.: N.C.C.D.

de Jong, E. 1986. *The Bilingual Experience. A Book For Parents*. Cambridge: Cambridge University Press.

Dodson, C.J. 1983. "Living with two languages". *Journal of Multilingual and Multicultural Development* 4 (6). 401-414.

Döpke, S. 1984. "George Saunders: Bilingual Children: Guidance to the Family" *Polycom* 36 (March). 21-22.

Döpke, S. 1986. "Discourse structures in bilingual families". *Journal of Multilingual and Multicultural Development* 7 (6). 493-507.

Döpke, S. 1988. "The role of parental teaching techniques in bilingual German-English families". *International Journal of the Sociology of Language* 72. 101-112.

Döpke, S. 1990. "Are mothers really the main mediators of language?" In *Learning, Keeping and Using Language*, ed. by M.A.K. Halliday, J. Gibbons and H. Nicholas. Amsterdam: John Benjamins.

Döpke, S., T.F. McNamara and T.J. Quinn. 1991. "Psycholinguistic aspects of bilingualism". In *Bilingualism and Bilingual Education*, ed. by A. Liddicoat. Melbourne: National Languages Institute of Australia

DuBois, J.W., S. Cumming and S. Schuetze-Coburn. 1988. "Discourse Transcription". In *Santa Barbara Papers in Linguistics Vol.2.*, ed. by Sandra A. Thompson. Santa Barbara: University of California.

Ellis, R. and G. Wells. 1980. "Enabling factors in adult-child discourse". *First Language* 1. 46-62.

Ervin, S. 1964. "Imitation and structural change in children's language." In *New Directions in the Study of Language,* ed. by E.H. Lenneberg. Cambridge, MA: M.I.T. Press

Ervin-Tripp, S. and W. Miller. 1977. "Early discourse. Some questions about questions". In *Interaction, Conversation and the Development of Language*, ed. by M. Lewis and L. Rosenblum. New York: Wiley

Fantini, A.E. 1985. *Language Acquisition of a Bilingual Child. A Sociolinguistic Perspective*. Clevedon: Multilingual Matters.

Foster-Meloni, C. 1978. "Code-switching and interference in the speech of an Italian-English bilingual child". *Rassegna Italiana di Linguistica Applicata* 10 (2-3). 89-95.

Friedlander, B., B. Davis, and H. Wetstone. 1972. "Time-sampling analysis of infants' natural language environments in the home". *Child Development* 43. 730-740.

Fullard, W., S.C. McDevitt and W.B. Carey. 1978. "Toddler Temperamental Scale". Unpublished test form, Department of Educational Psychology, Temple University, Philadelphia.

Furrow, D., K. Nelson and H. Benedict. 1979. "Mothers' speech to children and syntactic development: some simple relationships". *Journal of Child Language* 6. 423-442.

Furrow, D. and K. Nelson. 1986. "A further look at the motherese hypothesis: a reply to Gleitman, Newport and Gleitman". *Journal of Child Language* 13. 163-176.

Gallagher, T.M. 1977. "Revision behaviour in the speech of normal children developing language". *Journal of Speech and Hearing Research* 20. 303-318.

Garcia, E.E. 1980. "The function of language switching during bilingual mother-child interaction". *Journal of Multilingual and Multicultural Development* 1 (3). 243-252.

Garvey, C. 1977. "The contingent query: a dependent act in conversation". In *Interaction, Conversation and the Development of Language,* ed. by M. Lewis and L. Rosenblum. New York: Wiley.

Giattino, J. and J.G. Hogan. 1975. "Analysis of a father's speech to his language-learning child." *Journal of Speech and Hearing Disorders* 40. 524-537.

Gleason, J.B. 1973. "Code switching in children's language". In *Cognitive Development and the Acquisition of Language,* ed. by T.E. Moore. New York: Academic Press.

Gleason, J.B. 1975. "Fathers and other strangers: men's speech to young children". In *Developmental Psycholinguistics. Theory and Applications,* ed. by D. Dato. Washington, D.C.: Georgetown University Press.

Gleason, J.B. and S. Weintraub. 1978. "Input language and the acquisition of communicative competence". In *Children's Language. Vol.1.,* ed. by K.E. Nelson. New York: Gardner.

Gleitman, L.R., E.L. Newport and H. Gleitman. 1984. "The current status of the motherese hypothesis". *Journal of Child Language* 11. 43-79.

Golinkoff, R.M. and G.J. Ames. 1979. "A comparison of fathers' and mothers' speech with their young children." *Child Development.* 50. 28-32.

Graves, Z. and J. Glick. 1978. "The effect of context on mother-child interaction: a progress report". *The Quarterly Newsletter of the Institute of Comparative Human Development* 2 (3).

Gumperz, J.J. 1982. "Conversational code switching". In *Discourse Strategies.* Cambridge: Cambridge University Press.

Harding, E. and P. Riley. 1986. *The Bilingual Family: A Handbook for Parents.* Cambridge: Cambridge University Press.

Hoffmann, C. 1985. "Language acquisition in two trilingual children". *Journal of Multilingual and Multicultural Development* 6 (6). 479-495.

Howe, C. 1981. *Acquiring Language in a Conversational Context.* London: Academic Press.

Hubbel, R.D. 1977. "On facilitating spontaneous talking in young children". *Journal of Speech and Hearing Disorders* 42. 216-231.

Jefferson, G. 1972. "Side sequences". In *Studies in Social Interaction,* ed. by D. Sudnow. New York: Free Press.

Jespersen, O. 1922. *Language, Its Nature, Development and Origin.* London: Allen and Unwin.

Käsermann, M. 1980. *Spracherwerb und Interaktion.* Bern: Huber.

Katchan, O. 1985. "Early bilingualism: friend or foe?" Paper given at the annual conference of the Applied Linguistic Association of Australia, Brisbane. Published in *Knowledge and Language,* ed. *by* J. Kurcz, G.W. Shugar and J.H. Danks. North Holland: Elsevier.

Kavanaugh, R.D. and M. Jen. 1981. "Some relationships between parental speech and children's object development". *First Language* 5. 103-115.

Keenan, E.O. and B.B. Schieffelin. 1976. "Topic as a discourse notion: a study in the conversations of children and adults". In *Subject and Topic*, ed. by C.N. Li. New York: Academic Press.

Kielhöfer, B. and S. Jonekeit. 1983. *Zweisprachige Kindererziehung*. Tübingen: Stauffenberg Verlag.

Klann-Delius, G. 1980. "Welchen Einfluß hat die Geschlechtszugehörigkeit auf den Spracherwerb des Kindes?" *Linguistische Berichte* 70. 63-87.

Lamb, M.E. 1975a. "Fathers: forgotten contributors to child development". *Human Development* 18:245-266.

Lamb, M.E.. 1975b. "Infants, fathers and mothers: interaction at eighteen-months-of-age in the home and in the laboratory." Proc. Meet., Eastern Psychological Association.

Langford, D. 1981. "The clarification request sequence in conversations between mothers and their children". In *Adult-Child Conversations. Studies in Structure and Process*, ed. by P. French and M. McLure. London: Croom Helm.

Leopold, W.F. 1939-49. *Speech Development of a Bilingual Child. Vols. 1-4.* Evanston, Illinois: University of Illinois Press.

Leopold, W.F. 1957. "Ein Kind lernt zwei Sprachen". *Sprachforum* 2 (3-4). 248-252.

Leopold, W.F. 1957-8 "American children can learn their German mother tongue." *The American-German Review* 24. 4-6

Lieven, E.V.M. 1978. "Conversations between mothers and young children: individual differences and their possible implications for the study of language learning". In *The Development of Communication*, ed. by N. Waterson and C. Snow. Chichester: Wiley.

Lieven, E.V.M. 1984. "Interactional styles and children's language learning". *Topics in Language Disorder* 4 (4). 15-23.

Luria, A.R. 1961. *The Role of Speech in the Regulation of Normal and Abnormal Behaviour*. New York: Liveright.

Masur, E.F. 1982. "Cognitive content of parents' speech to preschoolers". *Merrill-Palmer Quarterly* 28. 471-484.

Masur, E.F. and J.B. Gleason. 1980. "Parent-child interaction and the acquisition of lexical information during play". *Developmental Psychology* 16. 404-409.

McClure, E. 1981. "Formal and functional aspects of code switched discourse of bilingual children". In *Latino Language and Communicative Behaviour*, ed. by R.P. Duran. Norwood, N.J.: Ablex.

McDonald, L. and D. Pien. 1982. "Mothers' conversational behaviour as a function of interactional intent". *Journal of Child Language* 9. 337-358.

McLaughlin, B. 1978; 2nd, ed. 1984. *Second Language Acquisition in Childhood*. Hillsdale, N.J.: Lawrence Erlbaum.

McLaughlin, B., D. White, T. McDevitt and R. Raskin. 1983. "Mothers' and fathers' speech to their young children: similar or different?" *Journal of Child Language* 10. 245-252.

Menyuk, P. 1963. "A preliminary evaluation of grammatical capacity in children". *Journal of Verbal Learning and Verbal Behaviour* 2. 429-439.

Metraux, R.W. 1965. "A study of bilingualism among children of U.S.-French parents". *French Review* 38. 650-665.

Moerk, E.L. 1972. "Principles of interaction in language learning". *Merrill-Palmer Quarterly* 18. 229-257.

Moerk, E.L. 1974. "Changes in verbal child-mother interactions with increasing language skills of the child". *Journal of Psycholinguistic Research* 3 (2). 101-116.

Moerk, E.L. 1976a. "Motivational variables in language acquisition." *Child Study Journal* 6. 55-84.

Moerk, E.L. 1976b. "Processes of language teaching and training in the interactions of mother-child dyads". *Child Development* 47. 1064-1078.

Moerk, E.L. 1980. "Relationships between parental input frequencies and children's language acquisition: a reanalysis of Brown's data". *Journal of Child Language* 7. 105-118.

Moerk, E.L. 1983a. "A behavioural analysis of controversial topics in first language acquisition: reinforcements, corrections, modelling, input frequencies, and the three-term contingency pattern". *Journal of Psycholinguistic Research* 12 (2). 129-155.

Moerk, E.L. 1983b. *The Mother of Eve - As a First Language Teacher*. Norwood, N.J.: Ablex.

Moerk, E.L. 1985a. "A differential interactive analysis of language teaching and learning". *Discourse Processes* 8. 113-142.

Moerk, E.L. 1985b. "Picture-book reading by mothers and young children and its impact upon language development". *Journal of Pragmatics* 9. 547-566.

Moerk, E.L. and C. Moerk 1979. "Quotations, imitations, and generalisations. Factual and methodological analyses". *International Journal of Behavioural Development* 2. 43-72.

Nelson, K. 1981. "Individual differences in language development". *Developmental Psychology* 17. 170-187.

Nelson, K.E. 1977. "Facilitating children's syntax acquisition". *Developmental Psychology* 13. 101-107.

Nelson, K.E. and J. D. Bonvillian. 1978. "Early language development: conceptual growth and related processes between 2 and 4 1/2 years of age." In *Children's Language Vol. 1.,* ed. by K.E. Nelson. New York: Gardner.

Nelson, K.E., M.M. Denninger, J.D. Bonvillian, B.J. Kaplan, and N. Baker. 1983. "Maternal input adjustments and non-adjustments as related to children's linguistic advances and to language acquisition theories". In *The Development of Oral and Written Languages,* ed. by A.D. Pelligrini and T.D. Yawkey. Norwood, N.J.: Ablex.

Newport, E., L. Gleitman, and H. Gleitman. 1977. "Mother, I'd rather do it myself: some effects and non-effects of maternal speech styles". In *Talking to Children: Language Input and Acquisition,* ed. by C.E. Snow and C.A. Ferguson. Cambridge: Cambridge University Press.

Ninio, A. 1980a. "The ostensive definition in vocabulary teaching". *Journal of Child Language* 7. 565-573.

Ninio, A. 1980b. "Picture-book reading in mother-infant dyads belonging to two sub-groups in Israel". *Child Development* 51. 587-590.

Ninio, A. and J. Bruner. 1978. "The achievement and antecedents of labelling". *Journal of Child Language* 5. 57-73.

Oksaar, E. 1976. "Code-switching as an interactional strategy for developing bilingual competence". *Word* 27. 377-385.

Oldenburg, J. 1986. "The transitional stage of a second child - 18 months to 2 years". *Australian Review of Applied Linguistics* 9 (1). 123-135.

Olsen-Fulero, L. 1982. "Style and stability in mother conversational behaviour: a study in individual differences". *Journal of Child Language* 9. 543-564.

Peal, E. and W.E. Lambert 1962. "The relation of bilingualism to intelligence". *Psychological Monographs* 76 (27). 246-281.

Penfield, W. 1967. "The learning of languages". In *Foreign Language Teaching. An Anthology,* ed. by J. Michel. London: Macmillan.

Pieper, U. 1984. "Is parental language sexually differentiated?" *Studia Anglica Posnaniensia* 17. 71-80.

Poplack, S. 1980. "Sometimes I'll start a sentence in Spanish Y TERMINO EN ESPANOL: towards a typology of code-switching". *Linguistics* 18. 581-618.

Porsché, D. 1975. "Urteile und Vorurteile über Zweisprachigkeit im Kindesalter". *Linguistik und Didaktik* 23. 179-189.

Porsché, D. 1983. *Die Zweisprachigkeit während des primären Spracherwerbs*. Tübingen: Gunter Narr.

Rebelsky, , F. and C. Hank. 1971. "Fathers' verbal interactions with infants in the first three months of life". *Child Development* 42. 62-68.

Rodd, L.J. and M.D.S. Braine. 1970. "Children's imitations of syntactic constructions as a measure of linguistic competence". *Journal of Verbal Learning and Verbal Behaviour* 10. 430-443.

Rondal, J.A. 1980. "Fathers' and mothers' speech in early language development". *Journal of Child Language* 7. 353-369.

Ronjat, J.A. 1913. *Le Development du Langage Observé Chez un Enfant Bilingué*. Paris: Champion.

Rosenblum, T. and S.A. Pinker. 1983. "Word magic revisited: monolingual and bilingual children's understanding of the word-object relationship". *Child Development* 54. 773-780.

Ruke-Dravina, V. 1965. "The process of acquisition of apical /r/ and uvular /R/ in the speech of children". *Linguistics* 17. 56-68.

Sacks, H. 1967-72. Unpublished lecture notes. University of California

Sacks, H., E. Schegloff and G. Jefferson. 1974. "A simplest systematic for the organization of turn-taking for conversation". *Language* 50. 696-735.

Saunders, G.W. 1982a. "Infant bilingualism: a look at some doubts and objections". *Journal of Multilingual and Multicultural Development* 3 (4). 277-292.

Saunders, G.W. 1982b. *Bilingual Children. Guidance for the Family*. Clevedon: Multilingual Matters.

Saunders, G.W. 1988. *Bilingual Children: From Birth to Teen*. Clevedon: Multilingual Matters

Schmidt-Rohr, G. 1933. *Muttersprache. Vom Amt der Sprache bei der Volkwerdung*. Jena.

Shatz, M. and R. Gelman 1977. "Beyond syntax: the influence of conversational constraints on speech modifications". In *Talking to Children: Language Input and Acquisition,* ed. by C.E. Snow and C.A. Ferguson. Cambridge: Cambridge University Press.

Slobin, D.I. 1968 "Imitation and grammatical development in children". In *Contemporary Issues in Developmental Psychology,* ed. by N.S. Endlerr, L.R. Boulter, and H. Osser. New York: Holt, Rinehart and Winston.

Slobin, D.I 1973. "Cognitive prerequisites for the development of grammar". In *Studies of Child Development,* ed. by C.A. Ferguson and D.I. Slobin. New York: Holt, Rinehart and Winston.

Slobin, D. I. and C. A. Welsh. 1971. "Elicited imitation as a research tool in developmental sociolinguistics". In *Language Training in Early Childhood Education,* ed. by C.S. Lavatelli. Evanston, Illinois: University of Illinois Press.

Smith, C. S. 1970. "An experimental approach to children's linguistic competence". In *Cognition and the Development of Language,* ed. by J.R. Hayes. New York: Wiley.

Smolak, L. 1987. "Child characteristics and maternal speech". *Journal of Child Language* 14. 481-492.

Snow, C.E. 1977. "The development of conversations between mothers and babies". *Journal of Child Language* 14. 1-22.

Snow, C.E. 1978. "The conversational context of language acquisition". In *Recent Advances in the Psychology of Language,* ed. by R.N. Campbell and P.T. Smith. New York: Plenum Press.

Snow, C.E. 1983. "Saying it again: the role of expanded and deferred imitations in language acquisition". In *Children's Language Vol. 4,* ed. by K.E. Nelson. New York: Gardner.

Snow, C.E. and B. Goldfield. 1983. "Turn the page, please: situation-specific language learning". *Journal of Child Language* 10. 551-569.

Søndergaard, B. 1981. "Decline and fall of an individual bilingualism". *Journal of Multilingual and Multicultural Development* 2 (4). 297-302.

Stella-Prorok, E.M. 1983. "Mother-child language in the natural environment". In *Children's Language Vol. 4,* ed. by K.E. Nelson. New York: Gardner.

Stubbs, D.M. 1983. *Discourse Analysis.* Oxford: Basil Blackwell.

Swain, M. 1972. "Bilingualism as a first language". Ph.D. thesis. University of California, Irvine.

Taeschner, T. 1983. *The Sun is Feminine. A Study of Language Acquisition in Bilingual Children.* Volterra, V. and T. Taeschner. 1978. "The acquisition and development of language by bilingual children". *Journal of Child Language* 5. 311-326.

von Raffler-Engel, W. 1965. "Del bilinguisme infantile". *Archivio Glottologico Italiano* 50. 175-180.

Weisgerber, L. 1966. "Vorteile und Gefahren der Zweisprachigkeit". *Wirkendes Wort* 16. 73-89.

Wells, G. 1980. "Apprenticeship in meaning". In *Children's Language Vol. 2.*, ed. by K.E. Nelson. New York: Gardener.

Wells, G., M.M. Montgomery and M. MacLure. 1979. "Adult-child discourse: outline of a model of analysis". *Journal of Pragmatics* 3:337-380.

Wells, G. M. MacLure, and M.M. Montgomery. 1981. "Some strategies for sustaining conversation". In Conversation and *Discourse,* ed. by P. Werth. London: Croom Helm.

Wells, G. and W.P. Robinson. 1982. "The role of adult speech in language development". In *Advances in the Social Psychology of Language*, ed. by C. Fraser and C. R. Scherer. Cambridge: Cambridge University Press.

Zierer, E. 1977. "Experiences in the bilingual education of a child of preschool age". *International Review of Applied Linguistics* 15 (2). 143-149.

Zimmermann, I.L., V.G. Steiner and R.E. Pond. 1979. *Preschool Language Scale*. Columbus, Ohio: Belland Howell.

APPENDIX: Transcription Symbols

,	continuing intonation
.	stopping fall in tone
?	rising inflection
!	animated tone
-	halting or abrupt cut-off
—	incomplete intonation unit
CAPITALS	emphasis
<l text l>	clearly slower and more accentuated than the rest of the same speaker's contribution
<r text r>	faster than the rest of the same speaker's contribution
<p text p>	quieter
<f text f>	louder
_text mark	no interval between adjacent utterances, or to continuous flow of speech in spite of visual separation through intervening interruption
{ text } 1	overlapping utterances
+	short, unmeasured pause

(2.4)	pause, measured in tenths of a second
=	extension of sound or syllable
(xx)	incomprehensible
(text)	correctness of understanding is doubtful
[text]	phonetic transcription
((remark))	clarifications concerning characteristics of speech or the conversational scene
C	child
M	mother
F	father
S	researcher

Index

Q

R

S

T

W

Weintraub 11, 188
Wells 83, 84, 86, 96, 97, 99, 100, 145, 189, 195, 196
Welsh 144
Wetstone 188
White 188

Y

Yu 5

Z

Zimmermann 29, 34, 76, 174. *See also* Tests: Preschool language scale

DATE DUE